HOLY LITERARY LICENSE:

The Almighty Chooses Fallible Mortals to Write, Edit, and Translate GodStory

Other Works by Robert Flynn

North to Yesterday

In the House of the Lord

The Sounds of Rescue, the Signs of Hope

Seasonal Rain

A Personal War in Vietnam

The Last Klick

When I was Just Your Age
(with Susan Russell)

Wanderer Springs

Living With the Hyenas

The Devil's Tiger
(with Dan Klepper)

Growing Up a Sullen Baptist

Tie-Fast Country

Slouching Toward Zion

Paul Baker and the Integration of Abilities
(with Eugene McKinney)

Echoes of Glory

Burying the Farm

Jade: Outlaw

Jade: The Law

*Lawful Abuse: How the Century of the Child
Became the Century of the Corporation*

HOLY LITERARY LICENSE:

The Almighty
Chooses Fallible Mortals
to Write, Edit, and Translate
GodStory

Robert Flynn

Author of Growing Up a Sullen Baptist

WingsPress

San Antonio, Texas

2016

*Holy Literary License: The Almighty Chooses Fallible Mortals
to Write, Edit, and Translate GodStory*
© 2016 by Robert Flynn

Cover: "Holy Venus!" by Bryce Milligan
(with apologies to Botticelli)

ISBN: 978-1-60940-465-9 (paperback original)

E-books:
ePub: 978-1-60940-466-6
Mobipocket/Kindle: 978-1-60940-467-3
Library PDF: 978-1-60940-468-0

Wings Press
627 E. Guenther
San Antonio, Texas 78210
Phone/fax: (210) 271-7805
On-line catalogue and ordering:
www.wingspress.com
Wings Press books are distributed to the trade by
Independent Publishers Group
www.ipgbook.com

Cataloging In Publication:

Flynn, Robert, 1932- author.
Title: Holy literary license : the almighty publisher chooses fallible
    mortals to write, edit, and translate GodStory /
    Robert Flynn, author of Growing up a sullen Baptist.
San Antonio, TX : Wings Press, 2016.
LCCN 2016033172
ISBN 9781609404659 (pbk. : alk. paper); ISBN 9781609404673
(kindle/mobipocket ebook); ISBN 9781609404680 (library pdf)
Subjects: LCSH: Bible--History--Miscellanea. | Bible--Criticism,
    interpretation, etc.--Miscellanea. | Flynn, Robert, 1932-
LCC BS447 .F59 2016
DDC 220.6--dc23

LC record available at https://lccn.loc.gov/2016033172

To David Middleton,
colleague, friend, fellow pilgrim

CONTENTS

Acknowledgements

I want to acknowledge and thank the following people for their assistance, complaints, questions and encouragement that made this book possible. Colin Bass, Joseph S. Blair, Rev. Kyle Childress, Sybil Pittman Estess, Rev. Mark Hart, Barbara Higdon, Mark Noblitt, Edgar Twedt, Lori Tyler, Garrett Vickrey, Leslie Williams.

I also want to thank the writers of the hymns, some of whom wish to remain anonymous, and a special thanks to Jerome Malek for giving permission to use his composition for William Blake's poem, "The Lamb."

If this book upsets your pretty picture of life and death eternal, organized and disorganized church history and heaven that is smaller than NASA's photograph of our universe, you can thank the people named above.

If this book is more than you can tolerate you may blame me.

Author's Foreword

My brother Jim will not read this book. He died before the book was in a form where I could have sent it and gotten his opinion. If he weren't dead this book might have killed him. No, it wouldn't have but we would have argued about it. We were brothers, separated by two years. He was the older bother (a Freudian slip that I have made several times). The older brother in the biblical sense, too. As I am. He was not inclined to wander or wonder into the unknowable. We argued about everything. Cars, tractors, fountain pens, churches, movies, cities. God. Nothing was too grand or too trivial.

We did agree on a few things. We saw the film "Gentlemen's Agreement," and neither of us believed there was discrimination against Jews in America. We didn't know any Jews. As far as I know neither of us had ever seen a Jew, but they were relatives of Jesus, Moses, the apostles and our other heroes. How could Americans be prejudiced toward them? We didn't believe the Jews killed Jesus. We believed we did. We were taught that Jesus died for our sins. We believed the movie was a veiled attempt to show the discrimination against African-Americans. We both knew the resentment, the anger, the outright hatred toward black people; he more than I.

My family did not use the N-word, except as Negro which we carefully enunciated. Once when we were together I used "niggardly" in a sentence and it had the desired effect. Jim angrily accused me of bigotry while I innocently claimed it was a legitimate word. He knew that as well as I. He also knew why I used the word. I don't think I have used it since.

My older daughter, Deirdre, reminded me recently of an incident in a Deep South city. We were walking in a park.

Either my wife, Jean, or I held Brigid's hand. Brigid was a toddler. Deirdre danced and skipped ahead of us, as usual taking up the whole sidewalk. For some forgotten reason I called Deirdre "Spook." When an African-American family approached us I called "Spook, get off the sidewalk." The family stepped into the street. I apologized, explaining that I was yelling at my daughter. It didn't matter because they would have stepped into the street anyway. They knew the unwritten rules but I had humiliated a man in front of his family. My shame equaled his.

Decades later Jim pastored a church in east Texas that is closer to Alabama than to West Texas. One Sunday on his way to church Jim asked some black children why they weren't in church. They told him they didn't have a church so he took them to his. There were more of them the next Sunday. Soon their parents began coming to the church and then wanted to be a part of the church, to become members. Jim said yes and the congregation said no. He left east Texas to pastor a church in California.

I felt a sense of vocation or call when I was very young. Jim's call came much later when he was attending an agricultural college. He was going to take over our father's farm. I still kind of question the good Lord's judgement in revealing my call when I was so young. I didn't know what it meant or what to do with it. I wanted to know what I would be doing the rest of my life, forgetting that even Jesus struggled to discover his mission.

I was occasionally preaching when I was 14 and people tolerated the stupid things I said. For the most part. For a time I held services at the county jail. The prisoners would listen to anyone to pass a bit of endless hours with nothing to do. My father didn't like organized religion. His church was the Masonic Lodge but he always went with me when I spoke anywhere nearby. He was the only one who laughed out loud when at my first jail service I greeted the prisoners by saying, "I'm glad to see so many of you here."

That wasn't the worst thing I ever said. I was curious about other countries and assumed I was to be a missionary. While working in my father's cotton fields after school and in the summer I dreamed of taking the Gospel to Africa, or maybe China after reading Pearl S. Buck. No, she was not the wife of "Bring Them Back Alive" Frank Buck who captured wild and dangerous animals for American zoos and wrote about his adventures. Pearl Buck was the first American writer and first American woman to receive the Nobel Prize for Literature. Toni Morrison is the second woman.

As a missionary, along with the Bible I was also going to teach Chinese or Africans how to make ice cream and play American football. I didn't see how I could be happy in either place without ice cream and football. After my first year in college I enlisted in the Marines because my country was at war with North Korea, and later, China. Despite my prayers, God did not send me to Korea where after killing an heroic number of Koreans or Chinese I might return to those defeated countries as a missionary. When despite my prayers I didn't go to Korea, it seemed to me the Almighty had closed the door to a missionary career.

I occasionally held revivals and thought maybe my calling was to be a professional and perhaps popular evangelist. That was before the days of televangelism. That plan died when I tried to sell roofing in Waco after the deadliest tornado in Texas history. Street loads of houses were without roofs but I didn't like the tricks and devices I was to use to persuade people to buy roofing. My income was based on the difference between the actual cost of the roofing and what I persuaded them to pay for it.

Professional evangelism seemed too close to making money by overpricing roofing to people who had already suffered tragedy. And that was before the days of televangelists.

The only option left was being a pastor. Jean married me in 1953 believing she would be a pastor's wife. The pastor who married us asked her if she felt a calling to be a pastor's wife. She said she didn't; she loved me and wanted to be my wife whatever I did. I was disappointed by her response.

After I completed my degree at Baylor we moved to Fort Worth so I could attend the seminary. I still consider it my apprenticeship in hell. That requires some explaining. I have said and written that in 1887 my father was born in a boxcar at the end of the track that came to be called Chillicothe, Texas. My mother repeatedly pointed out that it wasn't a boxcar. According to her, Dad was born in a Pullman outfitted as a residence for my grandfather, an Irishman from Cork County, who came to Texas to help build the Fort Worth and Denver Railroad. He had earlier worked in California where he met and married a schoolteacher from Vermont. Where is the romance, the color in a Pullman? I have seen the cave in which Abraham is said to have been born. I have also seen the stone beehive houses of Haran in one of which Abraham was said to have been born. The cave is the better story.

In 1896, my grandfather was murdered, leaving a widow and three young sons who fiercely clung to the section of land my grandfather had bought with borrowed money. They lost contact with both their Irish family and their Vermont relatives. There was little time for school when there was so much work to be done to save the farm. Mostly they were taught at home by their mother.

In the Irish tradition of marrying late, sure and begorrah, my father was 45 when I was born. My mother was two and a half decades younger. Dad was the only one of my grandfather's three sons young enough to be drafted in World War I. Although he had little formal education, he kept a diary of his days in the trenches and the nightmares of going "over the top" into German machine guns. My father and I were very close and, when I enlisted in the Marines, he asked me to keep a diary. He never told me why he wanted me do it and never asked to see it.

While I was in the Marines, every night I recorded the mostly boring events of the day. I continued writing after I returned to Baylor. I enrolled in a drama class because Jerry Coody said it was the best speech class he had taken. I actively didn't want to be an actor but Coody was a Native American, an All-American football player and a ministerial student. How could he be wrong?

Paul Baker, who taught the class, didn't encourage me to be an actor. Neither did anyone else. Baker did scrawl encouraging words like "not bad" on a written assignment and passed it to Eugene McKinney. McKinney, son of Baptist hymn writer B.B. McKinney, taught playwriting and religious drama. Those two men and their families would become a major part of my life.

Seminaries are breeding grounds for cheap "supply" preachers who would fill the pulpit for a pastor who was sick or wanted to be doing something else on Sunday. I supplied a lot of pulpits and found writing a sermon more enjoyable than preaching it. I wrote more than I studied. I read more about the creative process and story-telling that I did about the Bible. I desperately wanted to be a writer. That much of my disappointment with the seminary is on me.

I wrote a lot of sermons that I would never preach because we were told repeatedly by different professors that we should not preach what we were learning in the seminary because it would shake the faith of the church members who did not have the biblical background that we had. I understand that better now but at the time it seemed a betrayal of our calling. It wasn't our fault that congregations had been sheltered from the facts so long that we could not tell them what we believed to be the truth. If their faith was that shallow, it needed to be shaken, but gently and with love.

I preached at a small church that didn't have a nursery and unhappy infants were passed back and forth between parents until one took it outside. Older children sat with parents and tried the parents' and the congregation's Christian forbearance. It was during the Christmas season so I brought my "Keep Christ in Christmas" sermon. I even wrote a poem for the occasion. Mercifully there is no written evidence of either but the last two lines of the poem are still emblazoned on my brain. "For

Christ was nailed to a Christmas tree and Santa Claus washed his hands."

They didn't stone me. They didn't invite me back either. I had killed Santa Claus. Wives kept a tight grip on husbands as there were some clenched teeth and fists. Some men followed me to my car, escorting me from their property. I took that as a sign that I was not called to be a pastor. I didn't see how I could say what I wanted to say if children determined what could be said.

Had I tricked myself into believing I had a calling? Those were my days in the wilderness. Was my call as insubstantial as my memory of Uncle Boyd, my mother's younger brother, the one everyone loved, the one everyone said I looked like? Was I supposed to be like him? "Too good to live." That's what his best friend said about him. I tried to imagine what that would be like. So nice and well-behaved I walked out of this world and into the next.

With Jean beside me, I slept with a loaded pistol under my pillow. Jean believed it was to protect her as there had been a couple of rapes in our neighborhood. That was part of it, maybe a big part.

It wasn't as dramatic as it seems on paper but I knew that on some tomorrow I would have to face the question about my vocation. Could writing be fulfillment or was it betrayal? The pistol was insurance that I didn't have to face that tomorrow if I didn't want to. With that assurance I began to wonder if writing could be a vocation. Was I delusional?

It's hard to tell someone you want to be a writer. You can say you want to be a doctor, lawyer, professor, banker, CEO—and people will nod and wish you success. You can say you want to be an elementary school teacher and people will look askance, especially if they are in-laws. If you're a man, in-laws will be certain there is something wrong with you. You can say you want to be an astronaut and if you are a grown man who has never flown anything bigger than a kite they may doubt your ability but they won't laugh behind your back.

Tell others that you want to be a writer without any hard evidence of talent and you will be an object of ridicule. No one I talked to believed writing could be my vocation, although some allowed that it might be a vocation for others. I was supposed to be a preacher and writing was not preaching.

Hardest of all to tell was Jean. Jean had worked and taken night classes preparing to be a pastor's wife. Now I had to tell her that I had been wrong. As always Jean was a sweetheart. She said she would support me in whatever I wanted to be. As always Jean was the practical one. She wanted to know what we had to do, step by step. My plan was to return to Baylor, get a degree in drama, write plays and teach religious drama, playwriting and required classes.

Those days in the wilderness are how and when this book began. I taught at Gardner-Webb College, now University; Baylor another Baptist University; and Trinity, a Presbyterian University. I have written a stage adaptation of William Faulkner's novel *As I Lay Dying*, a two-part documentary on the religion of the cowboy for ABC-TV, ten novels, two collections of stories, two memoirs and a nonfiction book, *Lawful Abuse*, about the way this nation has treated children. I also edited two books and have contributed to at least 30 additional books.

My colleagues, my students, the schools, the churches I belonged to and the church members and everything I have written is part of this book. In retrospect it seems clear to me that writing was my vocation, perhaps teaching as well. Whether I have fulfilled God's purpose for me is a decision that only the Almighty can make.

And why did the Almighty make it so hard to get published?

Introduction

A Confession

Many years ago I was on a panel of writers, one of them a popular columnist known to be a fundamentalist Christian. It is necessary to draw a distinction between fundamentalists and evangelicals. All Christians who believe that salvation is by grace through faith without need of sacraments or works are evangelicals. That includes fundamentalists and the line between them is not clearly marked.

However, fundamentalists are best identified by the once ubiquitous bumper sticker, "The Bible says it, I believe it, that settles it." Fundamentalists tend to read the Bible literally, believe its simplest meaning and close the door to further exploration of its meaning to its first audience, its historical context, the intention of those who wrote the Bible, their rhetorical strategies, archeology, science, the fragility of the earliest known writings, problems of translation, etc. That's like settling for glasses that allow you to see words and ignoring the evidence revealed by microscopes and telescopes. The Bible, one of the world's great books of literature and religion, is not that simple for those who have studied it.

Evangelicals can't put their beliefs on a bumper-sticker, not even on the side of a freight train, but if they did it would begin:

> The Bible says it in some places and for some times. However, I will not offer burnt offerings, I will not stone a disobedient child, require abortion or infanticide if a man has sex with an aunt or a brother's wife, forgive a debt after seven years or require property to return to the original owner every 50 years.

However, I will read the Bible as a written guide to Christian faith and practice, and that begins the search for its meaning to its first audience, its meaning to me, and its meaning regarding the present world condition in the light of the life and teaching of Jesus Christ.

With evangelicals there is always a *however*.

In a nation where churches are unregistered lobbyists for special interests, it is essential that politicians, the public and the media correctly identify different denominations and splinter groups and their different interests. Politicians and those in the media learn the position of the Catholic church by asking the local Catholic authority. But how do they report the Protestant position? Usually by identifying the loudest and most widely known voice. That is often a TV personality who claims to have a large following such as Jerry Falwell, founder of the "Moral Majority," or Pat Robertson who has a large TV following. That personality is then identified as an "evangelical" although he or she is more likely to be a fundamentalist.

Many denominations and churches have both fundamentalist and evangelical members, so how is an underpaid and overworked reporter to know the difference? Many evangelical groups no longer identify themselves as evangelical because they do not want to be mistaken as fundamentalist, allowing fundamentalists to usurp the name for themselves. I believe that is wrong.

The fundamentalist on the writing panel publicly revealed that what he thought about before going to sleep at night was women and money. You probably have a few seconds or minutes to let your mind run free if your prayers don't put you to sleep. What you think about during those half sleep dreams may be the most revealing thing about you.

I was surprised that anyone would reveal such a thing. I was further surprised by his subjects. Women I understood but money? I have worried about money, but dreamed of great sums of it? No. In our student years Jean worked full time and took night classes and I was on the G.I. Bill and carried a class over-load to finish college as quickly as possible. We couldn't have done that if Jean hadn't known how to make biscuits and gravy. Sometimes that was all we had to eat. Once I brought the son of a state senator home for lunch and Jean opened a can of whole kernel corn she had been saving for a time when we might not have gravy.

Once we had to borrow milk intended for my young nephew who, with his mother, my sister, was waiting orders for shipment to Germany to join his soldier father. We didn't have enough milk for gravy for the three of us. We were young, had upward mobility and could see a promising future. That isn't true of many hungry Americans today.

In twilight sleep, the images that ran through my mind after prayer weren't about food or status but women and killing people. Let me hasten to add that in those half-asleep dreams I did not kill women and children, only bad men who should be killed to save democracy, the American way of life, my home, Christianity, not necessarily in that order.

In the beginning I killed horse thieves, cattle rustlers and Indians. The list expanded to include Germans and Japanese, especially Japanese because of their sneak attack on Pearl Harbor. Sneak attacks are usually the best attacks, like the Doolittle bombing of Tokyo, but that wasn't a sneak attack; it was a surprise attack. I was learning the rhetoric of war.

Pearl Harbor must be avenged. I heard that everywhere. I tracked the progress of the Marines across the Pacific on a map provided by a newspaper. I was thrilled by their heroism and prog-ress, but I feared the war would be over before I had a chance to exact my own vengeance on God's enemies.

I learned of Hiroshima at the bus station in Vernon, Texas. An old man said the war was over. America had dropped a new kind of bomb, an atom bomb, destroying a Japanese city and the war would soon be over. I didn't know what an atom was and had heard an "Adam" bomb. I thought it was the beginning of a new world. And it was. We were naked to our own weapons. Edward R. Murrow said it best, did the atom bomb mean midnight or 00:01?

I could think of no scenario in which I could destroy an airplane carrying a nuclear weapon to destroy America without blowing myself up. I wanted to be a hero but I wanted to be around to enjoy the applause.

After Hiroshima I began killing Russians and other godless Communists in the minutes before sleep came. After the Communist threat subsided, I defended Israeli villages against hordes of Arabs. That ended when Jean and I went to Israel entering by the land bridge from Jordan. We liked Jordan. The people were kind, friendly. I saw no weapons anywhere, not on the police, not at the airport. But we cheered when we saw the Israeli flag at the border. It was almost like being home.

Israel was a shock. At the border was the largest, most formidable bunker I had ever seen even in war zones and former war zones. We were not allowed to enter Jericho because some kids were throwing rocks and Israeli soldiers were firing rifles. Signs warned motorists not to get off the road because the roadside was mined from Jericho to Jerusalem. On one side of the highway were abandoned Palestinian villages, the buildings and houses pocked by bullets and broken by artillery shells. On the other side of the highway were Israeli settlements with children playing in the streets.

I told Jean that we were seeing a new Northern Ireland. We had been to Ulster in 1972 during "The Troubles." When we entered a town, if the British soldiers were ducking from doorway to doorway we didn't stop. If they were playing with the children we did. We slowly drove through a roadblock with a machine gun set up beside the road to stop any car that didn't slow down. We and our car were undergoing a strip-search in Derry when we were suddenly ordered to go. An armored car was bearing down on us at high speed and we needed to clear the road.

The Troubles started centuries earlier when Scot Presbyterians were moved to Ulster to replace dispossessed Irish Catholics. The Scots were fiercely loyal to Britain, and their descendants who outnumbered the native Irish fought to keep their birthplace a province of Britain even after the other four Irish provinces gained independence. Sometimes the quarrel over whose land it was became violent.

Israeli children born in occupied Palestine would remember the villages as home and would fight to the death to save their birthplace. Just as the Palestinians do. America occupied Germany, Japan, South Korea, South Vietnam, Afghanistan and Iraq, but moved no Americans to live there as the British had moved Scots to Ulster as early as 1610. I have found no new targets. There is an abundance of bad people but no bad people whose death would save democracy, Christianity and the world.

One of the seductive things about writing is discovering things you don't know you knew until it appears before your eyes on screen or paper. It was only a few years ago while writing about my childhood religious experience that I confessed to myself that one of the reasons I had enlisted in the Marines was for a license to kill. I assure you I was not the only one who didn't enlist in the Marines to learn a trade. I wanted to "kill Commies for Christ." I would not only be saving South Korea, America and Christianity, if I were a killer of davidic measure I would be saving myself from insignificance. I could return to Baylor as an American David who had killed many to save all that Baylor held dear. When I spoke sinners would listen.

I didn't go to Korea. That was more than an embarrassment; not killing and risking death was a humiliation and I was a failure. I prayed more that I would be sent to Korea than for anything else at that time but God was unimpressed.

Not going to Korea also meant I did not feel like an authentic Marine. I once introduced Tim O'Brien, author of *The Things They Carried*, before a public reading and backstage we talked about Vietnam. I told O'Brien that I went to Vietnam as a reporter because I did not feel like an authentic Marine since I had never been shot at. O'Brien said he understood that.

For a time in Vietnam I embedded myself with Golf Company, Second Battalion, Fifth Marines led by Captain Tilley (now Col. Tilley, ret.) and Gunny Shivers (now Lt.Col. Shivers, ret.) who had received a battlefield commission. Because I was with squad and platoon-size units I carried a rifle and under fire I returned fire. I don't believe I killed or injured anyone. Or harmed either side. To some that will seem an unorthodox baptism.

That's a wretched, forlorn confession: that an American raised in a Christian home and educated in a Christian culture believed something was missing if he hadn't faced giving or receiving sudden or prolonged and miserable death. In America killing someone is a rite of passage that plays not only in the Marines and Special Forces but street gangs, mobsters and a handful of law enforcement officers.

In the book and movie, *Jarhead*, a Marine spotter in a sniper team in Iraq is not allowed to reenlist because he didn't report an arrest on a drug charge. He sees two Iraqi officers and asks for permission to kill them. Permission denied. Topside wants to call an airstrike. He pleads for a chance to kill the men. Denied. His sniper pleads for him. Denied. He is going to leave the Marine Corps having been in a war but having never been shot at or killed anyone. That failure is devastating.

Another confession: I was going from my office to the kitchen to get a fresh cup of coffee when Jean told me to turn on the TV in the den, any station. When I did, I saw a World Trade Center tower burning after being hit by an airliner. I watched paralyzed because I knew what it meant. I didn't think, "What a lousy pilot." Then I saw an airplane make a well-executed turn and line up to hit a second tower. My first thought was, "I have to reenlist." My second thought was what are the Marines going to do with a 68-year-old corporal.

An anonymous admiral is supposed to have said, "The Army and Navy are Military Services, the Air Force is a corporation, the Marine Corps is a religion." I sometimes joke that the Marine Corps is my second religion out of fear that it may be my first. I confess with some shame but more pride that if the Marines said they needed me anywhere in the world I would pay for my own ticket.

From Where Did Dreams of Killing Come?

My father served in the "War to End All Wars." They didn't come close. Dad's nightmares awoke me some nights as he dreamed of tinkling cans meaning Germans were in the wire, or being lost in No Man's Land at night, afraid any movement would draw fire, maybe from his own trenches, but lying there until daylight meant discovery and almost certain death.

Dad didn't talk much about his experiences in the trenches. I have a short clipping without a dateline from an unknown newspaper that someone had clipped and kept for Dad. "Twenty-Six Come Back Out of 210 in Company." That was Dad's company 30 minutes after going "over the top." He told me once that it was like he was following a white light as shells, bullets and dead men fell around him. But after that 30 minutes the 26 men were in the German trenches. With a wounded German soldier unable to withdraw. An officer from another unit was sent to lead them and they continued the attack.

Most of my life I have wondered if I could have advanced under those conditions and then attacked again. When I enlisted a female cousin told me not to let the Marines change me, but change was what I wanted.

There Were Other Inducements:

In World War II both the news media and entertainment media were the propaganda wing of the federal government promoting enlistment in the war effort and rationing on the home front.

Even before Pearl Harbor there were war movies, some of them about World War I, others about American volunteers in the Royal Air Force of Britain, making sure that we knew who the good guys were. Both the Jewish Bible and Christian Bible declared that vengeance belonged to God because human beings are incapable of doing justice. After Pearl Harbor the theme was the "terrible swift sword" of American vengeance. The press headlined Japanese duplicity, cruelty and torture, encouraging hatred. Film violence surged with multitudinous murder. Newsreels of flaming Japanese being flushed from caves or enemy airplanes falling out of the sky brought cheering from the audience.

My church was heavily invested in the war. Like most churches we had a banner with blue stars for those members in the military, red stars for those who had been wounded or were missing, and Gold Stars for those who died. The banner was taken down when the Gold Stars became too burdensome to bear.

Our boys were heroes, our enemies were God's enemies. H. Rap Brown was only partly right; violence is more American than apple pie.

A Marine who had fought the Japanese in the Pacific announced in church that he was going to Japan as a missionary. That brought no amens in our church. We had prayed and sacrificed for him. We did not want our enemies to turn to our God.

Holy Story Not Holy Words:

At a World Voices Festival by International PEN I heard a Muslim Arab woman tell of her novel, a love story about men and women. She was living in France because many in her country were angry with her for defiling the sacred language of the Koran. She had used Arabic, her native language, to describe human lust and carnal love.

Like the Bible, the Koran has been translated into many languages but Arabic is the sacred language. The woman could have written her book in French without upsetting anyone but she wanted to use her native language to make the book accessible to all those who read Arabic.

To many Jews, Hebrew is the sacred language of the Jewish Bible. There are many words about love, lust, incest, rape, idolatry to fertility gods and minority sexual practices.

The language of the Christian Bible was written in Hebrew and Greek with a sprinkling of Aramaic. Few American Christians regard those languages as sacred. We prefer a Bible written in English. But not just any Bible written in English.

The Power of Language:

Anyone who has hunted wild turkeys knows that they have mating calls, warning calls, assembly calls. By imitating the mating call of a hen a hunter can lure a love-stricken gobbler into shooting range. You can also use calls to locate a well-camouflaged wounded gobbler that responds by warning his love, his rivals and you of imminent danger.

According to the Bible Adam gave animals their names. To a degree, if you name something you own it and have power over it. What do you call someone who wants to kill citizens of your country although he is a citizen without a uniform and maybe without a country? Is he a patriot who is seeking justice for people with whom he identifies? terrorist? gunman? militant? warrior? freedom fighter? revolutionary? rebel? crusader? detainee? suspect? During World War II, Filipino groups fighting Japanese occupation of their country were called "guerrillas" by the news media but French and Yugoslavian groups fighting German occupation were called "partisans," perhaps because most of them were Communists. Menachem Begin and Nelson Mandela, who both received the Nobel Peace Prize, were earlier called terrorists by politicians and the news media.

The Power of Words:

My childhood faith embraced the King James Bible with a reverence that bordered on superstition. The unfamiliarity of the language in the KJV made it mysterious and otherworldly. I still am uncomfortable when someone puts a glass or tray on a Bible. That seems peculiar to those who read multiple versions of the Bible on their telephone, but I, and others like me, wanted to preserve the magic and mystery of the Bible. To do that we tried to erase all evidence of human hands and minds in the creation of the Bible. We wanted to believe the sacred scriptures fell directly from God's lips. And in English.

I was intensely interested in the Bible from an early age. My church memorized scriptures that could be used effectively in evangelism and in arguments regarding the superiority of our church. Also to maintain our separation from similar churches that had the same words but not the energy and enthusiasm we had. You have to go to bed early to keep up with Baptists, no late night TV or scummy cable shows. We had drills and competitions as to who could find a prooftext the fastest. We called it "sword drill" to prove our benign intentions.

Our focus was not on the story but on the sacred words. Already I knew that some of the sacred words had been expurgated in the sense that they could not be used in polite society or read aloud in church.

The original words of the writers:

In college I studied Greek so that I could read the New Testament in the language of the writers. I was disappointed to discover that there were no original texts, that all we had were copies of those texts, often in fragments, and that the texts did not always agree.

When the Revised Standard Version (RSV) of the Bible appeared there was confusion that rose to rage. The RSV was easy to read and painstakingly accurate but two versions of the Bible that contained the same stories but used different words defiled the Holy King James Bible. Now there were other words that made our memorized words less authoritative, as though the spirit and power were in the words themselves.

The Written Word of God:

In the temptation of Jesus, both Jesus and the tempter quote scriptures (Matt. 4: 7; Luke 4: 12). The tempter asked Jesus to throw himself from the highest part of the temple to demonstrate his majesty. Rev. Kyle Childress, pastor of Austin Heights Baptist Church, Nacogdoches, Texas asked, "If the Bible is the Word of God and it is always the Word of God, why doesn't Jesus do what it says?" Childress answers his question thus—"Well, because Satan is quoting the Bible...How and who uses the Bible makes a difference in how it is heard. In one case it might be God's Word and in another it might not. Whether the Bible is God's Word or not depends on who the speaker is and who the hearer is. It depends on context, purpose, motivation, and so on...He (Satan) is saying that the Bible is good in and of itself. It has authority and power whether God is connected to it or not. The Evil One is perfectly happy for us to have the Bible and use the Bible, just as long as we leave God out of it" (EKKLESIA Project, 3/10/11).

When I was a student at Baylor, a Waco preacher burned a copy of the RSV in the pulpit. Burning one copy is not going to destroy a book but it may change people's attitude toward that book, even the Bible. It seems to me that there has been prejudice against the RSV from the beginning. There had been other versions of the Bible of course but this was the first one to threaten the authenticity and authority of the "sacred" words of the KJV.

The RSV made way for a floodgate of translations and now one can read them on an iPad or iPhone. But others still cling to the KJV as their lifejacket in a rising sea. In the first decade of the 21st century my wife and I greeted some guests at one of our church services. They were looking for a church home and had but one question: Did we use the King James Bible? We did, but not exclusively, and our pew Bible was the New International Version (NIV). They did not return.

As if to make the subject absurd someone placed on YouTube a preacher in Arizona stating from the pulpit that he had just discovered that the King James Bible used "pisseth" and that's the word his church would be using. It wasn't clear why or how often that word would appear in church services or church restrooms but he and his flock would be true to the sacred words of King James' authorized Bible. A good American might ask by what authority a king authorized a Bible but so far it hasn't come up.

I was quite young when I was shocked to discover a word in the Bible that I was not allowed to use at home and that I had never heard read aloud in church, "eat their own dung and drink their own piss" (II Kings 18: 27; Isa. 36: 12). The NIV refined it to "eat their own excrement and drink their own urine," but in the KJV "pisseth" appeared in I Sam. 25:22; I Kings 14: 10, 16: 11, 21: 21; II Ki. 9: 8. That may be why many churches use other versions for a Pew Bible. A bored teenager might discover such words while flipping through the Bible. The way some look for suggestive hymn titles while adding "between the sheets." Sure you did.

There were other such words and passages in the Bible that were never read aloud or discussed in church so it was years before I learned that it was a picturesque description of those to be put to the sword when a city was captured—any male old enough, young enough or healthy enough to stand while urinating.

King James had a way with words. Although I have never seen a musical note that didn't scare me, a friend and I composed a hymn for the choirs of the churches that used the KJV in worship but did not realize the full richness of the language, such as that found in Exodus 26.

Hymn of Joy for the Strong Heart

Robert Flynn J.W. Kelam

Tune: BOBBYJEAN

Clinging to the words:

I, and my fellow church members, were chagrined that we had to read a translation and yet we did not *want* to know about the all-too-human political and religious cunning and finagling in determining the exact wording of the text, or the grimy story of the maneuvering and manipulation in deciding the biblical Canon. We were horrified by stories of scribes miscopying sacred texts, sometimes adding comments, and how much of the Bible was oral tradition, perhaps changing from tent to tent and tribe to tribe before it was written down.

For most of human history the spoken word was considered more authentic than the written word. Genghis Khan would totally destroy a city and everyone in it then go to the next city and say, "I am Genghis Khan and what I did to your neighboring city I will do to you unless you become my slaves." Or, he might ask for tribute in terms of precious metal, young boys and girls.

After a number of cities had surrendered, the conquerer grew tired of returning to them for tribute so he sent a messenger who said, "This is the sword of Genghis Khan and unless you pay more tribute he will use it to destroy this city."

Jewish religious leaders had long interpreted the written law (Torah), but were not permitted to record their interpretations because Jews believed it was important to perpetuate living traditions. When the Romans destroyed the Temple, outlawed the nation of Israel and scattered the Jews, it was necessary to write the interpretations of the scriptures to have a common practice among the dispersed people.

Later, when messages were written they required the stamp or seal of the king or other authority for authenticity. Tradition tells us that Homer wrote the *Iliad* and the *Odyssey*. Some scholars claim there was more than one Homer. We don't know who wrote *Gilgamesh*, circa 2500 BC, one of the oldest stories of mankind.

We don't know who wrote much of the Bible; we only have traditions regarding who wrote the books. Some of the books had more than one writer. Later writers added new insights or there were two versions of the same story, and editors or copyists tried to include both (the creation story) or weave them together (the flood story). Pretending the Bible is one book causes readers to believe the creation story was the first story written. It wasn't. I find it gratifying that the writers of the Bible did not have the egotism or the proprietary instincts of modern writers. The Bible writers believed what they did was for the glory of God and preservation of the tribe (Jewish Bible) or of the church (Christian Bible).

Few of us know or care about the prophet Jeremiah, other than that he was the "weeping prophet," or Hosea who was the first person to decry the double standard in sexual matters (Hosea 4: 14). What's wrong with not knowing about the writer? It removes the human element from the Bible, and how human understanding of the Divine changed before the canon was decided—and after it was decided. It made the Bible a static thing like a statue or an idol.

I believe we need the two creation stories (Gen. 1 and 2) to understand both the goodness of humans made in the image of God, and the terrible things done by humans made of mud. We shouldn't be too concerned that the meaning of words changes over decades and centuries and that there is some shifting of meaning between versions of the Bible. Jesus revised the Ten Commandments in the Sermon on the Mount. "You have heard...but I tell you..."

It isn't vital that we know who wrote the various books of the Bible, but I believe that we lost the sense of the Bible being a library of different voices, different revelations and different thoughts about the same story when the translators attempted to keep all translations in one "voice"—so that it seemed to be the voice of God. Or, in the beloved King James Version, the language of Shakespeare. We enshrined the words rather than glorifying the Story made flesh that dwelled among us.

The Duplicity of Words:

Different writers used different voices or rhetorical styles, sometimes including poetry in prose passages. That is most noticeable in the prophets but it is only recently that translators have indicated it. I believe the Bible also contains satire. The book of Jonah uses humorous exaggeration to expose wrong-thinking and sacred cows for a redemptive purpose. There is also irony, meaning the opposite of what is said, in the book of Ecclesiastes.

Everyone understands that "Thank you for stepping on my foot," doesn't mean what the words mean. But sometimes it's difficult to recognize irony. There was famine in Ireland, children died of hunger in their beds, mothers died unable to feed them. Fathers walked the roads looking for jobs or food. English landlords and English politicians viewed them with contempt: they had too many children, to feed them would encourage laziness, to give a man a living wage so he could feed his family would make them less dependent, less subservient to their employers.

In 1729, Jonathan Swift, an Anglican priest, wrote "A Modest Proposal, For Preventing The Children of Poor People in Ireland From Being A Burden to Their Parents or Country, and For Making Them Beneficial to The Public." His ironic proposal was that since Ireland had too many children and England had a shortage of meat that Irish children be sold for food. "I grant this food may be somewhat dear (expensive), and therefore very proper for Landlords, who as they have already devoured most of the Parents, seem to have the best Title to the Children."

Although written only 300 years ago I had college students who did not recognize the irony.

When I was in the seminary a friend was a "supply" preacher at a Baptist church in a small town west of Fort Worth. The morning service had gone well. For the evening service he read as his text, "Vanity of vanities, saith the Preacher. Vanity of vanities; All is vanity" (Ecc. 1:2).

A deacon stood up in a back pew and said, "Brother Preacher, I don't believe that's in the Bible." My friend averred not only was it in the Bible, it was in the King James Baptist Bible."

Whereupon, the good deacon said, "If it is, it ought not be."

The words are even worse in the NIV. "Meaningless! Meaningless!" says the teacher. "Utterly meaningless! Everything is meaningless." I had the same problem with Ecclesiastes as the good deacon. It was beautifully written but why was it in the Bible if nothing in this life mattered? My problems were increased when I learned that scholars agreed that the end of the book was added later.

I now believe that the writer intended irony. "Eat, drink and be merry for tomorrow you die" was current philosophy even then. The writer implied that if you follow that to its logical conclusion, life has no meaning. The writer even states that plainly in the text. "A man may have a hundred children and live many years; yet no matter how long he lives, if he cannot enjoy his prosperity and does not receive proper burial, I say that a stillborn child is better off than he" (Ecc. 6:3).

It's unfortunate that the voice of the writers is obscured in biblical translations because writers and storytellers, especially poets and singers, are aware of the shape, sound and rhythm of words, and try to use them, along with meaning, effectively. Singers are less concerned than poets with the visible shape of words, but words in print do have a shape. In what was called grade school I was told that a Frenchman visiting America said the most beautiful English words were "cellar door." Almost everyone I knew had a storm cellar and there was nothing pretty about cellar doors. It took years of writing to learn that "infantile paralysis" sounds pretty. And who doesn't like to say "Walla Walla, Wash" and "Timbuktu?" Shape, sound and rhythm are lost in translation along with shades of meaning.

Words are not perfect things on which to base perfect understanding. If you know anything about animals, stables and child birth, the stories of Jesus' birth are not pretty. However, most of us imagine the lovely scenes that artists have provided. The Romans used three kinds of crosses, X, I, and T. No, that wasn't the origin of the XIT brand in Texas. The Bible doesn't tell us which kind was used to crucify Jesus, but artists portray the T model and that best suits our theology, pointing out to the world and up to God, the Way of the Cross.

The Importance of Names:

You should have learned the importance of names from Rumpelstiltskin. My wife's name was actually Norma Jean but she was always called Jean and she was a Jean. My brother's wife was also named Norma Jean but she was always called Norma and she was a Norma. No one ever got them confused.

God has different names in the Bible because no name can contain God. The meaning of men's names is explained in the Bible. In secular literature names are carefully chosen because the name is usually the first clue to the character of the person you are creating. As stories develop and characters grow and change, their names often have to be changed. When you get the name right, that's how you and the reader remember the character. How many people have forgotten the name of Goliath or Scarlett O'Hara? People who have never read *Moby Dick* remember the first line, "Call me Ishmael."

In my first novel, *North to Yesterday,* I created an evil slave-owner named James Laurie, Mr. Jim. Jean proofread the book twice; my mentor and colleague Eugene Mckinney read it at least twice. Treysa, his wife, also read it. None of us noticed that "James" and "Laurie" were also the first and last names of the president of Trinity University where Eugene and I taught—until another colleague stopped me on the campus to say she thought it was brave of me to name a slave owner after the president.

Dr. Laurie was the finest president I ever worked with, and "with" is the word he would have used. From the president to the groundkeepers and janitors we were all working for the good of the university. He and his delightful wife came to our parties, the only president to do so. Once I had to clean her shoe of horse dung she had stepped into in the front yard. Perhaps that's why no other president accepted our invitation.

Once, seeing that we were on the same flight, Dr. Laurie gave up his seat in first class to sit with me in last class to ask my opinion on issues facing the campus. He came to Paris to see my stage adaptation of Faulkner's *As I Lay Dying* in the Theater of Nations competition.

Dr. Laurie called me to his office to ask me about using his name, curious rather than offended. I explained that I didn't think of it as his name. I was unable then or now to explain why I thought James Laurie was a good name for a slave owner. But it was.

I also used the name of a colleague and friend for a scoundrel, the name of the daughter of another friend for a prostitute, and the name of the grandfather of a woman I knew in public school. The characters of the novel existed in a different world and their names were appropriate for that world.

Jesus is the Greek version of the Hebrew name Joshua. Joshua, a hero of the Jewish Bible, was first called Hosea (Saves) when he led the counterattack against the Amalekites (Ex. 17). His name was changed to Joshua (God Saves) when he was one of the good spies who believed the Hebrews could conquer Palestine (Num. 13, 14). If the English translators had used Joshua in the New Testament rather than Jesus, would that have made a difference to you? The unfamiliarity makes a difference, of course, but the two names don't look the same and they don't sound the same. Imagine substituting Joshua for Jesus in your favorite hymns. "Joshua fit the battle of Jericho," but "Jesus loves me this I know."

Scholars believe Jesus spoke Aramaic, and some Aramaic words such as "abba" and "mammon" have survived in the New

Testament Greek and many English translations. Greek permitted a far wider audience than Aramaic. But would it matter if the Bible quoted Jesus as saying, "Allah," the Aramaic word for God rather than "Theos," the Greek word? I think we would be less inclined to deny that Muslims worship the same God we do.

Would it matter if the scribes and translators had not changed Junia, a woman's name, into Junias, a man's name? Paul mentioned her as one of note "among the apostles." (Rom. 16: 7, KJV) The Greek text says Junia, but religious and political correctness persuaded translators to change a woman into a man to deny that a woman was an apostle with authority over men. That has made a huge difference in women's place in church for two thousand years.

What if a name is also a noun? Faith was once a popular name, as was Grace, and Noble, Pleasant for men. If it's capitalized it's a name but the earliest scriptures we have are translations copied in all caps or all lower case and were written from margin to margin with no punctuation—requiring scholars to determine where a sentence begins and where it ends. Genesis 1: 27 doesn't say that Adam and Eve were created in God's image but that male and female were. The Hebrew word for male is adam, and in Genesis I, is translated as man.

Adam doesn't become a name until Genesis 2: 19 when it is not translated but transliterated (letters from the Hebrew alphabet changed into corresponding letters from the English alphabet). We don't know why translators did that but it complicates our understanding of whether Adam was a particular person or represented all men. Eve doesn't have a name until Chapter 3: 20, leading some, like John Calvin, to believe the story of Eden is allegorical. (Using a story to represent something else, like Hebrew slaves in Egypt to depict the plight of slaves in America or the story of David and Goliath to illuminate the battle of American colonials against the British Empire.) Read the creation story translating adam as man rather than turning the noun into a name and see what difference it makes.

When Jean learned that our grandson, Colin, had an imaginary friend, she asked Colin the name of his friend. 'He doesn't have a name," Colin said. "He's imaginary."

Dad believed instead of fighting the Germans, he and the other doughboys should be in Ireland fighting the British for Irish independence. One of the reasons Dad disliked the English was because they had changed his name. Because of repression of the Irish in Ireland and America the Flynns had dropped the O' from their name. The first time we were in Ireland I ordered some packages to be shipped home. They arrived addressed to Robert O'Flynn. I preferred that.

Uncle Boyd had a name. That's all I had of him. My only memory was Mother's memory, one she told me more than once. One morning I said, "I dreamed Uncle Boyd was here last night."

"Your Uncle Boyd was here last night."

"I dreamed I saw him."

"You did see him. He got you out of bed and held you in his lap." For some reason I was Uncle Boyd's favorite, probably because I was the youngest.

"I dreamed he showed me his pistol"

"He did show you his pistol."

Mother's family said I looked like Uncle Boyd. In his photographs he looked slender, happy, a little cocky with self-love. He was the best loved member of his family. The only one who could make Grampa laugh. The only one for whom Gramma made excuses.

Human Beings Have Their Fingerprints
All Over The Bible:

The word "spirit" has several meanings. In the Bible, whenever the word "Spirit" is capitalized it means the Holy Spirit.

Lower case "spirit" may refer to man's spirit or to an evil spirit. But who decided that?

We are God's hands to feed the hungry, care for the sick, defend the defenseless, even the least of them. We are God's feet to carry hope to the world, to carry children to safety, to carry us to places of terror and temptation. We are also God's hands and God's tongue to tell the GodStory, and we are flawed in all these things. "There is a crack in Everything. That's how the light gets in" (Leonard Cohen).

Who Capitalized and Punctuated the Christian Bible?

Jesus and his disciples passed a man blind from birth and his disciples asked who sinned, this man or his parents (John 9: 1-4). A literal English translation of the story in all caps without punctuation or spacing reads:

ANDPASSINGHESAWAMANBLINDFROM
BIRTH ANDASKEDHIMHISDISCPLIESSAYIN
GRABBIWHOSINNEDTHISORHISPARENTS
THATBLINDHESHOULDBEBORNANSWER
EDJESUSNEITHERTHISSINNEDNORPARENTS
HISBUTTHATSHOULDBEMANIFESTED
THEWORKSOFGODINHIMMEITBEHOOVE
STOWORKTHEWORKSOFHIMWHOSENT
MEWHILEDAYISCOMESNIGHTWHEN
NOONEISABLETOWORK

Or with spacing and capitalization but without punctuation:

And passing he saw a man blind from birth and asked him his disciples saying rabbi who sinned this or his parents that blind he should be born answered jesus neither this sinned nor parents his but that should be manifested the works of god in him me it behooves to work the works of him who sent me while day is comes night when no one is able to work

It's possible to space and punctuate the story to say that God made the man blind from birth so that Jesus could pass by and give him sight, thus glorifying God.

It's also possible to space and punctuate the story thus: "And passing he saw a man blind from birth and asked him his disciples saying, Rabbi, who sinned this or his parents that blind he should be born? Answered Jesus, Neither this sinned nor parents his. But that should be manifested the works of God in him, me it behooves to work the works of him who sent me while day it is. Comes night when no one is able to work."

Being born blind wasn't fair. That's a complaint every child makes. I was good and something bad happened. The moral explanation is that being good is not going to prevent disease, stop a wayward car or a drunk driver or give you undamaged children. The philosophical explanation may be that east of Eden, it is not a loving, caring world. The scientific explanation will likely be in genetics, infection or something amiss in the complex procedure that conception, gestation and birth are.

The man was born blind and God was revealed through him. The story is not about him or his blindness or his parents or sin. It's about God's Kingdom. When we pray, "Thy Kingdom come, Thy will be done," we enlist as a verb in GodStory. Our success or our failure, our health or our illness is part of God's kingdom that is and is coming.

Thy Kingdom Come:

Antioch, where Jesus' followers were first called "Christian," has been destroyed many times by earthquake and fire. Yet when a tsunami struck Indonesia with enormous loss of life, some who claim to read God's intent and purposes said it was because Indonesia is the country with the largest Islamic population.

Dr. Donald J. DePaolo, a geochemist at the University of California, Berkeley said that the "geological process that caused the earthquake and the tsunami is an essential characteristic of the earth...and has something very directly to do with the fact that the earth is a habitable planet." Robert S. Detrick Jr., a geophysicist at the Woods Hole Oceanographic Institution said, "There's no question that plate tectonics rejuvenates the planet." William Broad wrote that "some experts refer to the regular blows as the planet's heartbeat" (*New York Times*, 1/11/05).

That's the scientific, and for me the theological, explanation for "natural disasters." Sodom and Gomorrah are going to suffer for it, but without "natural disasters" or "acts of God" there would be no life on earth. My childish notion of "fairness" is not big enough or bold enough to understand the One who laid the foundations of the earth (Job 38: 4).

We owe a debt to the faithful translators and scribes who prayerfully and dutifully gave us the Bibles that we have. But they were human like ourselves. That doesn't make the Bible less valuable. Without the human element putting God's revelations of the Divine on a lower shelf with brief but brilliant insights into the Majesty and Glory of the Divine we would still be worshiping rocks and rivers.

Faith and Certitude:

It wasn't until I began writing stories and understood something of how stories come into being that I began seeing what had long been hidden to me, the inside structure of the continuing story of the library that is the Bible, the way an architect sees both the covered structure of a building as well as the grand design. The structure of the Bible is more like a Russian Orthodox Church with its bows, bulges and bulbs, more

St. Basil, than Notre Dame.

My intent, and my prayer, is that I may rattle your certitude to deepen your faith. I would like to trouble your certainty that you and your church, denomination or religion know all there is to know about creation, grace, and redemption; that you have a lock on the Bible that is superior to that of anyone else; and that God can be contained in the Bible or any and all other sacred texts.

We all walk in darkness by the light of faith. Absolute certainty is one of the most dangerous things on earth. In the 20th century, absolute certainty caused the deaths of 1+ million Armenians; 12-14 million Ukrainians; 6 million Jews, Gypsies (Romany), and Jehovah's Witness; 30 million Chinese; 1-2 million Cambodians; and 1 million Rwandans. Today's suicide bombers and Muslim martyrs are certain their cause is just and are willing to die for it. For that reason I will tell you of a battle between faith and certitude.

Five Smooth Stones:

When David went to battle Goliath he took five smooth stones. Five? Why not four? Three? Wouldn't two stones show more faith in God? No. David didn't lack faith; he lacked certitude. Look over one shoulder as far as you can, then as far as you can see over the other shoulder. Somewhere beyond the horizon on one side is faith and the other certitude.

Goliath had certitude. He was absolutely certain he could kill any Israelite who faced him. Goliath insulted the Israelite soldiers every morning and every evening. His voice roared over the hills. He had a bearer carrying his shield before him, turning it from side to side to flash light on Goliath's cruel, cocksure face. Goliath waved his sword over his head and the mountains rang with cheers.

David came forth with five stones and a slingshot. If David had certitude he would have twirled his sling like a child while the high places echoed curses, jeers and ridicule. He would have held up one smooth stone, showing that was all he needed to defeat this giant. Certitude comes with pride and showmanship. Faith comes with humility.

All humans live somewhere along that continuum between faith and certitude in news, history, religion, politics, geography, science, math, whatever. Scientists and mathematicians seek certitude by continually testing their theories. Futurists have visions and dreams that cannot yet be tested and look for means to prove their belief. Some religious people require certitude. If you keep all the laws, check off all the commandments, fulfill all the requirements, then you can be certain that you will go to eternal bliss, or at least purgatory, and not the bad place.

Some people live by faith. They accept few things as certain and many things by faith. I have little confidence in news, a little more in history by reputable writers, and a great deal in the arc of human history that includes fossil, archeological, astrophysical, chemical, and biological history, with many questions, theories and things unknowable.

Leslie Weatherhead, a Methodist/Congregationalist English preacher wrote a book titled *Christian Agnostic.* I thought all Christians were agnostics in the sense that we don't know much about God, but we have faith in our knowledge of God through the life and teaching of Jesus Christ. The many things we don't know and can't understand aren't a stumbling block. That is the human condition and we try to walk by faith, not by certitude that cannot easily adjust to facts that change.

A Life of Change:

After a writing session I had taught at some conference, during the Q & A that followed, a woman asked, "Are you still married to the same woman?" I assumed she was or had been married to a writer or was considering marrying a writer. I said I had been married only once but my wife hadn't always been the same woman. Jean had come into the room in time for the question and I could tell she thought my answer was inadequate.

Jean had taught high school English and wrote biographies for young adult readers. She knew some people were terrified when they had to think through things for themselves. They wanted yes or no answers. I explained that I hadn't always been the same husband. We both had changed. Our relationship had changed. We probably wouldn't have stayed together if we had remained the two shallow, overly idealistic, scared people who had vowed to love each other as long as we both lived.

The Moral of the Story of David and Goliath:

I was trained as a United States Marine and a Southern Baptist preacher. Both taught that you defend by attacking. In Korea there were "China" Marines in the First Marine Division who had served in China before World Two, during World War II and after World War II. They spoke Mandarin and some had Chinese wives. They had identified three separate Chinese Armies in North Korea by intercepted radio messages. Actually there were four Chinese Armies in North Korea. Gen. MacArthur refused to believe it, claiming they were a few Chinese volunteers and ordered the Marines into what they knew was a trap.

Gen. Oliver Smith, C.O. of the First Marine Division, slowed movement as much as he could to maintain unit integrity without being charged with insubordination. When the Chinese sprang the trap, the U.S. 8th Army lost unit integrity and "bugged out" in the longest retreat in U.S. military history. Gen. Smith ordered the Marine regiments to linkup.

Gen. "Chesty" Puller, C.O. of the Fifth Marine Regiment, told his Marines "There are Chinese behind us, in front of us, and on both sides of us. We are surrounded. They won't get away from us this time." And the Marines attacked. Reunited they attacked toward the sea where they were picked up by the U.S. Navy. MacArthur said, "If I had another division like this First Marine Division I could win this war."

To the Marines, the moral of the story of David and Goliath is that to defend the sacred home land you attack with whatever you have, rocks or rockets, bullets, bombs or ballistic missiles.

To fundamentalists the moral is, to defend The Christian Nation you attack those who spell God's name differently, those whose names look funny, those whose hue is not pink enough, men who don't look or act like men, women who believe they have the same rights as men, Christians who don't defend Christmas, and public schools that excommunicated God permitting this apostasy.

HOLY LITERARY LICENSE

CHAPTER ONE

Reading the Bible and Going Crazy:

The Kid I Don't Remember:

When my parents asked what I wanted for my 9th birthday, I said I wanted a Bible. We had a family Bible, of course, with births, deaths, marriages recorded. My mother said I would have a Bible someday but she thought I was too young to be reading the Bible by myself. My father believed too much Bible-reading made people crazy.

I don't know that boy, or why he was adamant about a birthday Bible, but I was there and I still have the Bible. I began with Genesis and read it all the way through. And I proved that my father's opinion was correct. My Bible-reading drove him crazy. Why can't snakes still talk? Is that why their tongues are split? What does begat mean? What is a concubine? How did a rabbi cut his concubine into 12 pieces? Head and two shoulders are three. Upper legs and lower legs make seven. How did he cut her into 12 pieces? How did he mail the pieces to twelve tribes?

I could have read through the Bible faster and understood it better if the Revised Standard Version had been available. Perhaps my father would not have always left the room when I opened my Bible to read it.

When I was 13 or 14, I took a free Bible class by mail. I bought a Scofield Reference Bible as a resource. Every week I received a new lesson and a test over the last lesson. I made an A on each lesson, even the dispensations. I knew more about the Bible but I didn't believe it could be reduced to numbers and equations.

One year in high school the Bible was taught as an elective. The first semester was taught by my Baptist pastor and I loved it. The second semester was taught by a pastor who was still tangled up in Ham who saw his father Noah naked. Noah pronounced a curse on Canaan, Ham's son, that he and his children would be servants (Gen. 9: 18 to 10: 32). Noah's curse still applied to black people anywhere in the world, but especially in Chillicothe, Texas. That seemed unfair then and it does now, but Noah's curse on Ham's descendants, but not Ham, has been used for centuries to excuse bigotry and oppression of people of color.

I majored in Religion at Baylor and minored in Greek. We translated the Gospel of John. I learned a lot about the Bible at Baylor, less so in the seminary where I studied Old Testament history while translating Ephesians. But the best teacher I had for reading and understanding the Bible is the writing process.

The Bible is Written in Retrospect:

The writers and storytellers whose words are in the Bible had a reason for telling or writing those words and they used their perspective and various rhetorical devices to inform and persuade their audience.

Writing allowed me to see a bit of the insight, the intent, the methods of writers including those whose writing is in the biblical canon. The first thing writing taught me was the shortcomings of language. There are not enough words.

Recently there was a story about scientists who had discovered an object in space that they couldn't describe because they didn't have anything to compare it with. "The theorists have a lot of work to do now," a scientist said. I liked the story because it reminded me of the task of the Gospel writers. If you can't describe a strange object in space, how do you describe God?

The Problem of Language:

The Gospel writers had to tell of an event unique in history with words that were not singular but ordinary. Think of the birth of your own child. Didn't you think he/she was unique? And he or she was. Had there ever been anyone like your child? No. How did you explain that to others? You couldn't without the template of a noble child born in ordinary circumstances: welcomed with gifts from people who recognized the child's worth, raised among those who did not acknowledge the child's magnificence. Nevertheless, your child would ride into town with flags waving, people cheering, and bands trying to be heard over the hosannas. And then the cross. Like Mary you worried about your child's uniqueness and what it would cost him or her. You harbored those thoughts in your heart.

There had never been anyone like Jesus. How could writers tell of his birth in a unique way? They couldn't. The universal longing to touch the eternal had already created the story, a story that required transfiguration. Jesus was of royal blood, like Cinderella or Siddhartha, but born into low estate like Muhammad. He stood apart from others, like Saul or Samson or David. Rather than going mad like Saul because his own disowned him, finding redemption in self-destruction like Samson, or planting the seed that would undermine all that he had created like David, Jesus triumphed over death and created a new foundation for a new life.

I marvel at the gospel writers who were writing about what they believed was a time like no other time when the sublime walked among them, talked to them, ate with them, yet was beyond anything they could understand. No matter how much inspiration and insight into holy matters God gives you, you can only express it in the ordinary limited language that you and your audience understand.

Duality in the Bible:

You can't clearly express a thought that you don't clearly hold. I believe that's why there are two stories of creation, two stories of destruction and two stories of the birth of Jesus. Even today with all our miraculous instruments, including a telescope in space, we don't have a solid grip on creation. "Space seethes with an enormous enigmatic energy, and, each second, trillions of cubic light-years more of it materializes from nothingness" (Bob Berman, *Astronomy*, November 2007).

You have more knowledge of science than the writers of Genesis. Would you like to explain Berman's statement? I believe Berman is right and that the "enigmatic energy" is the God of creation still creating—but I can't get a grasp on light-years or nothingness. Where does nothingness come from? According to my little understanding of Einstein's theory of relativity and less understanding of quantum physics and even less understanding of antimatter, the Big Bang theory should have produced equal amounts of matter and antimatter that would have crossed each other out. The Big Bang would have been a hollow pop creating nothing. "Recently the Fermilab's particle accelerator discovered that the collisions of protons and antiprotons produced pairs of muons that were about 1 percent more muons than anti-muons." (Taubes, G., "Theorists nix distant antimatter galaxies," *Science*, 278:226, 1997: Hellemans, A., "Putting antimatter on the scales," *Science*, 280:1526, 1998: Antia, M., "Ready to takeoff, antimatter experiment takes some flak," *Science*, 280:1339, 1998: Cohen, A.G., De Rújula, A., and Glashow, S.L., "A matter-antimatter universe?," *The Astrophysical Journal*, 495:539–549, 1998)

I don't understand muons that exist for a fraction of a second before decaying, but to nonscientific me that's the work of the Creator God in a far more sophisticated way than I can manage, and so I marvel at the inspiration of the writer of Genesis One. You have more knowledge of science than the writers of Genesis.

Would you like to explain creation as God (Job 38:4) challenged Job to do?

I marvel equally as much at the inspiration of the Gospel writers. The Redeemer God returned to creation not as a Super Human, like the God of the second creation story, but as a helpless baby. How do you write that? Mark didn't. John wrote about the Word or the story rather than the nativity. Matthew recorded the facts as he believed them. Luke was more concerned with the story than with the details. Some scholars have noted that Luke and Acts were written like a novel with a beginning, a major character who fails, and an end where the followers of the one who failed persevere to save the world. That's the same plot as the film "Viva Zapata" and dozens of other hero tales.

If I could, I would want to write the Nativity story the way Luke wrote it, knowing that was also the way others wrote about the birth of their gods. The Hindu god Vishnu descended into the womb of Devaki and was reborn as her son, Krishna. Buddha chose who his mother would be. He entered her womb from the side in the shape of an elephant.

The Koran contains several miraculous births including that of Jesus. Sufism states that the poet Kabir was born of a virgin widow who was a Hindu. The Egyptian god Horus was created by parthenogenesis, asexual reproduction in which embryos occur without fertilization. The word comes from two Greek words, partheno "virgin" and genesis meaning "birth."

Greek and Roman mythology tell of many gods born of a god and a woman including Perseus, Ion, Romulus, Asclepius, Helen and Leda. Alexander the Great and Caesar Augustus claimed to be born of god and woman. How many ways can you write about a unique birth when unique has no good synonyms but only descriptions such as "the only one." And *unique* permits no modifiers. But my intent would be the same as Luke's.

Luke is generally believed to be a gentile writing to gentile Christians, many of whom are likely to have known of Greek and

Roman myths. But Luke's nativity story is not informed by Greek and Roman myths but by Jewish writings (The Old Testament) and Jewish traditions, as John Shelby Spong has pointed out. *(The Birth of Jesus)* Regardless of the intended audience, Jews would understand Luke's story and Bible scholars would revel in it, but that would not detract gentiles.

How would you describe the resurrected Jesus walking among his followers, and then leaving this world? It would depend on your intent, what you wanted the story to say and how to say it in the simple language of people who fished, farmed, and herded animals, many of whom couldn't read and didn't know the words used in the royal courts. The Gospel writers' first audience believed the world was flat, heaven was above and hell was below. Wouldn't you write that Jesus ascended into heaven, although John Shelby Spong has pointed out that if Jesus ascended at the speed of light he would not yet have escaped our galaxy?

The first audience knew there were three dimensions. It wasn't until the 20th century that Einstein pointed out that there was a fourth dimension: space/time. Now physicists believe there are 14 dimensions. That's further than my imagination can stretch although I know that some creatures see or hear dimensions that most humans don't. Scientists with powerful instruments see and hear things of which most of us have little understanding. They also declare the existence of things they can't see because those things have to exist in order for our understanding of the universe to work. Is their existence real? For example, dark matter must exist in order for Newton's theory of gravity to work. Scientists rarely, if ever, speak of "final theories." Scientists walk by faith, and so do we. Scientists also recalibrate.

Figurative Language:

Writing taught me the value of figurative language. Literal language means understanding a word in its simplest sense and it has its purposes. Laws, rules and punishments are written to be read literally so there is no misunderstanding of the meaning. It's difficult to misunderstand "Hang by the neck until dead." "Until dead" had to be added later because some condemned were hanged but didn't die and had to be released.

In 2013, I was on a research trip in Cuba. Every morning, bleary-eyed, I went through the breakfast buffet line in the Havana hotel making my selections from the items that never varied. I was familiar with the offerings and didn't realize until the third or fourth day that the name of each item was printed in Spanish below the item. I was startled to see perro caliente. Hot dogs had been there every morning, and I had eaten dog in Southeast Asia but reading the literal meaning in Spanish was a shock.

Words have power. When you view food suspiciously, not only as to taste but as possibly hazardous to your stomach's mental attitude, then the words have an added impact. When learning a language, the most basic meaning is the one you learn first. Later, you understand that "hot dog" means tubular sausage or maybe an athlete showing off.

But language is not big enough or broad enough to describe God or spiritual experience literally. That's why your conversion experience may seem unique to you—but when others speak or write of their own, it sounds very similar.

Most of the important ideas in the Bible are stated as metaphors. "The Lord is my shepherd" is not literally true unless you grow wool and slept last night in a pasture. If you have ever worked sheep you know that "sheep-like" may be true but it is not a compliment. Figurative or extended meaning of a word is often the most difficult to understand.

God is described as a rock, a light, the word, refuge, fortress, dwelling place. There were times and places where a rock was literally worshiped as a god. Was that the intention of the writer? I think not. He meant that God was like a rock. But how is God like a rock? You can easily start an argument over that. God is immovable like a great rock. God is like a rock that you can throw to destroy your enemies, the way David destroyed Goliath.

The richest scriptures and those with the most depth are figurative. A house built on sand cannot stand. A city on a hill cannot be hidden. Literally, that's something that a child can understand. Why would such ordinary thoughts be in a sacred text? They wouldn't. It's the extended meaning beyond the literal that is valuable.

If you're inclined to prefer literal interpretations of the Bible, read Hebrews 7: 9-10. Levi existed in the loins of his great-grand-father. Is that where fundamentalists believe life begins? Not since Nicodemus has there been such a literalist.

"Men love darkness rather than light because their deeds are evil," extends beyond purse-snatching and mugging. "The Lord is my lamp. Thou will light my candle: the Lord my God will enlighten my darkness." Literally, it would be better to carry a flashlight. Don't demean figurative language. There is no other way to describe God except as a Super Human.

Intent:

I don't recommend reading the Bible from the beginning to the end, especially for children. I don't remember how long it took me to read the Bible my parents gave me when I was nine. I do know that much of what I was reading was just words because I didn't understand the text, the historical and cultural context, or the intent of the writer.

The writers of the Jewish Bible attempted to explain a people who were no people until God remembered His covenant with Abraham, Isaac, and Jacob (Ex. 2: 24). Did God have a senior moment? Was the Almighty still resting on the sixth day? No. It must have seemed a long time to generations of Hebrews but Moses may not have been the first called to lead the Hebrews.

He was the first to do so. Perhaps God waited until the Hebrews became numerous enough with leaders wise enough to escape Egypt, survive the desert and conquer the land the Lord had "given" them.

How did a Benjamite child living in Babylon learn what it meant to be a Benjamite? Several years ago, Susan Russell Marcus, a group of children, and I worked on a research project that resulted in a book of oral histories titled *When I was Just Your Age*. The children asked the subjects questions such as, "What was your birthday like when you were my age? When you were my age, who did you want to be like when you were grown?

One of the projects was to interview members of the Kickapoo Traditional Tribe of Texas, the Native American tribe that has most successfully resisted acculturation. They have dual U.S. and Mexican citizenship with a reservation in Mexico. In Texas they lived in traditional wickiups under the bridge from Eagle Pass, Texas, to Piedras Negras, Mexico. They worked as migrant laborers often in the Great Lakes region that was their original home. The Kickapoos had kept moving to avoid assimilation with other tribes and especially Europeans.

The grandmothers and grandfathers, as the elders are called, spoke Kickapoo with a smattering of Spanish. The mature field workers spoke mostly Spanish with a smattering of Kickapoo. The children attended English-language schools in Texas or traveling with their migrant worker parents in northern states, and Spanish-language schools in Mexico. The children were fluent in both.

To interview them we had to speak to the children who would translate our words into Spanish for their parents who translated Spanish into Kickapoo. It was a difficult interview. In light of their different languages, different dress, different customs in Mexico, Texas, and the places they worked as migrants, how did they hold on to their tribal ways and avoid assimilation?

"How did children learn what it meant to be a Kickapoo girl or boy?" "From the stories the grandmothers and grandfathers tell us," they said. "Tell us the stories," we pled.

"No," they said. "If you know the stories you will be Kickapoo too."

They were right. Reading the stories of Tolstoy, Chekhov, Dostoyevsky makes us a bit Russian. The stories of Gabriel García Márquez, Tomás Rivera, Isabel Allende, Jorge Luis Borges make us a bit Latino. The stories of Chaim Potok, Isaac Bashevis Singer, Franz Kafka make us a bit Jewish.

The stories of the tribes that worshiped the one true God, the stories of Abraham, Isaac and Jacob, of the Exodus, being led to a holy land that was theirs by conquest, but also by covenant or contract with obligations on both sides; stories of the judges, the kings, captivity in Babylon, the return to Jerusalem, the rebuilding of the wall for national security, rebuilding the Temple and ethnic cleansing still teach Jews what it means to be Jewish.

There were hero tales of Gideon, Samson, Saul, David, Deborah, Jael, Rahab the prostitute and Ruth the Moabite. And cautionary tales of Uzzah who was struck dead for touching the Ark of the Covenant to keep it from tipping, of ten cowardly spies who saw only fear in the promised land, Samson, Saul, David, Solomon, who became the Pharaoh of Israel, Achan, a soldier who took souvenirs in the battle of Jericho and was stoned to death along with his children and animals. Their bodies were burned so there would be no trace of them in the Promised Land. All that remains are their stories.

Michal, who accused David her husband for dancing naked before the Ark in the presence of the serving girls, became barren. Jezebel who worshiped a fertility god and tried to kill the prophet Elijah,was eaten by dogs. Delilah who made Samson weak and Eve who caused Adam to sin were among the warning stories for women.

Forty-two children were killed by two she-bears for taunting a prophet, calling him "old bald head." No, they weren't killed for telling the truth but for disrespecting a prophet. Was it appropriate?

It's a cautionary tale. Maybe the cries of the children provoked the bears.

The stories of Daniel, Shadrach, Meshach and Abednego were the definition of a Jewish child.

The primary warning was the story of King Ahab and Queen Jezebel who turned Israel from the worship of Yahweh to worship of the fertility gods Baal and Asherah (1 Kings 16: 31-33). Jezebel encouraged Ahab to build a temple to Baal at his capital, Samaria, and to erect a phallic Asherah pole. That drove the prophet Elijah to madness.

Believing the sexual union of Baal and Asherah produced fertility, followers practiced ritual sex as a kind of prayer to encourage the fertility gods to produce bumper crops. Asherah was worshipped near trees and Asherah poles (Deut. 12: 2,3; 2 Kings 16: 2-4; 17: 10). Both male and female prostitutes were employed (I Kings 14: 23-24, 15: 12, Hosea 4: 14.) However, money earned as a male or female shrine prostitute could not be used to repay a vow to Yahweh (Deut 23: 18). That was worse than adultery; it was idolatry.

When Tamar, in the lineage of Jesus, posed as a prostitute to seduce Judah, her father-in-law, she was mistaken for a temple prostitute or priestess (Gen. 38). The marriage of Ruth, a Moabite, to Boaz and the birth of their son, Obed the father of Jesse, the father of David was accepted in the same way as Tamar and Judah's son (Ruth 4: 7-22).

The writers of the Jewish Bible had to explain how their genocide was different from that of other tribes and nations, why the first born of the father had the birthright (Deut. 21: 17) but that they were the people of Abraham, Isaac and Jacob. In addition to stories as explanation and example, the writers wrote history, records, laws, rules, customs, religious sacrifices, dietary restrictions, virginity testing, circumcision as tribal marking, and the uses and restrictions regarding property that defined the tribes that were to become a nation. Much of this did not apply to gentiles, including gentile Christians.

The Christian Bible attempted to define what "Christian" meant by defining who Jesus was with stories of his birth, his discovery of his call to messiahship in the Temple when he was twelve, his acceptance of his call when he was baptized by John, his anguish in the desert as he attempted to understand how he was to accomplish his mission, his acts of feeding the hungry and caring for the sick, his dining with outcasts, preaching deliverance to the poor, setting his face toward Jerusalem when he knew what the outcome was likely to be, praying that another way could be found, facing his betrayer, his accuser, his denier. Praying that they would be forgiven for what they did. Dying naked and forsaken. Rising from the grave and revealing himself to those who had believed in him.

What does it mean to be a Christian? Do these things in remembrance of him.

My parents taught me what it meant to be a member of their family. My mother's ideal was outlined with Thou Shalt Not. My father told stories, many from newspapers, some personal. Some boys derailed a train for the excitement of it. Two people were killed and the newspaper or Dad speculated their last seat would be in an electric chair. I had imagined the thrill of seeing a train derail but had mentioned it to no one. How did Dad know?

Two boys plotted to rob someone. A younger boy, perhaps a brother, tagged along. A car stopped to offer them a ride and one of the older boys sat beside the driver and the other sat behind the driver. When they reached a place where no houses were visible, the one behind the driver grabbed him by the throat and the one beside him grabbed the steering wheel. The driver was killed. The two older boys would be executed, Dad or the paper speculated, but the younger boy who had no part in the crime might spend the rest of his life in the penitentiary because he did nothing to stop them. I would likely have done what the younger boy did. How did Dad know?

Dad had seen a wounded German soldier beg for mercy. Dad also told me of the cruelest thing he had ever seen. A boy his age had cut a live turtle out of its shell. I have never forgotten the mental picture of that turtle awkwardly struggling against the pain and indignity. I don't remember whether he told me that story before or after the possums.

Possums were more than a nuisance on a farm during the Depression. They were a danger to livelihood as they ate eggs, baby chicks, hens, meat we had hanging in the barn, vegetables in the garden on which we depended for food. Dad had killed a possum and it had babies riding on its back. Mother told me to kill the possums. It wasn't a pleasant task but I decided to make it educational. I would find different ways to execute them. I drowned one by holding it under water. I beheaded one. I was hanging one by the neck when Mother came around the corner of the barn and told me to stop playing with the possums and kill them. I bludgeoned the rest of them to death.

Neither Mom nor Dad ever mentioned the execution of the possums to me but in my mind there was a connection between the possums, the squirming of the turtle and the wounded German. I was the tender-hearted one of the family, the one who cried when our pets died, the one who tried to save a turtle with a broken shell that allowed screwworm flies to lay their larvae that ate live flesh inside the shell. I cleaned out the larvae and closed the broken shell with tractor grease. I never found the shell so I believed the terrapin lived and I still do.

I was one who cried when Dad let me drive the car to the highway to get the mail and I knocked down a wooden frame holding five mail boxes. Mother scolded me but Dad said he would repair the frame and he did.

However, there were Dad's last words.

My grandfather was murdered in 1896 when my father was eight-years-old. Grandfather, Grandmother and 13 other Flynns came to Texas to build the Fort Worth and Denver Railroad. My father was born in 1887 at a railhead called Chillicothe. A year later Grandfather homesteaded a section of land in Wilbarger County that still belongs to the Flynn family. Dad supposed that Grandfather quit the Fort Worth and Denver to farm and during a hard year needed cash. The only railroad job he could get was with the Sherman, Shreveport and Southern. Grandfather had taken the train to Fort Worth to see his brother and on the way back missed the train from Greenville to Campbell.

It was a few miles and as Grandfather walked down the track toward Campbell a young man joined him. When they reached a wooded area where a creek ran under the railroad, the young man stepped back and shot grandfather in the head and robbed him. Years later I walked down the track to the place where Grandfather died. It was still a lonely and secluded place.

Jean and I read newspaper accounts of the murder and trial and visited the small town where the oldest buildings had two fronts. One faced the railroad and when a highway was built parallel to the railroad, the backs of the stores were knocked out and new fronts were built to face the highway. A two-story frame house that had once been a room-and-board house for Grandfather and other railroaders still stood.

We were guided to an old man who remembered that Grandfather was a big man like my Uncle Bill and was known for lifting something heavy. The old man couldn't remember whether it was a rail, a crosstie, or a keg of railroad spikes. He also remembered his father had sent a hired hand with a wagon and mules to Greenville to pick up something. There were no roads and the hired hand followed the wagon tracks that paralleled the railroad tracks and found my grandfather's body. It caused great excitement in Campbell as everyone wanted to hear the story.

The murderer named Cook was found in a saloon and had Grandfather's railroad watch in his pocket. He was found guilty but wasn't hanged because his family swore he was 16 years old. Dad and his brothers said the family lied. After some years one of the Texas governors who sold pardons for campaign funds pardoned Cook. Dad's early life had been hard as he, his two brothers and their mother who had been a school teacher worked, worried and prayed as they hung on to the land. Dad kept track of the man through the years and swore he would kill him if he saw him.

Would Dad have done it? When I was too young to remember it, Dad was awakened by the rattling of the double doors to the truck barn. He was sure he had latched the doors so they didn't rattle in the wind. He took his six-shooter, slipped out of the house, slipped through the gate to the fence around the house and slipped into the barn. The truck was jacked up and a tire was loose where someone had tried to steal it. A man ran toward a side door and Dad shot at him. He returned to the house, got the lantern and went back to the barn where he found blood on the ground and the barn wall. Dad spent the rest of the night looking for the man, afraid he might bleed to death in a fallow field. I thought it was the bravest thing I had ever heard of. If the wounded man was armed and angry or scared he had a lighted target to shoot at.

Dad's last words to me were, "Put your arm around me." When I did, he died. Dad's last words to Jean were, "Don't tell Bob where Cook is." I was astounded by Dad's words. I asked Jean to repeat them when I had doubts about myself and they were always the same. Did Dad see something in me that made him fear I might for love of him fulfill his mission by killing an old man I didn't know? I had carelessly thought of how I would have done it, present myself suddenly, tell him who I was and why I was there. I never pictured myself doing it.

I don't know whether it was Grandfather or Uncle Boyd or something else but I had a "premonition" that I would die by gunshot. It lasted from childhood until I went to Vietnam.

Audience:

The audience to whom you are writing deserves some consideration. You want the reader to stretch a bit to understand but not so much the audience gives up in frustration. Have you recently read Numbers Chapter 5 or 1 Chronicles 1-4, with all its begats? Record-keeping is important to Bible scholars, cultural historians and many Jews, but unlikely to entertain or educate most Christians. That's also true of the dimensions of the temple. The dimensions of Noah's ark have provided believers with centuries of arguments with much entertainment but little insight.

It is equally true of the language of Revelation, another biblical book that you may not have read recently. You can make the symbols mean many things, especially if you pretend the book was not written to be meaningful to its first audience but was intended for you and your time in history. When I read my astrological predictions it's always when the prediction is out of date. That's so I can watch myself shape yesterday's, last month's or last year's prediction to fit, fully aware that one-twelfth of the world's population were supposed to have the same kind of day or year that I did. Why then do I read such foretelling when it's no longer foretelling? Because some days that's the only good news in the newspaper. Except for the ads that promise wonders of various dimensions depending on the cost.

I can read Revelation and parts of Ezekiel and some other books the same way I read my astrological forecast trying to fit recent personal or international events to a prophecy written for others. But I don't. Parts of those scriptures are applicable to me and to my time on earth, but only in the huge context of God's relationship to the Divine creation. Symbols grow out of the theme of the book and sometimes the audience sees symbols that the writer does not. Read Freudian interpretations of common fairy tales and see what you missed.

Writers and thoughtful readers have to differentiate between the factual and the truthful, between literal language and figurative language, between writing styles such as historical, political, imaginative, symbolic, poetic, ironic, sarcastic, etc. The most important thing is not to lose the intent of the writer, not to lose the story in arguments over individual words.

A Christian, a Muslim and a Jew met every day to pray for peace in the land that is holy to all three. For weeks, months, years they prayed until one day in despair and desperation they cried out, "Will there ever be peace in the Holy Land?"

"Yes," responded a loud voice from above. "But not in my lifetime."

If you think that's a joke, you missed the point. God is the problem in the Holy Land. Does that require the death of God? No. It requires that three religions give up their exclusive right to the Almighty, their claim that God loves them and their land more than the others.

When you recite the Lord's Prayer, who is the "our" in "Our father who is in heaven?"

CHAPTER TWO:

Absolutes and Never Minds

To fully enjoy the depth of the Bible we must differentiate between fact and truth.

I taught creative writing for many years. In those classes I told students that fiction was changing the facts to tell the truth. You would have to read a lot of Russian history to see Czarist Russia as clearly as you can by reading Tolstoy, Dostoevsky, Gogol or Chekhov. The same is true of Faulkner and the South between the World Wars.

Many years ago I read of an explorer who took a film projector and screen to a tribe that had never seen photographs, much less a film. He showed them an American movie. Afterwards they couldn't tell him the plot or the point of the story. They wanted to know what happened to people who walked off the screen. Where did they go? Sometimes a whole city appeared looking very solid and then changed into a small room. What happened to the city?

That's the way some of us read the Bible. We become so concerned with the incidentals that we miss the truth. We debate what kind of fish swallowed Jonah and miss the point of the parable: Your enemies are not God's enemies. God wants to save them, not destroy them. Could that also be the reason that God did not destroy Nazi Germany to save the Jews, Gypsies and Jehovah's Witness? Or destroy the Soviet Union to save Russian and German Christians? Or destroy the Confederacy to free African Americans from slavery?

Facts:

"I think that only daring speculation can lead us further and not accumulation of facts." —Albert Einstein

"Facts are constituted by older ideologies, and a clash between facts and theories may be proof of progress." —Paul Karl Feyerabend

"Death and vulgarity are the only two facts in the nineteenth century that one cannot explain away." —Oscar Wilde

Fact or Fiction:

Facts are such slender things, hard but pliable, absorbing colors, giving back refracted darkness or light, lingering long after most of the relevance has been bled away by more immediate facts. Yes, I know that scientifically darkness can't be refracted, but it can be mirrored. We are talking about fact and fiction and mirrored isn't the right image.

We cling to facts because we want something solid to hang on to. But facts change. The fact that eggs are bad for you forced many egg farmers out of business but now the fact is that eggs are good for you. Coffee is bad for you; coffee is good for you. Leeches are again used in medical practice. "Columbus" is not the right answer to, "Who discovered America?"

Darwin's theory of evolution challenged the idea that humans descended from a single couple such as Adam and Eve but some scientists are inclining back to an original couple.

Einstein proved the shortest distance between two points is a curved line. That's not what I learned in high school. When I was in school there were twenty plus elements in the periodic table. The last time I checked there were almost 300. The only time I ate fish on Friday was when I was in the Marines. No one does that anymore and today's rations contain shrimp, that Jews can't eat, and tuna that they can. Pluto was a planet, was not a planet, is now a small planet. Facts that appear in newspaper and especially TV reports are not the same as the facts that appear in history books. And the greater the distance in time between the reporting of the facts, the more unreported facts come to bear on the meaning of the reported facts.

It's a fact that if you step off a tall building you are going to go kersplat. Most of the time. Every few years there is a story in newspapers about someone who did that but was saved by an awning, a sign, a truck loaded with mattresses that broke the fall. The explanation for the fall is Newton's "theory of gravity." There are scientists who are reexamining Newton's theory because they believe that while gravity works, Newton's theory of how it works is wrong. Today's fact is yesterday's magic and tomorrow's joke.

A scientist said, if it can't be disproved it's not science. Meaning that the same process by which a scientific theory is proved can be used to disprove it. That's why the means of proving a new theory is replicated around the world to see if it is consistently proved. One failure means the theory is wrong at least in part. That's also why I find attempts to prove that God exists silly. The Bible says God is unsearchable (Ps. 145: 3). That doesn't mean God can't be found; it means that God can't be researched. You can't put God under a microscope or examine God with a telescope in space.

Facts change, facts are reinterpreted, factual truth can't rise above known facts, limiting imagination, creativity, insight. Fact tends to be restricted to local life and time, the four corners of the earth. No biblical prophet could have written, "God is my copilot" or poet have sung:

> Life is like a mountain railway
> With an engineer that's brave
> We must make this run successful
> From the cradle to the grave
> Heed the curves and watch the tunnels
> Never falter, never fail
> Keep your hands upon the throttle
> And your eye upon the rail

No one listening to the poet could have understood what he said. There are still places in the world where those words would not be understood. Like song lyrics, facts are so slippery that post-modernists invented the literary construction "true facts."

Confronting Truth:

Here's a scary thought. Not only do "facts" change, there is more than one kind of truth.

When I enrolled in Baylor I was confronted with, "What do you know and how do you know that you know it?" by a freshman wannabe philosophy major who had attended the first day of class. I was a 17-year-old high school graduate and I knew almost everything I needed to know. I went to college to get my facts reinforced.

I smarted off that I knew 1+1=2, expecting a laugh. A sick sophomore math major said that was true only in a base 10 system. In a base 2 system, 1+1=3. In a base 12 system ... that was something I didn't need to know. If a base 10 system was good enough for Moses it was good enough for me.

I knew that you had to be "born again." It was probably a religion major who asked if I thought that was literally true. Well, no, I knew that was a metaphor but Jesus used it so it was a metaphor that was okay.

I knew that God is love. Had I suffered much? That kind of superiority belonged only to a G.I. Bill military veteran who should have been home with his wife and kids. We were a Christian family who behaved well so we really hadn't suffered. The eligible male members of my family served in the war but they all came home except one cousin's husband who had received a posthumous Silver Star. Another came home from the war but died soon afterward.

I had never worried about food security during the Depression. I was born on my father's farm. In addition to row crops like cotton, corn, wheat, and sugarcane, we had two gardens, one of them irrigated. My mother canned vegetables that we would eat during the winter. We also had chickens, cows, pigs, and for a time sheep. We slaughtered our own chickens and pigs and sent calves to the butcher. We could pay with wheat to have our wheat turned into flour, and with corn to have corn turned into cornmeal. We sent wool to Fort Worth and it was returned to us in blankets. I still have one of the blankets. We sold or bartered eggs, butter and, in a good year, black eyed peas, but cotton was our money crop and we needed little cash.

I had attended a two-room school with children who had no breakfast, brought no lunch and were willing to suffer a switching to steal someone else's lunch and eat whatever it was. That wasn't hunger, that was theft, and had to be punished. The lower four grades had a flip chart with maps of the U.S. and Texas and one of a human with the body cavity exposed in garish colors so that we could learn the location of organs. I hated when it was displayed at the front of the room because my perverse eyes kept looking at it and my stomach saw it and recoiled. When lunch break came and we marched by rows to the cloak room to retrieve our lunches one boy would go to the chart and kiss the organs hoping it would make me so sick he could have my lunch. Sometimes it worked but I never thought of those who had no lunch as suffering or thought of sharing my food.

That's the way things were—until I came home from the Marines and the first night met Jean who was a friend of my sister and would a year later, in 1953, become my wife. Jean would be a rising senior in the fall, the first in her family to get that far. Her father had been a sharecropper and food security required every member of the family to work. Jean and her siblings had to skip school when work was available for their age. Mostly, they chopped cotton and pulled cotton bolls, lying down in the field when the school bus passed. Jean said she prayed it wouldn't rain because then she couldn't work and had to go to school where she was embarrassed about where she had been and what she hadn't learned. When it rained she prayed it wouldn't stop raining because then she would have to skip school and work in the field.

When Jean's father gained a job with the city water board the family made a huge step upward. Jean worked for the Middle School principal before and after school and as a waitress on Saturday and Sunday. She dreamed of escaping the cotton fields and marriage to a cotton farmer by learning shorthand and typing and becoming a secretary. She bought a typewriter, giving weekly payments to her father.

One day a man came and repossessed the typewriter while she sat and cried. Her father had pocketed her payments. She cried for more than the typewriter. She lost her dream of ever being the person she wanted to be.

I was more casual with money, knowing that my father would prevent someone taking something essential from me. Checks from the V.A. came to me in Waco and I mailed them to my bank in Vernon. Sometimes a weekend or holiday meant a check I wrote reached the bank before the deposit did. It wasn't a problem. Deposit the check again and the money was there.

The first week we were married my $9 check for our first groceries bounced. Jean was very upset about it. Before the job in Vernon her father had written a check with insufficient funds to pay for it and spent a few days in jail while the children dropped out of school to earn money to pay for it. When they returned to school, the other children asked, "What kinds of birds are there?" And answered their own question: "There's blackbirds, there's red birds and there's jail birds."

The first week we were married happily (to be read both ways, happily married and happily Jean took over) Jean took over everything that had numbers, especially those in proximity to dollar signs.

Jean taught me the hard work and the hard life of the poor, those Jesus called the "least of these." I had also pulled bolls for a penny a pound and chopped cotton ten hours a day, 50 cents an hour, five dollars a day. I wasn't helping feed my family, I was earning money for college. Although neither of my parents had finished high school we children understood that we were expected to go to college. That is a big difference.

One of those hot 100-degree days chopping cotton I calculated that $5 dollars a day for 365 days would be $1725. I could go to college without having to work outside of school. Then I remembered I wouldn't be working seven days a week but five, and some days I would be in school. I was never very good at math.

I hadn't suffered and I didn't know of anyone who had except those fighting the war overseas.

A law student, of course, asked if my beliefs were founded on my experience or was I buying my parents' pre-stressed belief system? I went in search of a more interesting bull session, one debating whether communion should be open to all Baptists or just the members of my local church.

I had left Baylor and enlisted in the Marines because I believed I could save America and Christianity (they were almost identical in my mind) by killing Communists, and for other reasons including a desire to separate my belief from that of my parents. My belief system did change with more doubt about what I really knew and more faith that I didn't need a lot of certitude. What I needed was a closer relationship with the Divine.

Kinds of Truth:

Truth is even more complicated than math systems. When told that the French peasants were rioting because there was no bread, what did Queen Marie Antoinette say? If you answered, "Let them eat cake," you would be wrong. Marie Antoinette said no such thing. That story is not factual. But is it true? I would say yes, because you would have to write a lot of words to show the ignorance and contempt of the French nobility to the plight of the poor. That's why that quotation is still popular. It's also not true that you use only 10 percent of your brain, although for some of us that might be an exaggeration.

During the 1968 Tet Offensive in Vietnam, a village was occupied by the Viet Cong and an American officer is quoted as saying, "We had to destroy the village to save it." No one has ever stepped forward to claim that remark, so I suspect it may not be factual—but it is true and in modern wars it is universally true. The cities of Stalingrad and Manilla were virtually destroyed by those defending them. The Americans declared Manilla a free city and withdrew its military to spare it. When the Americans returned, the Japanese did defend it and blew up some buildings themselves. Countless villages, towns and small cities have been wiped out by bombs and artillery shells. Palestine is a virtual history museum of villages destroyed to save them.

Transcendent truth is considered the highest kind of truth by those who believe that "truth." "The Lord is my shepherd" is transcendent truth that goes beyond the literal meaning of words and material life experience to express a universal truth using the language of the common people. I believe that it is transcendent truth but there is absolutely no way to prove it on this planet.

Absolute truth, aka dogma: Doctrines and creeds are based on facts; faith and tradition and can be argued. Dogma is true because some authority said it was true. It can't be proved, disproved or argued; it must be believed—"God is love." Sometimes that authority is yourself—"There is a God." But if dogma can say there is a God, dogma can also say there is no God.

Factual truth, aka literal truth, is based on proven facts and the exact meaning of words. Factual truth tends to be limited to a particular time and place. Spare the rod and spoil the child (Prov. 13: 24). My mother, and the two teachers in the school I attended, believed in switching the back of our legs with a small branch of a tree. It stung momentarily and convinced us that we had done wrong. Today you could be arrested for doing that.

"I have never seen the righteous forsaken nor his seed begging bread" (Psa. 37:25). I have seen that, even in the richest nation in the world. The psalmist must have lived in Solomon's court, a particular place at a particular time.

Factual truth can't adequately express spiritual truths because we don't have the language or vocabulary for it. The biblical writers had astonishing insights into God and people but tended to express it in figurative language. "Man born of woman is of few days and full of trouble. He springs up like a flower and withers away" (Job 14: 1, 2). That doesn't mean that we literally sprout or bloom or that it's your mother's fault that you wither like a flower or that a test tube baby wouldn't share the same fate.

Self-evident truth is what we believe because that's the way things appear to our limited eyesight. The earth is flat. The shortest distance between two points is a straight line. Everyone is born either a male or a female. The universe revolves around wherever I am standing. Heaven is above the earth and hell is below it. "Things that are equal to the same thing are equal to each other," Euclid said, but that is not always true with generic candies and medicines.

From a distance a straight line appears curved. That's why the pillars of the Parthenon are not of the same height so that the line appears to be straight although it is not. Jean and I rafted the Rio Grande in the Big Bend and at one point the raft seemed to be going uphill because of the layers of rock that appeared to be slipping into the river.

Sensory perception is not infallible. I was in the irrigated garden with my parents. Dad pushed a hand plow and mother planted peas. My brother and sister were in the house doing homework before it was dark. I was too young for school and probably in the way in the garden. I wore a tee shirt, short pants and was barefooted. As the sun inclined toward evening I said I was cold. My parents wanted to finish their work before it was dark and ignored me. When I whimpered, Mother told me to go to the house, but I didn't want to go to the house. I wanted to be with my parents. When the whimpering continued Dad told me to close the gate and it would be warmer. The garden was enclosed by barbed wire to keep cattle out of it but it had a wooden gate so that it was easier for Mother to open and close when she was carrying things into or out of the garden. I closed the gate and I was warm.

Anecdotal truth is what we usually mean by "witnessing." You may testify that there is a God because you have met the Deity; you have experienced divine guidance because God is in your heart. It may be true to you, it may be true to those who know you best, but it is day-to-day truth and one slip can wipe out your authority.

In 1936, the Baptist World Alliance met in Berlin where Hitler loudly proclaimed himself a Christian. Lloyd Allen, professor of church history at McAfee School of Theology, wrote of that meeting, "Most of the BWA delegates spoke out for soul liberty, the kinship of all humanity and the separation of church and state, but too many Baptist leaders did not." The *Watchman-Examiner* printed a letter by a Boston pastor who wrote, "It was a great relief to be in a country (Nazi Germany) where salacious sex literature cannot be sold; where putrid motion pictures and gangster films cannot be shown." John Sampey, president of Southern Baptist Theological Seminary, expressed gratitude to Hitler for prohibiting German women from smoking cigarettes and wearing red lipstick in public. Southern Baptist Convention President M.E. Dodd defended Hitler's persecution of the Jews, who he declared were guilty of "self-aggrandizement to the injury of the German people."

Some Christians admired Hitler for his morality. He did not smoke or drink and he abhorred pornography and homosexuality. He called his nation to repentance. Decades before Jerry Falwell, Pat Robertson and 9/11, Hitler called his nation to repentance:

"Providence withdrew its protection and our people fell...And in this hour we sink to our knees and beseech our almighty God that He may bless us, that He may give us the strength to carry on the struggle for the freedom, the future, the honor, and the peace of our people. So help us God." Hitler's family values: "And marriage cannot be an end in itself, but must serve one higher goal, the increase and preservation of the species and of the race. This alone is its meaning and its task." His faith-based charity: "With a tenth of our budget for religion, we would thus have a Church devoted to the State and of unshakable loyalty."

Hitler declared, "Today Christians...stand at the head of Germany...I pledge that I will never tie myself to parties who want to destroy Christianity. We want to fill our culture again with the Christian spirit...We want to burn out all the recent immoral developments in literature, in the theater, and in the press—in short, we want to burn out the poison of immorality which has entered into our whole life and culture as a result of liberal excess during the past..few years."

God seemed to favor Hitler and Nazism because of their rapid rise to power. "I would like to thank Providence and the Almighty for choosing me of all people to be allowed to wage this battle for Germany." "I follow the path assigned to me by Providence ... there is a God.... And this God again has blessed our efforts during the past 13 years" (February, 1940). "Hence today I believe that I am acting in accordance with the will of the Almighty Creator: by defending myself against the Jew, I am fighting for the work of the Lord."

I think Hitler may have been the person best known as a Christian in the 20th century. Millions of Christians around the world admired him. Before Pearl Harbor some German-American Bunds taught German propaganda, as did Defenders of the Christian Faith, Knights of the White Camellia, Sentinels of the Republic and the Christian Front. The America First

Committee accepted funding from Germany. On February 23, 1933, the Associated Press ran a wire story under the headline, "Hitler Aims Blow at 'Godless' Move." The article described Hitler reaching out to Catholics for support in his attack against the "spread of atheism," citing a papal encyclical admonishing priests to "serve the religious interests of the nation."

The major churches in Germany supported Hitler. In Austria priests were authorized to display the swastika. Some bishops wrote "Heil Hitler" on official letters. A parish newspaper declared "One people—one Reich—one Fuehrer—one God." Bishop Alois Hudal helped Franz Stangl, commander of Treblinka death camp, and other war criminals, including Adolf Eichmann, to escape. Hudal explained, "The Allies' War against Germany was not a crusade, but the rivalry of economic complexes for whose victory they had been fighting. This so-called business...used catchwords like democracy, race, religious liberty and Christianity as a bait for the masses. All these experiences were the reason why I felt duty bound after 1945 to devote my whole charitable work mainly to former National Socialists and Fascists, especially to so-called 'war criminals.'" That statement sounds eerily familiar today.

Hitler is the rebuttal to anecdotal truth. Jesus warned against those who called him Lord and even worked in his name but did not do God's will (Matt. 7: 21,22).

Other Kinds of Truth:

Experiential truth is what seems true because it is consistent with our experience. It is often found in fables such as "The Fox and the Grapes." There is no evidence that foxes think like human beings, but we all know what "sour grapes" means. We recognize the "truth" of the fable because it conforms to and informs our experience of what it means to be human. Truth is also found in the best fiction, drama and poetry. In 1869,

Heinrich Schliemann discovered the buried city of Troy using *The Iliad* as his guide. *The Iliad* was written in the 8th century B.C. The city, at least, was true.

Although never an activist, William Faulkner's fiction made the plight of blacks and non-blacks in the South real to people far from the South and undergirded the civil rights movement that still battles racism in America.

The Icelandic Sagas of Eric the Red and his son, Leif the Lucky, and others, are reminiscent of the hero tales of Samson and David from the Old Testament. They have been recognized as literature for centuries because of their depictions of human nature—love, family, courage, adventure but also greed, power, jealousy and revenge. Recently, scholars have discovered that much of the sagas is true but embellished to make the story more attractive and the point of the story more powerful. Eric the Red did form a settlement in Greenland and named the island Greenland to attract more settlers. Leif the Lucky did discover America centuries before Columbus and left artifacts of his visit that have been found.

I bought the traditional (small) diamond engagement and wedding rings for Jean only to discover she had always dreamed of a gold band. Some years later, because Valentine's Day was on the weekend, I gave Jean a gold band. I think it was the gift that Jean loved most, other than our children. I also gave our two daughters a Valentine present, but all we remembered was Jean's excitement. On Monday, our younger daughter's first grade teacher called Jean. Brigid had been so exuberant that the teacher asked her why she was so excited. "My parents got married," Brigid said. Brigid got the facts wrong but the story right.

Confronting the Unknown:

The car was off the road. My seat was reclined but I sat up and saw something gray coming toward me.

I was placed in an ambulance. I was unable to move my head because there was some kind of brace on it. "Did you pick up my wife?" I asked. They had. "Are you here, Jean." "I'm here." "Are you okay?" "I'm okay."

I was in a room of curtains. I could hear talking in an adjacent room. "Are you here, Jean?" "I'm here." "Are you okay?" "I'm okay." I was living scenes with no intervals or transitions.

Someone stood beside me. I couldn't see him because I couldn't turn my head but I think he was a Highway Patrolman. "What happened?" he asked. "I don't know. I was asleep." "Who was driving the car?" "I was." "Your wife said she was driving." "That's right. We changed drivers in Stephenville." "Did the car roll over?" "No." "It rolled over twice." "Did you know you were outside the car and walking around when the ambulance got there?" "No." That was strange because I woke myself one night earlier saying, "Get out of the car. Get out of the car." I had told Jean about it the next morning.

Someone stood beside me, probably a nurse. "We are going to medevac your wife to Scott White Trauma Center. Your grandson is going to pick you up and take you there by car." I think he said "airevac" but I heard medevac. Jean must have given them Colin's telephone number because I didn't know it.

There was talking in the hall. "Have you ordered a second helicopter?" "Yes, it's on its way."

Someone was beside my bed. "They medevaced your wife and a second helicopter is on the way to get you."

They placed me on the hard deck of the helicopter. A male and a female sat on a bench at my feet. The male hovered over me. I wondered where he put his feet as there was no room for anyone but me. Part of the structure pressed into my back and ribs. I tried to move but couldn't. "Can you take off the brace?" "No. Are you in pain?" My neck and shoulders hurt. It wasn't a sharp pain but a dull ache that I thought was bearable. "No." I responded. "This is the first helicopter I have been in that had doors instead of machine guns in the openings," I told him. He may not have heard as the noise of the engine and the whine of the blade winding up was deafening.

The flight seemed interminable as I repeatedly fell asleep and was awakened by the dull pain. I tried to raise my head to speak to the attendants but was unable. The male hovered over me. I wondered if he was standing on me because there was no room on the deck for feet. "I'm paying for this trip but you get the scenery. It's not fair." "That's how it is," he said. He had no sense of humor.

I was lifted from the helicopter and placed on a gurney. As they rolled me into the hospital I saw Colin at the door and knew everything would be okay.

When I woke up, Colin was beside the bed, along with others. I asked where Jean was. At the other end of the hall. I asked why we weren't in a room together. Afraid they would get the medications mixed up.

Food appeared at my bed. I don't know if I ate any. Maybe a doctor stood before me. I also stood. I asked when I would be released. "You'll have to spend one night in regular care first." Maybe a doctor stood in front of me. I don't know the length of time between those episodes or whether it was the same man. I was being released. "Why am I being released early?" I asked. "We need the bed." I thought there had been a multiple car wreck or a serious accident at nearby Fort Hood. "If you need the bed you should pay me for it," I said.

Colin and I went to see Jean. Her eyes were open but she didn't seem to see either of us. Colin took me to a motel and I fell asleep. Colin brought something for breakfast and then took me to the hospital while he searched for a motel in walking distance from the hospital. He took me to the motel, explained that I must leave the hospital through the same doors I entered, turn left, take the first right and after some distance I would see the motel. He had to go to Lampasas to retrieve the contents of the car. Colin drove me back to the hospital. I asked how the car looked. "It was totaled," he said. That was reassuring. Of all that happened, I believed that was substantial.

In Jean's room I mostly slept and when I was awake Jean wasn't. When I started back to the motel I got lost. I retraced my steps to the front of the hospital and tried again. The second time I reached my destination although I had almost turned back to the hospital before I saw the motel.

The next morning Colin and I returned to the hospital. When Jean saw me she said, "I thought the nurses lied. I thought I had killed you." "No," I said, relieved that I wasn't the driver. How could anyone bear a burden like that no matter how innocent?

"They said you were okay but they wouldn't put us in the same room," Jean said. "You didn't come see me. I thought you were mad at me because of the accident." "No." How could she even imagine that? "I could have killed both of us," she persisted. "No," I said. "You saved our lives." "I want to go home," she said. "As soon as they release you," I promised.

When my head began to clear some days later I told Colin how relieved I was to see him waiting for me at the airlift emergency door to the hospital. He said the first time he saw me I was in Intensive Care and unresponsive.

If I didn't see Colin at the door how much of what I remember is true?

CHAPTER THREE

Truth as Mythology

This chapter is not about fanciful Greek or Roman myths where immoral gods toy with human beings. I do not mean a widely held but false belief such as an "urban legend." I'm referring to a story or idea that is held to be true although we know that it is without factual basis because the myth tells the greater truth.

Scientists tell us that there are some things that are so small or so distant that no one has ever seen them but they have to exist in order for our world to work the way they believe it works. In the same way, there are some universal myths or stories that people need to know or create in order to answer universal questions, understand their own existence and give meaning to their mortality. I believe they are similar to Carl Jung's "collective unconscious." Every tribe, every nation, every family has a creation story to explain how it began, where it came from and what that means. Many family stories are similar to that of Abraham, sagas of the "old country," the ones left behind, the heroes who braved the unknown and began a new life, and what that means.

Jean left her family more than I left mine. Her mother was always welcoming to my whole family but she saw education as Jean's way of divorcing her family, speaking a different vocabulary, introducing new ideas, traveling to strange places. If Jean had not helped with the cooking, the cleaning up, and keeping the little ones happy and out of the way, her family would have accused her of putting on airs. Her mother told her, "If I hadn't been there when you were born I would believe you were someone else's child." It wasn't until the grandchildren completed high school, pursued higher education and still came home that the wound healed.

The Creation of My Family Story:

My first night home from the Marines, I found that everyone I knew was married or in school. I went to Midweek Services with Mother and my sister Bettye. That's when I met Jean. There was no enchanted evening, no bells, I don't even remember meeting her but I did. She was in a group of young people that my sister socialized with. The group, including Bettye and my mother, went for coffee together. Mother was unofficial den mother of the group. That was a source of annoyance since I had no den mother, and no young women friends most of the time I was in the Marines.

I had a few days before summer school began and nothing to do so I spent most of my days walking around the country with a rifle and a Ka-Bar on my belt. Fences were to keep livestock out or in, not to control people. In the evening I went out with Bettye and her friends.

One evening, it may have been the second or the tenth, there were more people than car seats. I gallantly sat down so that a young lady could sit on my lap. A young lady who liked me but to whom I was not attracted saw my lap as an invitation. In defense I pulled another lovely lady on my lap. That was Jean. I don't remember what the gang did. We never did much, maybe just drive around. Sometimes we took hotdogs and .22 rifles to Pease River, built a fire out of driftwood and shot rats attracted by the food. At some point that evening while sitting on my lap Jean kissed me.

Jean always said that I kissed her but it doesn't matter. From that moment we were a couple. I've seen that in the movies a hundred times and I have never believed it. But for us it wasn't just the kiss. We liked being together. When I left for summer school we promised to write. It's scary how seemingly insignificant moments change your life. Jean's family had moved to California but Jean had stayed behind to finish high school and lived with her cousin Patsy Ree, and Patsy's husband. If Jean had gone to California with her family I might never have met her.

I was at Camp Pendleton so long I helped establish a Southern Baptist Church in Oceanside. There was already a Baptist Church but they read the scriptures with a different accent. A beautiful blonde came to the church. I know, that's a lot of beautiful women I found attractive. Maybe I saw all young women as attractive. The blonde and I began seeing each other after church when I had liberty to leave the base. If I had remained in the Marines much longer I would have gone to Korea or tried to marry her, or maybe both.

I had been assigned to a replacement draft and had completed combat training. Shortly before the draft shipped out for Korea, a few of us were pulled out and given other assignments. I decided I would stow aboard the next ship with the next draft from Pendleton. I told a sergeant my plan. I had met him in the church also and we became close friends. He also thought the blonde was gorgeous but I met her first and he respected that. Sarge said I would never be able to stow aboard on my own but that he would go with me and together we could do it.

That put the plan on a different battlefield. Sarge had been in the landing at Inchon and had fought in the battle of Seoul and the Chosin Reservoir, three of the toughest battles in Marine history. How could I ask him to risk his life again after what he had been through? Once the ship left the harbor it wasn't turning around. We would go to Korea but we would go in the brig and we would both likely lose a stripe. Sarge might lose three. I had only two to lose.

I completed my active duty service, went home and met Jean.

Baylor was on the quarter system and I signed up for summer school classes at 8, 9, and 10 am. Friday, at 11a.m. I was on my way to Vernon. Al, a friend from my freshman year, had been in the Navy Reserve and we didn't know anyone at Baylor. Al had dated a girl who attended Waco High School and he thought she might be in town and might have a friend. Al had written her name and telephone number on the wall beside the telephone in the temporary, one-story army barrack that had been converted into a male dorm. The front door was locked but all the windows were open. I was taller than Al so I climbed in a window and discovered why all the windows were open. The inside had been painted, including the space where the telephone and adjacent numbers had been.

I sat in the window while we conjured up another plan. A campus cop came around the corner and ordered me out of the window. I jumped to the ground and explained why I was in the window. He didn't listen but accused us of breaking and entering, and maybe vandalism after he had examined the building. He ordered us to report of the Dean of Students.

We explained to the Dean what had happened and that Al had not been in the building at all. The Dean didn't buy any of it. Less than 24 hours after returning to classes I had 24 demerits. One more and we would be excommunicated from Baylor. The Dean also said he was writing a letter to our parents and to our pastors telling them what we had done and warning them that expulsion was likely. I didn't worry about getting one last demerit. I worried about what my parents and pastor would say. I asked if he would give us time to return home and explain what had happened. He said he would.

Al was from Dallas and had a car. It was a 500+ mile round trip to Vernon. I could take a bus from Waco to Fort Worth and then another bus from Fort Worth to Amarillo, getting off in Vernon. I could take a bus from Waco to Dallas, walk two blocks to another bus station and catch a bus to Amarillo. I could hitchhike from Waco to Fort Worth, hitchhike across Fort Worth to U.S. 287 and catch a ride to Vernon. Hitchhiking was free and faster but with uncertainties that included the weather and drivers. The bus was slower and cost money, but I could complete reading assignments and some writing assignments, and Jean would know when I would arrive.

"What have the Marines done to you?" Mother asked when I walked in the door. A lot of things, but breaking and entering wasn't one of them. A first-year law student would have put an end to the whole thing in the Dean's office. My mother insisted on taking it seriously but I refused. It was silly. It wasn't even a prank.

My pastor also asked what the Marines had done to me. I told my story and he seemed to believe it but worried what it would do to my reputation. I told Jean and she thought it was funny.

That became the pattern for the following months. I would try to get home by the time Jean got off work, maybe have lunch with her Saturday and see her after work. Most of those dates included our mothers after Jean's family returned to Vernon. We sat together in church on Sunday, ate lunch with my mother or Jean's family, then I hitchhiked back to Waco, maybe after a service at the jail. The longer we were together the more we argued. I tried to tell her my requirements for a pastor's wife. She tried to tell me who she was. She would do anything I needed her to do but I had to respect her for who she was, not who she would become with my guidance. People sometimes ask how I proposed. I didn't.

Jean and I were in Dad's pickup arguing as usual. Our friends were waiting a respectable distance away to follow us into the house which was up an outside staircase. One friend came over and said, "Why don't you two stop arguing and get married." I said I thought I had Jean talked into it but now I wasn't so sure. I pulled out the diamond ring set that I had bought and handed it to her. I don't think she said yes. I don't think she kissed me. She put the engagement ring on her finger, ran over to show it to our friends and then ran upstairs to show my mother.

We married three days after Jean graduated from high school. We spent one night in a small town named Iowa Park that had no park. The next day we loaded up our belongings and rode with a friend back to Waco and the three room cottage that had been a maid's quarters behind a large house. It was a shotgun cottage, front room, bedroom. A third room had been divided between a bathroom and a kitchen. I couldn't imagine that we would ever need more room than that. I didn't want to give Jean much space.

Ever after, Jean told new pastors that she met me in church and had resented the church ever since.

"A myth isn't true on the outside but it is true on the inside because a myth is archetypal in its content, it is true for all times and all places. A myth offers the kind of archetypal wisdom and transformational power that only a myth can provide." Carl Jung wrote that. Also: "We are so captivated by and entangled in our subjective consciousness that we have forgotten the age-old fact that God speaks chiefly through dreams and visions."

Universal questions asked by every child and that every religion and that most writers attempt to answer are: Where did I come from? Why am I like this? Why do I eat too much and drink too much and do things that I know aren't good for me? What is going to happen to me?

Religion, Folklore and Myth attempt to answer those questions.

For a long time I avoided knowing about myths for fear that a myth might have the same plot as the Gospel of Mark. Wouldn't that lessen the story of Jesus? Like others I eventually faced that fear and found faith in the story.

The American Creation Story:

Almost every nation and sometimes every tribe in a nation has a creation myth of how our tribe came into being in this particular place in which this mountain, this water source, these trees or rocks, this land was given to us by Providence and is sacred and will forever belong to us. The names of the Native American tribes were given to them by others, usually their enemies. Most Indian tribes called themselves "the people" in their own language, and that was echoed in the U.S. Constitution, "We the people of these United States..."

The American Myth:

The American myth is that the land was formless and void and Adams and Eves, tired of the divine right of Kings and Pontiffs to regulate their lives, and tempted by freedom and opportunity, crossed a body of water to find them. Under a gracious, benevolent Providence, young George Washington defeated Goliath George III and won independence. Multiple versions of Moses came down from the mountain top with a Declaration of Independence, a Constitution, a Bill of Rights.

There were years in the wilderness led by days of manifest destiny and nights of eminent domain enforced by genocide against ignorant savages who worshiped false gods. The nation split in two, with citizens of one kingdom carried into captivity by rancor, individualism, dreams of supremacy only to return to union for wars of aggression and acquisition until they became an exceptional nation above the rules and laws we require other nations to obey.

Out of that came our national motto *E pluribus unum* (From Many, One) and our Constitution, "We the People, to form a more perfect union..." who are sometimes a well-regulated militia and sometimes a well-armed mob.

Missing from that story is that, among the first European pilgrims to come to America seeking religious freedom were the French Huguenots (Calvinists), who landed in Florida, formed a colony and celebrated the first Thanksgiving. King Philip II of Spain ordered his military to "hang and burn the Lutherans." It has always been hard for Catholics, and some Protestants, to understand the differences between the Protestant denominations.

After slaughtering the Calvinists, the Spaniards began their own religious settlement open only to Catholics. Harder to understand than the differences between Christian denominations is the anger of Christians who want freedom of religion only for themselves. In Boston, the Puritans prohibited Catholic priests and executed some Quakers. The colony of Georgia was formed as a barrier against the Spanish Catholics in Florida. Fewer than twenty years before the Civil War, anti-Catholic riots in Philadelphia cost the lives of a dozen people.

Genesis One:

For a story teller, the first paragraph of a story has unlimited possibilities. The story can be set any time, even before time, and any where, including space, a land with fairies, elves, unicorns, hobbits. You can have a glass house on the sun. The Statue of Liberty can rise from a swamp in Death Valley. Squirrels can invent, jackrabbits can walk upright and armadillos can talk with a Spanish accent. A writer also faces unlimited questions. How are you going to make a house on the sun believable? Who cares if squirrels can invent? What does it mean that the Statue of Liberty is in Death Valley? How did it get there?, etc.

The first paragraph and to a lessening degree the following paragraphs establish the internal logic of a story, the laws, limits and rules that apply. If physical laws in the story are not the same as the physical laws of the earth that we know at the present, then you must inform the reader early on. Readers don't want to be told that a battle is won because, "Oh, by the way, one character can stop the sun." Once you establish the norm, whatever it is, the rest of the story must be consistent.

A rich man dies and goes to Hades and Lazarus, a beggar, dies and goes to Abraham's bosom. The rich man sees Lazarus. That's the premise. The rich man wants Lazarus to dip his finger in water and touch his tongue but there's a gulf between them (Luke 16: 19-33). That's the internal logic. That doesn't mean in heaven you can see people suffering in hell. Gloating would be a sin. If you couldn't gloat, seeing the misery of your enemies would turn heaven into hell.

"In the Beginning God:"

That's the premise. The beginning of what? Not God. Although my mind can't grasp something that has no time, no beginning and no end, that is God. It's not even the beginning of creation. It's the beginning of the story and the story begins with God. With that premise, the story has limitless possibilities. Can God stop the sun? (Josh. 10:12-14) Yes, God can but it would make a wreck of the universe the Almighty created and is creating.

Do I believe that God stopped the sun? No, I believe that the writer was telling us in prose what Deborah sang. "The stars from their courses fought against Sisera" (Judges 5:20). God was involved in the battle but the stars maintained their courses.

Rev. Garrett Vickrey, pastor of Woodland Baptist Church, San Antonio, Texas has pointed out that in the second temptation of Jesus the devil uses as a proof-text Psalm 91. "Jesus knows the Psalm. And he knows this proof-text is taken out of context. It's not specifically about the Messiah. It's about those who trust God with their lives; it's about those who are faithful to God. It's poetry. The devil quotes it as prose."

You don't read poetry and prose the same way. You don't believe it the same way either. I once quoted Wordsworth to an adult Sunday School class, "The child is father of the man," and asked if it was true. No. I asked if there was a way in which it could be true. No. I explained the meaning of the line. If that's what the poet meant he should have said that.

Craig Barnes wrote, "The pastor is the parish poet," explaining that "Poets are devoted more to truth than to reality; they are not unaware of reality, but they never accept it at face value" (*The Pastor as Minor Poet*, M. Craig Barnes).

Most poetry and song lyrics make no attempt to explain the circumstances or report the facts. That's the terrain of journalism, history and biography, and facts and conclusions are not the same in those.

Poets and songwriters attempt to reveal the truth. Deborah also sang that the usually shallow river of Kishon fought against Sisera. Or, as another prophet stated it, "The arc of the moral universe is long, but it bends towards justice." Martin Luther King, Jr.

This is God's Story:

The Bible is not the story of mankind or the story of Israel. Or the story of America. Those are subplots, maybe even footnotes. Creation was for the pleasure of God, not the pleasure of humans. That's the logic for the rest of the story. If the story had begun with creation that would put too much importance on how rather than Who. "Creation began when..." If you believe that God created everything then what does it matter how the Almighty did it? Let the scientists tell their story.

If the story had begun with the creation of human beings, that would have made it the story of mankind. "Human life began when..." People would have the self-importance that we assume. If it's our story we have the right to complain that we feel pain, grief, fear, that we are born with imperfections, that we die. If it's our story we have the right to exploit, even destroy, the rest of creation. We have the right to regress rather than progress in our knowledge of God, of our relationship with God, and our understanding of "our" universe. I know an ordained minister who wishes the Renaissance had never happened, that Darwin had never been born, that science and religion still told the same stories. When the scientists pointed out that the religionists got it wrong, the religionists punished them, sometimes with death. Today when the scientists discover that the religionists got it wrong, the religionists ignore them. That's known as progress.

If I believe that this is God's story and that God is love I can be relieved of a lot of religious anxiety. Of American anxiety. Of Dow-Jones anxiety. That may require that I pray more and pose less. And it requires a powerful lot of faith. I confess that there are days when I pray more to my computer than I do to God. If you will just let it work this time I will never do it again.

Our Earth was Not Created From Nothing:

Some translations of Genesis 1:1-3 read as though they were the description of a planet destroyed by something like a natural or nuclear catastrophe. "At the beginning of God's creating of the heavens and the earth, when the earth was wild and waste, darkness over the face of Ocean, rushing-spirit of God hovering over the face of the waters, God said: Let there be light" (Shocken Translation).

"The earth was without shape or form, it was dark over the deep sea, and God's wind swept over the waters" (Common English Bible). "The earth was completely empty. There was nothing on the earth. Darkness covered the ocean, and God's Spirit moved over the water" (Easy to Read Version). "The earth was without form and an empty waste, and darkness was upon the face of the very great deep. The Spirit of God was moving (hovering, brooding) over the face of the waters" (Amplified Bible). "The earth was a shapeless, chaotic mass, with the Spirit of God brooding over the dark vapors" (Living Bible).

We worship a divinity to whom there is no such thing as time, not even eons. The Creator also has what we would call unlimited intelligence and unimaginable creativity. It may be arrogant to believe that we are the first in creation or the only god-like objects in a universe for which we have not found limits. One scientist believes that rather than searching distant stars for life forms we should be studying the earth for ancient civilizations that existed before our own, earlier creations that were formed and then destroyed by a "mind" that had endless time in which to create, experiment and enjoy.

There is a scientific theory that the universe and everything that we and scientists know about and imagine are in a gigantic black hole. I have almost no understanding of black holes but I can imagine a black hole being what many of us think of as the "mind" of God in which our universe and our planet and our planet's time are but a tiny speck. We have to imagine God in human terms because that is all we are capable of but I think of God as a great story teller who thought or spoke the universe and every living thing into being with a mind beyond our comprehension and time beyond our creation. How many stories can God be creating in multiverses or black holes beyond our own? Maybe the tiny triumphs and tragedies that occupy our minds and consume our lives are not that important.

For me writing a novel is similar to chiseling an image out of stone with careful carving, delicate planing, skillful sanding and much hacking and chopping. When I release the story from its matrix of choices and decisions I see the mold for other stories this one might have been. God doesn't have to make those choices. I've chopped and carved on three novels at the same time, switching from one to another. Time is a human invention. God Eternal doesn't have to turn from one universe to another

The Bible tells us that we are a revised version (Gen. 6-8). There may be editions after humans destroy ourselves. C.S. Lewis wrote of other beings on other planets in his novels *Out of the Silent Planet* and *Perelandra*.

Other Stories:

The family story I knew best about Uncle Boyd was that he was picking cotton and in the adjoining field were teepee-shaped shocks of sorghum. Uncle Boyd had stashed some home-brew in one of them and, growing tired of the frequent trips to wet his throat, he put the jar of home-brew inside his shirt to hide it. Grampa was a tee-totaler who hated beer more than taxes and taxes more than Oklahoma where his older son had moved.

The jostled beer blew up cutting Uncle Boyd's stomach. Uncle Boyd concealed his sin until at the end of the day he got back to the house and Gramma saw his bloody shirt. Gramma's concern over Uncle Boyd's cuts saved him from Grampa's belt but not his words. Grampa's voice always seemed to have a sneer and his words left one naked and bloody.

How did that story measure someone who was too good to live? Someone who would walk from this world into another?

In a 2008 interview with the Vatican newspaper, Father Jose Gabriel Funes, director of the Vatican Observatory said, "In my opinion this possibility (of life on other planets) exists. Just as there is a multiplicity of creatures on earth, there can be other beings, even intelligent, created by God. This is not in contrast with our faith because we can't put limits on God's creative freedom." He further said, "some aliens could even be free from original sin," concluding "there could be (other beings) who remained in full friendship with their creator."

My first surprise upon reading the story was that after its history of problems with astronomers the Vatican has an observatory and astronomers. But the happier surprise is that the Vatican is so open to thoughts that trouble mainstream Protestants and secularists.

Another astronomer working at the Vatican Observatory told the BBC in relation to the search for Earth-like worlds by the Kepler Space telescope, "We Jesuits are actively involved in the search for Earth-like planets. The idea that there could be other intelligent creatures made by God in a relationship with God is not contrary to traditional Judeo-Christian thought. The Bible has many references to, or descriptions of, non-human intelligent beings; after all, that's what angels are. Our cousins on other planets may even have their own salvation story—including other examples of the incarnation of the second person of the Trinity. We are open to whatever the Universe has for us."

Funes thought it possible that the human race might be the "lost sheep" of the universe and that the most likely explanation for the start of the universe was the "big bang" theory that it sprang into existence from dense matter billions of years ago. "As an astronomer, I continue to believe that God is the creator of the universe and that we are not the product of something casual but children of a good father who has a project of love in mind for us," he said.

Another Vatican astronomer said, "I believe there's all kinds of weird stuff out there."

When you pray to "our Father in heaven" do you pray to a super genie hovering over your bed or is your mind filled with a Majesty that envelopes space and eternity and inhabits universes and realms you can't imagine?

And on the seventh day God rested:

Genesis One concludes, "And God saw every thing that he had made, and, behold, it was very good." You will notice that translators put the seventh day in a different chapter from the six days of creation because it is not part of the poem of creation. Chapter Two has a different author, generally called the Priestly or P writer who writes in prose and concerns himself with ceremonial rules such as resting on the Sabbath. You also see his hand in the mixed account of destruction where one writer says the animals are two by two (Gen. 6: 19) and the priestly writer writes that there are seven clean and two unclean animals (Gen. 7: 2). If there were only two clean animals, blood sacrifice would make reproduction impossible. Also, there is a contradiction. After the flood God says that everything that lives and moves will be food for humans (Gen. 9: 3).

The Sabbath was created for man not God (Mark 2: 27, 28). The God of Genesis Two is not the majestic God of Chapter One who thought the universe into existence. The God of Chapter Two is a humanoid God who is a bit lazy and creates a human to tend his garden, discovers as an afterthought that he gave mates to the beasts of the fields and the fish of the sea but not the servant he had created. This Divinity not only rests on the Sabbath, the Almighty rests during the heat of the day and goes walkabout only in the cool of the evening. He can't find the Divinely created humans and doesn't know they did wrong until they hide.

I don't believe God rested after the sixth day any more than I believe that God forgot about Noah and the ark. God remembered Noah (Gen. 8: 1). That God "remembered" his covenant (Ex. 2: 24) doesn't mean God is forgetful. God has no future. God has no past. God IS. God is always in the present tense. "God remembered" is a literary construct meaning that the time was right.

In Genesis 1, God is a creative unity with a masculine and feminine side. One of the names of God is Shekhinah, a feminine word that means "presence" as in the temple or tabernacle. It is through the Shekhinah that humans can experience the Divine. The Shekhinah is often represented as a bride or princess. Some believe the erotic phrases in the Song of Songs represent the longing of the male and female elements of the Godhead. (Jewish Virtual Library)

When God is with you, in your presence, God is female. That is the God in the first creation story, a poem. The second story of creation is a folk story, an oral tradition to explain how leopards got their spots and why men dominate women. Man is made of mud. Woman is made of bone. That is why men are so often dirty and crumble when tears are thrown at them. Women are clean, utilitarian and shine like bone. (That is a folk explanation of why men and women are the way they are.)

Why does it matter that one of the names of God is feminine? Religions that have male gods subordinate women.

The Myth of Innocence:

There appears to be a universal story of an ideal place and time, a peaceable kingdom where there were no predators, no flies and mosquitos, no grassburs, goatheads, nettles or prickly pear. Not even carrots had to die because trees bore all the fruit that anyone could eat. In the Bible that ideal is the Garden of Eden where food was plentiful delivered by the hand of God.

The story of Eden is short but it is a brilliant universal story and has had a huge impact on human thinking. The story begins when God makes man of clay and creates Eve as a secondary character. To be a story there must be a problem to be solved, an issue to be resolved, a question to be answered—a fall from the status quo triggered by the serpent, followed by the restoration of the previous norm or the triumph of a better way and happily ever after.

Theoretically, children are born "innocent," that is: without knowledge, and knowledge that is both good and evil corrupts them.

I have published two short memoirs, so I know the fragility and unreliability of memory. That is especially true if you are the only one who could know of the experience. In what I believe to be my earliest memory I was sitting in a clear piece of ground at the edge of a field outside our yard. The small clearing was surrounded by goatheads (aka puncturevine). No matter how they fall the seeds of the ground-clinging vine will have a point sticking up to puncture bicycle tires and bare feet.

A small kitten tried to come to me, stopping to bite the goatheads from its feet. When it reached the clearing, I picked it up, picked out remaining goatheads, stroked it and then put it outside the clearing. The kitten returned. I picked it up, stroked it and put it outside the clearing. I don't know how long this process was repeated but I was tormenting a creature that I loved. I knew it was wrong and I continued it.

What I believe is my earliest memory is the knowledge of good and evil. How did I know it was wrong to cause pain to another creature? Why did I feel guilt? Why did I torment a kitten and why did I stop?

Flash forward a few years to when I was in high school. A young couple in the town where I lived spent Christmas Eve drinking and quarreling. They were still at it when their son toddled into the room to see what Santa had brought him. The parents employed large grilling forks that they had used to turn the turkey to drive him away. He cried in pain and confusion but the more they tortured him the more he turned to them for comfort wanting to be hugged, to be held in their laps but consumed by their own misery they continued poking him with the forks to drive him away until he died.

That's almost a parallel to my childhood memory. They had to know it was wrong but didn't stop. One of the things that troubles me most today is that "good Americans" learned that the federal government had tortured suspected terrorists to force them to confess lies and falsely identify "other terrorists" to be tortured for the same reasons. "Good Americans" did nothing, and perhaps will tell their children that they didn't know their government had descended into depravity.

In 1989, I was in Cambodia and visited Tuol Sleng, a former high school in Phnom Penh that had been turned into a torture chamber by the Khmer Rouge. Suspects were tortured until—to stop the torture—they confessed they were enemies of the regime. But that was only the beginning. They didn't work alone; who were the others? Was their brother one of them? Their father? Their mother? In the former school was the photograph of a three-year-old girl who had been killed because a tortured parent had identified her as an enemy of the Khmer Rouge.

Don't say you wouldn't do that to your child until you have been tortured. That's why torture is depraved and unreliable. You will say or do anything to stop the torture.

Distance:

Perhaps you don't want to read any more details about cruelty to pets and children.

When writing stories there are three kinds of distance—physical, temporal and emotional. A writer decides how close she wants the reader to be to the story—beside the shepherds hearing the angels announce the birth of Jesus or at a distance observing his death on the cross? Do you prefer reading stories in which you are an observer—history and biography—or stories in which you are a participant—the Prodigal Son or the Good Samaritan?

The story of Jesus in the desert is immediate and real to me and to others who have accepted what we believe is a call or vocation but have struggled with how to accomplish that mission and have sweated long and lonely nights of doubt as to whether we have fulfilled God's purpose for us. The night before Jesus was crucified, when he questioned whether the way he saw before him was the only way, I am there.

Many artists and writers have attempted to close the emotional and temporal distance with their work. For a little while you are on a hillside in Israel with shepherds hearing the angels sing. Or the cobblestoned streets of Paris during the French Revolution.

Those whose family name is numbered in the book of Numbers likely feel some closeness to the account. I do not. I am emotionally close to Genesis One, the Psalms, to some of the visions of Isaiah, to the frustration and sorrow of Jeremiah as his people listened to false prophets and his beloved country fell into ruin. Seeing parts of the magnificent Gates of Babylon helped me imagine how the gates must have looked to Judean captives. Being physically closer made me emotionally closer.

I feel closer to the story of the rabbi whose wife is raped to death in Gibeah (Judges 19) than I do to the similar story of Sodom (Gen. 19), probably because of the implacability of the mob, the coldness of the rabbi who wants his wife to get up and pack the donkey for the trip home the next morning, and the poignancy of the wife dying with her hand on the threshold of safety. According to "Ask a Rabbi," a Jewish concubine was a wife who came without a dowry. I used "wife" because it is emotionally closer and warmer than concubine, even when they mean the same thing.

Walking the ancient streets of Jerusalem that Jesus walked closed the emotional, physical and temporal distance between me and Jesus carrying his cross. I believe that's why pilgrims go to Bethlehem, Mecca and the Tomb of Rachel. In Turkey I visited the museum of the Persian poet, Rumi, that also contained a hair from the beard of Muhammad in a glass case. Muhammad asked his followers not to do such things but Jesus asked his followers not to pray in public and to do their charity in secret.

Some Muslims kissed the glass case or put their hand on it. I put my hand on the glass case to close the emotional distance between me and Islam. I also visited the church where St. Nicholas was priest. His bones had been moved to Italy but his sarcophagus remained in his church. In America St. Nicholas is remembered as Santa Claus but he is the patron saint of Russia and Russian tourists filled the small church and crowded around the sarcophagus to kiss and touch it. I touched it to close the emotional distance between me and St. Nicholas since Santa Claus had turned cold.

Later, I saw nothing in Russia to convince me that Russians weren't Christians despite the brutality done to them and by them in World War II. Faith was suppressed by the Communist government but when the Iron Curtain came down, faith erupted faster than democracy in East Germany. Tolstoy and Dostoyevsky were two of the greatest Christian writers.

Walking distance from the church of St. Nicholas was a shopping mall and a statue of an overweight Santa Claus with the rosy cheeks of an alcoholic. Santa Claus was surrounded by American tourists hugging him, kissing his rosy cheeks and posing for photographs. That was the most offensive thing I saw in Turkey.

I washed my hands in the Ganges. Being from a semi-arid land I have long been aware of the life, power and importance of rivers. I watched a canoe race on an extinct river in the Australian outback where rivers no longer exist. The canoers carry their canoes as they race down the ancient river bed. Even in death the life of the river parties on. It's one thing to intellectually know about the Tigris and Euphrates but it's different seeing them.

The Ganges was ranked the fifth most polluted river in the world in 2007. Human garbage and animal waste is dumped in the river. Hindus burn their dead on pyres beside the Ganges and sweep the ashes into the river. Those too poor to buy wood for the burning sometimes slip unburned bodies of the dead into the river. I thought it might be irreverent or at least impolite to take pictures of the burning bodies but I was invited to stand above a pyre and take photographs of flames rising through the ribs and devouring the heart. I felt more religious than revolted by the sight. In a strange way it was like being devoured by the Spirit.

Hindus bathe themselves in the Ganges believing the Ganges is pure and purifying, ducking their whole body in the polluted water in a kind of baptism. Bathing in the Ganges is a test of faith. An old man completely immersed himself seven times. I watched two young Japanese women who were unable to get more than knee-deep in the river.

A dead cow floated in the water about thirty yards from where I washed my hands after a prayer. Did I feel cleaner? Physically no. I didn't put my hands in my pockets or touch any part of my body or clothing until we had returned to our hotel and I thoroughly washed my hands before undressing and showering. I washed my hands in the Ganges to number myself with people of faith across the ages and around the world. I am a stranger to the Hindu religion but I am not a stranger to Hindus. Namaste.

How close do you think the first folk-tellers and writers of the Garden were to the story? I think they felt very close physically, emotionally and temporally. "If you go up the river where you have been fishing or you cross that plain where your sheep feed and climb the high mountain you will see Eden. My great-grandfather once saw it." The story of Cherubim and a flaming sword guarding Eden might have been to discourage people from trying to find it.

I believe fundamentalists' attempts to date creation are to keep the story physically, emotionally and temporally close.

You may remember when your children discovered their personal nakedness and began closing doors. You may remember when you went through stages of defending your personal privacy. There were some things you told only one parent, only one family, one gender, one school, etc. Many of us have a daily fear that someone will hack into our computer, steal our identity, destroy our privacy.

It has been my untutored observation that most conversions in fundamentalist churches happen when children reach puberty and realize they have much to hide and that they need help with their new awareness and condition. Is it knowledge that makes us naked?

When the Romans outlawed Israel and destroyed Herod's Temple, Jews and Christians knew they were naked before military and political power. When Constantine declared Christianity to be the official religion of the empire, and the cross to be the sign by which they conquered, Christians knew they were naked before the temptation to subjugate and oppress others. A few years of life teaches you that you are naked to illness, disease, hunger, thirst, drought, flood, accident and injury.

When Copernicus discovered that the earth was not the center of the universe, people knew they were naked in a universe that was bigger and grander than their concept of God. With the atomic bomb, we knew we were naked to the power to destroy ourselves. When women were able to control reproduction men knew our authority over them was slipping. On 9/11, Americans discovered we were naked to our technology to enrich and empower ourselves when it was used against us.

Was There a Garden of Eden?

Members of The Church of Jesus Christ of Latter-day Saints (Mormons) believe that the Garden of Eden was located in present-day Jackson County, Missouri. I have an interest in archeology and was fascinated by what remains of Knossos in Crete where, according to myth, both Zeus was born and the intricate palace inspired the myth of the Labyrinth that was built to house the Minotaur.

Almost as fascinating were Athens and the Acropolis, the Roman theater in downtown Amman, the Roman aqueducts in Turkey as far as the eye could see in either direction, parts of the Gates of Babylon in the Archeological Museum in Istanbul, the stone city of Petra that appears as if by magic at the end of a narrow passage, the underground dwellings of Cappadocia and the churches carved into the fantastic hills of ancient ash and lava, Buddha's first seminary and the stupa marking the place of his immolation in India. I have been to Angkor Wat twice, the second time sardined with tourists from around the world, the first time just me, a dozen American veterans and scholars, and the monks because there were Khmer Rouge in the area.

I am not even an amateur archeologist. I view those scenes the same way as other tourists, sometimes with the help of guides and guidebooks. I go there to close the distance.

Even after seeing the Euphrates I have no interest in trying to visit Eden. What would you see if you discovered the Garden of Eden? There are no ruined shrines, no ancient temples, no crumbling castles, no broken statues. I'm pretty sure you wouldn't find the Tree of Life. Why would an archeologist bother to look?

Archeologist Juris Zarins believes he has found Eden. Much of the information below is from "Has the Garden of Eden been located at last?" by Dora Jane Hamblin *(Lambert Dolphin's Library)*.

Abraham journeyed to Egypt, Joseph journeyed to Egypt, the Exodus story is about Egypt, but there is nothing Egyptian about Genesis. The Sumerian word Eden meant fertile plain, Adam meant settlement on the plain. According to Zarins, humans had lived happily in a fertile land with food at their fingertips long before Genesis was written. About 5000 to 4000 B.C. there was a worldwide phenomenon that geologists and archeologists call the Flandrian Transgression that occurred at the end of the last glacial period. The melting glaciers caused a sudden rise in sea level. The Persian Gulf began filling with water and reached its modern-day level about 4000 B.C., swallowing Eden and all the settlements along the coastline of the Persian Gulf, moving into the southern regions of Iraq and Iran, driving human inhabitants from food security.

According to Zarins' reasoning, Adam and Eve represented hunter-gatherers who sinned by desiring food security through agriculture rather than trusting God to provide. That is repeated in the Exodus story of the Hebrews in the wilderness who were led and fed by God but wished they were back in Egypt (Ex.16: 3). It is reflected in Jewish law where every seven years the land was to lie fallow, no sowing or reaping, and people were to return to hunting, gathering and trusting God for food security. It echoes in Psalm 23: The Lord is my shepherd, I shall not be hungry. He maketh me to lie down in green pastures where there is grass for the sheep, he leadeth me beside still waters where there is no danger of a lamb being swept away. He prepares a table before me in the presence of mine enemies. From my tent I can see the lamplights in the Philistine cities.

The desire for food security resonates in Jesus's parable of the man who built bigger barns that he might rest in self-provided security (Luke 12:13-21), and in the words of Jesus: "Do not worry about tomorrow" (Matt. 6:34); "Ask not what you shall eat and what you shall drink" (Matt. 6:25); and "give us this day our daily bread."

The intended title of my first novel was "The Days in the Wilderness" because I wanted that reference to those happy days of slavery in Egypt and the free people who cried, "Would to God we were back in Egypt" (Ex. 16: 3).

The Desire for Security:

The Homeless do not worry about a collapse of the stock market.

What if the story of Eden were not about perfidious woman's weakness to temptation causing man to lust after her? In Orthodox Judaism, at funerals women follow the coffin because Eve killed Adam. Young girls are taught that they bleed because Eve shed Adam's blood.

What if the story were about being driven from the peaceful, secure Garden of Mom's cooking, Dad's allowance, driven east of Eden where we have to walk by faith refusing to bow to the false gods of food security, financial security, health security, personal security, national security and the false prophets of security from bad breath, body odor, ugly hair, inappropriate clothing, financial ruin, debt, seizure of our home, our car, our very life.

If Eden is my story, God placed me in a garden filled with good things and at least an equal number of bad things and the freedom to choose between them. My desire to have my own way, my proclivity to be attracted to that which is forbidden makes

Eden emotionally, physically and temporally close.

Rather than trusting God I work hard to provide my own security knowing that the stock market may crash taking my security with it, that I may die while worrying if my insurance is sufficient, that the child whose security I try to provide may vanish like a flower. The more I possess, the more I have to lose and the more I fear losing it.

Given the choice of a wholesome life, I usually go for ice cream, maybe with a slice of pecan pie beneath it. Given a choice between making the world a better place for all nations and all people and keeping my expenses low and my country strong, I sometimes choose to plunder the earth to keep gasoline and food cheap, oil royalty on the throne and debt-slaves in sweat shops.

To cover our nakedness to danger we seek more knowledge and learn to create new ways to save and destroy life in increasingly brutal battles of man against machine, man against nature, man against man, man against God.

The story of the loss of the illusion of individual security, of a benevolent nature, of warm-blankie technology, has been repeated in every culture and every human life. The story of innocence necessitated a story of a fall from innocence, philosophies of how far humans fell, and stories of restoration and the ultimate new life in a new dimension.

The Story of my Fall From Heaven to Earth:

Many families have a story of a fall from a loftier place to their present state. My story of a fall was from a romantic ideal to a disappointing reality. Although both our children were born in North Carolina and we met two of our closest friends there, those two years were not happy ones. I taught both Speech and Drama, directed at least one play a semester and produced a weekly radio show. In addition, I preached somewhere almost every Sunday. I had little time for writing and we had no money for anything but necessities.

Because of Jean's pregnancy I was for the first time the sole economic resource for the family and I felt the fear that many Americans feel. I lay awake at night with "what ifs"—what if there were complications to the pregnancy?—either of us needed medicine?—the car needed repair?—a new tire? I walked to school to save gas no matter how cold it was. Jean walked to the grocery store to buy groceries although neither of us had clothing for a North Carolina winter.

That first summer with no job we returned to Texas where the only job I could get was driving a tractor before tractors were air conditioned. The first day the temperature was reported to be 110 degrees. Although we were staying with Jean's mother, a former employer in Waco had somehow tracked Jean down. When I returned to the house after 10 hours of driving a tractor, Jean told me that she had been offered a job in Waco making more money than I was, thanks be to God. I would keep Deirdre who was six-months-old and write.

In Waco I introduced Deirdre to the Baylor Drama Department. On a bulletin board was a double page photograph in *Life Magazine* of a scene from Ramsey Yelvington's play, "A Cloud of Witnesses" that Baylor Theater had produced while I was gone. The following year they planned a stage production of Thomas Wolfe's novel *Of Time and the River*. Photographer Eliot Elisofon took a leave of absence from *Life Magazine* to work on lighting the stage production.

Exciting ideas, creative thinking were happening in the Baylor Drama Department but I was back in North Carolina writing a pretentious play with mythic characters that I didn't understand myself.

After the second year, I resigned from the school. Despite, or perhaps because of, the doctor's opinion that Jean could not have another child, Brigid was born 15 months after Deirdre.

We returned to Texas and moved into the farmhouse in which I was born. Jean had not graduated from college but I was sure that I would be able to get a job somewhere, maybe in a public school.

Our mothers worried more than we did. "How are you going to feed these babies?" That's something a lot of fathers hear, a lot of mothers hear and it destroys hopes and shreds dreams. It reduces happy, loving parents into drudges. What won't you do for a sick baby, a hungry child? What can you do when even payday loaners turn you away? Prostitution, shop-lifting, drug dealing, armed robbery. I had only a sniff of the fear that turns decent citizens into desperate and dangerous citizens. We had prospects. We knew this was the beginning not the end of the story. Without that what would we have done? I lost faith in politicians who promise that putting corporations on the public dole is the way to end poverty.

One day at dusk in 1959, a cousin drove over to say that Paul Baker wanted me to call him. I gathered the change in the house and drove to the closest public telephone in Chillicothe to return the call. Baker offered me a job in the Baylor Drama Department. I would teach playwriting, religious drama and fill in other classes.

That was my moment on the road to Damascus, the road to Emmaus, the road to our future. I would return to Baylor that I considered my and God's second home. I would work with my mentors Paul Baker and Eugene McKinney. Although I hadn't prayed for a sign, I believed this was a message on the wings of a dove.

When we were both students Jean had found fault with Baylor. Too much emphasis on football, although Baylor rarely had a winning team in those days. The buildings were too lavish, especially the Armstrong-Browning Building. The students were pretentiously pious, preferring being nice to being good. Jean called it "nasty nice." I defended Baylor with some anger. Jean accused me of idolatry. She believed I had made an idol of Baylor.

I loved Baylor. It was the kind of love that makes excuses for the beloved. Baylor strained at dancing on the campus and swallowed segregation.

My return to Baylor after two years in North Carolina was like I imagined the return of Nehemiah to Jerusalem after exile in Babylon. I believed I would spend the rest of my life at Baylor, teaching until retirement, reading in the library after retirement, sitting on a bench under a giant tree enjoying the day amid Baylor young people.

The first year had gone well. Jean was a full-time student and enjoying it. We had a baby sitter for Brigid. Deirdre went to a Baylor prekindergarten program. I retrieved her after class and we walked home where Jean had prepared lunch. I walked back to Baylor for class or other duties. I had adapted *As I Lay Dying* for the stage and a reviewer from *Saturday Review* had reviewed it favorably.

I had to teach in summer school because we needed the income. That also meant directing a play and I chose "The Skin of Our Teeth," by Thornton Wilder, but I needed a couple of extra players. I selected two mature high school students who had been in Baylor Children's Theater. The two students were black. Baylor Children's Theater was integrated but Baylor was not. I didn't see any problems with that. After working together a few days everyone forgot to identify each other by color. Which was what segregationists feared.

One afternoon during break one of the students returned to say, "I think you're in trouble." The cast had gone for coffee at Baylor Drug Store, adjacent to Baylor Theater, but couldn't get service. When they complained, the owner of Baylor Drug told them he was not having a sit-in at his drug store. The black students had gone as part of the group because they were part of the group. No one thought of it as a sit-in. The owner said he was calling the Baylor president, Abner McCall. The owner of Baylor Drug Store was a Baylor Trustee.

I called department chair Paul Baker, who was in New York, and told him what had happened. He said he would take care of it. And he did. The moment passed without becoming an event. Sometimes I think it should have become an event but likely I would have been without a job, the black students would have been arrested and probably not been permitted to return to high school and the college students might have been given 24 demerits.

Baylor that I thought of as my and God's second home slid to third place as I became homesick for the Marines. Marines were sometimes cruel but they weren't pretentious. "Did you see that gook when I lit him up?"

The "sit-in" seemed to have done no harm but no good either. "As I Lay Dying" became part of the repertoire of the Dallas Theater Center. I tried writing short stories, having had little success in putting another play on the boards. Jean graduated and was offered a job teaching English and Spanish at University High School.

There were distant disturbances. The fundamentalist wing of the Southern Baptist Convention was bellicose. They did not want Baptist schools and churches integrated. That wasn't a problem for churches. Baptist churches are autonomous. They can preach "God Hates Figs" or "God Hates Flab," and there is no authority to stop them. The schools were a different problem. The government couldn't force church schools to integrate but it could cut off funding for them, including tax exemption. And women were challenging their lower status, even in church.

A tenet of Baptist faith is that the Bible is the only creed. Issues could be debated with both sides choosing selected scriptures for their purpose. There was no bright line between dissension and heresy. The fundamentalists demanded a line in the sand with barbed wire and land mines to separate those who were inside and those who were out. The fundamentalists called it the "Southern Baptist Faith and Message." The inerrancy of the Bible in the "original autographs" was the perfect red line. No one had seen the original manuscripts, not even the latest ones, in a couple of millennia. No honest person could swear to that inerrancy but a dishonest person could demand that others take a loyalty oath to inerrancy.

Baptist schools from prekindergarten to universities were operated and governed by a local church, an association of local churches or a state convention and any of those organizations could employ the red line. No one knew whether pastors, teachers and professors would have to sign loyalty statements. Tenure meant nothing. Friendship meant nothing. Students brought tape recorders into classrooms to catch suspicious utterances. Some posed trick questions to catch others off guard. This was doctrinal cleansing.

President McCall called a faculty meeting. Some professors said they hadn't had time to study the document. It didn't matter. An English professor pointed out a grammatical error that should be corrected. Didn't matter. A Religion professor pointed out that in a single paragraph the document stated that "the Bible was written by men" and that the Bible "has God for its author," wording that could be used as a trap and should be clarified. McCall declared we were there to approve the statement, not to improve it. I was back in the seminary. Keep what you know to yourself. McCall said he didn't care what we believed. Baylor was going to endorse the statement. We weren't required to sign anything.

The Universal Myth of the Fall:

Judeans taken into captivity in Babylon not only heard Sumerian stories, they discovered the ideas of the Persian prophet and poet Zoroaster, Greek for Zarathustra. Through Judaism, Christianity was also influenced by Zoroaster. According to Zoroaster the one creator god, Ahura Mazda, existed in light and goodness, emphasized "good thoughts, good words, good deeds" and created the universe. Angra Mainyu existed in darkness and ignorance and created chaos, snakes and flies.

Evil invaded the earth. The forces of good trapped evil so that it could not escape and humans must struggle with evil in a violent place with half light and half night. Three prominent Persian kings, Darius the Great, Xerxes (Ahasuerus), and Artaxerxes, who are mentioned respectively in Daniel, Esther and Ezra, were Zoroastrians.

In Talmudic times, roughly from the Roman destruction of the Temple and denial of statehood to the Jews to Constantine declaring Rome a Christian empire, some Jewish teachers believed that death was punishment because of Adam's sin—but the dominant view was that humans sin because we are not perfect and not because we are inherently sinful.

Gnosticism does not have a concept of a fall from grace. The serpent freed Adam and Eve by giving them knowledge and they were forced out of the Garden so they could not eat of the Tree of Life and become a threat to the Almighty.

In the Koran, when God created Adam he commanded all the angels who do not have free will, and Iblis who does, to bow down to Adam, God's greatest creation. Iblis refused to bow to Adam and was banished from the Garden. Satan deceived Adam and Eve, they both ate from the tree, recognized their sexual shame and covered themselves. God forgave them and told them to leave the Garden. Earth would be their dwelling place for a short time. "Therein you shall live, and therein you shall die, and from it you shall be brought out (resurrected)." Surat al-A'raf: 24–25.

The Koran states, "That no burdened person shall bear the burden of another. And that man can have nothing but what he does. And that his deeds will be seen. Then he will be recompensed with a full and the best recompense." Surat an-Naim: 38-41

Eastern Orthodox and some Protestants reject the notion that we are "born in sin" because Ezekiel 18:20 states that a son is not guilty of the sins of his father.

In Adam's fall, We Sinneth All:

The *New England Primer,* 1685, the first primer designed for the American Colonies, represented the Puritan view of God, creation and childhood depravity.

Catholics and fundamentalist Christians believe that sin entered the world because the sin of Adam and Eve had corrupted the whole creation. It was the view of Augustine that, as sons and daughters of Adam and Eve, we participated in the first act of disobedience and are therefore born into the sin of Adam and Eve until freed by baptism. For that reason Catholics and some Protestants baptize infants without the knowledge or choice of the infants to erase original sin.

The Council of Trent, 1546, insisted that original sin is "not only by imitation" but didn't define exactly how it was transmitted. Thomas Aquinas saw original sin as the loss of the right relationship between humans and God resulting in "concupiscence" or uncontrolled desire not only relating to sexual matters but greed for money, power, control, transmitted from parents to children through the defective relationship between ourselves and God down the evolutionary chain.

Darwinism questioned whether it was necessary to take the story of Adam and Eve literally. There is no peaceable kingdom in evolution; it's survival of the fittest from the beginning.

Because of what I believe is my earliest memory, I am not concerned about original sin. I had my own Garden of Eden. I did wrong, I knew it was wrong, and I did it anyway. I didn't do it in defiance of God or my parents. I think I did it to demonstrate my power to do wrong, to be bad.

By the Breath of the Spirit:

In 1943, the Vatican issued "By the Breath of the Spirit" acknowledging different literary forms in the Bible other than factual and historical. What the new Catechism says is that human beings have an innate tendency toward sinning (concupiscence) that is the consequence of a historical fall but that the account of the fall in Genesis 2 and 3 uses figurative language.

Original sin is also the basis for the Immaculate Conception of Mary that has been the basis for political contention regarding the role of women in the Christian world, primarily in the Americas. In Catholic Europe Christians have largely shrugged past it.

The mother of Jesus was conceived in the same way as all humans but in order to be the "Mother of God" the mother of Jesus had to be free of original sin. Therefore, before she was born Mary was forgiven of original sin for her part in the birth of Jesus. But it couldn't be just the flesh that was forgiven but also the soul; therefore "ensoulment" had to happen at conception. Thomas Aquinas rejected the Immaculate Conception because if Mary had never been sinful she could not be redeemed by Christ.

Before 1854 fetuses that did not have human form could not receive religious rites. That was the year when the Immaculate Conception became doctrine. In 1870 when the pope became infallible, the Immaculate Conception became dogma. Mary became the new sinless Eve and Jesus the new Adam pure from original sin. Taken literally, that image has a strong ick factor.

Protestants don't believe in the immaculate conception of Mary and to many "Mother of God" is sacrilege or blasphemy. Into the 1970s, the major concern of fundamentalists and evangelicals was divorce, with more fundamentalists and evangelicals getting divorces than secularists. I never heard contraception or abortion mentioned in the pulpit.

There were no state or federal laws against abortion in America before 1821. Growing Catholic population and political power moved states toward stripping Jews and others of their religious freedom to plan their families in the way they believed best. Christian "sharia" laws criminalized contraception and abortion enforcing birth on demand. The Supreme Court overturned the last state law against contraception in 1965. That's an example of religious laws being extended to humanists, secularists and others by politicians despite the Constitution. By the time Roe v. Wade was decided in 1973, nineteen states explicitly permitted abortions in some circumstances. Then, as now, women with means were women with choice.

When Jean and I married in 1953, it was three days after her high school graduation, but we were both determined to graduate from college. Our Southern Baptist pastor warned us that should Jean become pregnant we should avoid Catholic doctors and Catholic hospitals because they would sacrifice a mother's life to save a fetus. Baptists thought that was ungodly and deplorable prejudice toward women.

Our married Baptist and evangelical friends received the same advice from their pastors. We assumed that because Catholics could not divorce, Catholic men preferred that the fetus be saved because they could always get another wife. We preferred the opposite.

Southern Baptists were an evangelical denomination with a vocal fundamentalist minority. During the 1971 and 1974 Southern Baptist Conventions, Southern Baptists were called upon "to work for legislation that will allow the possibility of abortion under such conditions as rape, incest, clear evidence of severe fetal deformity, and carefully ascertained evidence of the likelihood of damage to the emotional, mental, and physical health of the mother."

Prominent Southern Baptist fundamentalist, W. A. Criswell, pastor of First Baptist Church, Dallas, applauded Roe v Wade. "I have always felt that it was only after a child was born and had life separate from the mother that it became an individual person, and it always has, therefore, seemed to me that what is best for the mother and for the future should be allowed." W. Barry Garrett of Baptist Press wrote, "Religious liberty, human equality and justice are advanced by the Supreme Court abortion decision."

Baptists, including Southern Baptists, had been leading advocates of separation of church and state. Government support or intervention in religious matters was regarded as evil. When Lyndon Johnson signed the Civil Rights act, the political South took a sharp turn to the right. The fundamentalist South followed.

By 1980, fundamentalists had gained control of the Southern Baptist Convention with the support of Criswell and the tacit support of evangelist Billy Graham. Graham later declared, "It would disturb me if there was a wedding between religious fundamentalists and the political right. The hard right has no interest in religion except to manipulate it" (*Parade*, 1981).

The Bible began to say something different:

Fundamentalists began to believe that "ensoulment" was at conception, although less than half of zygotes (fertilized eggs) are implanted but are flushed from the body. Rather than being regarded as sacred lives by Catholics or fundamentalists, they receive no religious rites, provoke no public demonstrations or efforts to save them and are treated as human waste.

Catholics make no effort to use the Bible to support the dogma of immaculate conception or that ensoulment occurs at conception. Fundamentalists find a huge contradiction between basing doctrine on the Bible and "ensoulment" at conception. Adam first had a body in the image of God and then God gave him a soul.

When Judah believes that Tamar, his daughter-in-law, has committed adultery, he orders that she be taken and burned to death (Genesis 38). No thought is given to the fetus she carries. Exodus 21: 22 states that if a man causes a pregnant woman to have an abortion he must pay the father for the loss of his property, but if the woman is injured, it is life for life, eye for eye. The woman is a life; the fetus is not. Some try to force the interpretation that it refers to injury of the fetus but how many incubators did the Hebrews have in the Wilderness? As Dr. James O. Morse (U.S. Army, retired) points out, "Why even bother to fine the man at all if the child lived and suffered no injuries?"

In Ezekiel's vision of the Valley of Dry Bones, the scattered bones come together, tendons and flesh appear on them, skin covers them but they are not alive until Ezekiel prophesied for breath to enter them (Ezekiel 37: 7-10).

Some find it easier to talk about personhood and when a fetus becomes a "person." When a census was taken of the Levites, only males a month old or older were counted (Numbers 26: 62). In Leviticus, God tells Moses to place a value on humans—to pay for vows. "And if it be from a month old even unto five years old, then thy estimation shall be of the male five shekels of silver, and for the female thy estimation shall be three shekels of silver" (Lev. 27: 6). Not only did fetuses not have personhood, neither did babies until they were a month old.

Leviticus is the favorite book of the Bible for those whose religion requires lepers. "If a man has sexual relations with a man as one does with a woman, both of them have done what is detestable. They are to be put to death; their blood will be on their own heads" (Lev. 20: 13). However, Leviticus is a swamp with quagmires, crocodiles and venomous snakes.

"If a man marries his sister, the daughter of either his father or his mother, and they have sexual relations, it is a disgrace. They are to be publicly removed from their people. He has dishonored his sister and will be held responsible (Lev. 20: 17). Abraham, the father of three religions, married his father's daughter. "Do not take your wife's sister as a rival wife and have sexual relations with her while your wife is living." Jacob married two sisters.

"If a man has sexual relations with his aunt, he has dishonored his uncle. They will be held responsible; they will die childless. If a man marries his brother's wife, it is an act of impurity; he has dishonored his brother. They will be childless" (Lev. 20: 21, 22). Previous verses regarding sexual immorality required death by stoning or fire. How was the punishment of childlessness carried out without abortion or infanticide? Castration might work but only if none of the women were already pregnant.

If a husband is suspicious of his wife, whether with or without reason, he is to take her to a priest who will prepare bitter water that contains a curse and make her drink it. If she has been unfaithful her abdomen will swell and she will miscarry, be unable to bear children and become a curse (Num. 5: 11-31). Stoning is not required because there are no witnesses but she will be an outcast.

Abortion as punishment seems to be approved as the prophet Hosea prayed that God would punish the wayward Israelite women with abortions. "Give them, O Lord: what wilt thou give? Give them a miscarrying womb and dry breasts" (Hosea 9: 14).

In Numbers 31, God told Moses to take vengeance on the Midianites—and the Israelites killed all the Midianite men, burned their cities and took the women and children captive. Moses was angry because the Midianite women had been too submissive to Israelite men at Peor, bringing a plague on Israel, probably an STD (Numbers 25). Moses ordered the soldiers to kill all the male children and all the women. Neither pregnant women nor their fetuses were spared, but the warriors could keep virgin girls for themselves.

Ecclesiastes 6: 3 states that unless a man has a good life and a proper burial it is better that he be stillborn. Both Jeremiah and Job wished they had been aborted.

Jesus said that nonexistence was not the worst fate. "The Son of man indeed goeth, as it is written of him: but woe to that man by whom the Son of man is betrayed! good were it for that man if he had never been born" (Mark 14: 21).

Paul wrote "The spiritual did not come first, but the natural, and after that the spiritual" (I Cor. 15: 46). The writer of Hebrews wrote that Levi existed in the loins of his great-grandfather (Heb. 7: 9,10).

The Bible gives no support to those who believe ensoulment begins at the moment of conception. Neither does science.

There is no Moment of Conception:

According to David Barash, professor of psychology at the University of Washington, there is no Big Bang in conception, no precise moment in the complex process when a fertilized egg becomes a possible person. "A particular egg and sperm, each destined to contribute one-half the genome of a future human being, is produced via complex processes of oogenesis and spermatogenesis, respectively." Is this the moment when a soul appears?

The sperm cell migrates through a layer of follicle cells to reach the egg's zona pellucida that consists of three different glycoproteins, one of which acts as a sperm receptor and binds to its complement on the sperm's head. (Now?)

This induces the acrosome to spill its contents of enzymes, which enable the sperm to penetrate the zona and reach the egg's plasma membrane. (Now?) A protein in the sperm's membrane then binds to and fuses with the egg membrane, (Now?) triggering depolarization of the latter, which prevents other sperm from entering. (Now?) Granules in the egg's cortex release enzymes that catalyze long-lasting changes in the zona, achieving a longer-lasting block to other sperm. (Now?) Pseudopod-like extensions of the egg's interior proceed to transport the sperm into the egg. (Now?)

The nuclear envelopes around sperm and egg remain fundamentally distinct through the "fertilized" egg's first mitotic division. Only at this point, with two "daughter" cells already in existence, do the parental chromosomes unite, forming two nuclei. Paternal and maternal genes remain separate for at least 24 hours after sperm successfully breaches those follicle cells, and it takes an additional day or so before their combined influence directs cell function.

Science doesn't examine souls but it does minds and the two "daughter" cells have no neurons, and certainly no brain. Neither does a subsequent four-cell, eight-cell, or 128-cell descendant. Somewhere along the line between egg and baby, brain cells aggregate and start whispering to each other, whereupon a mind gradually coalesces. "Moreover, there is often a reciprocal diminution of self-hood and mental competence at the other end of life, as the Terri Schiavo debacle so painfully revealed" (*Los Angeles Times*, 7/18/05).

This description has been compressed and any scientific facts misstated or crushed beyond recognition are the fault of the author and not Dr. Barash.

Neither science nor religion can give us the exact moment a complex system becomes a person or ceases to be so. Nor can they tell us at what moment a sacred embryo that converts into a woman who becomes pregnant is reduced from a sacred life to a ward of the church or state. Why then has recent church dogma become such a political issue? 1870 may not seem recent to you, but that was 17 years before the birth of my father. Randall Balmer, professor, editor, and Episcopal priest provides the best answer in *Thy Kingdom Come*.

When President Eisenhower used the National Guard and the U.S. Army to enforce integration, leaders across the South knew that states could no longer resist integration. But churches could. Across the South and Midwest, fundamentalist and evangelical churches opened their own schools to whites only. Then Lyndon Johnson's Civil Rights and Voting Rights Acts limited states' authority to restrict voting and hand out stars and scars as the state saw fit. The Supreme Court stripped Bob Jones University, a segregated fundamentalist school, of its tax exemption. Followed by Rowe v. Wade. The South Must Rise Up Again.

Rowe v. Wade was not an immediate "dead babies" emotional issue with fundamentalists. Losing control of reproduction to a woman would give a woman authority over a man and that was strictly forbidden in their selected Scriptures. Ephesians 5: 22-25. Wives were to submit to their husbands. Husbands were to love their wives. They chose to ignore the previous verse. "Submitting yourselves one to another in the fear of the Lord." For men, love is a verb that requires little more than declaration. For women, a declaration of love means submission in its most literal sense.

To defend unborn life and male control of reproduction, fundamentalists attacked women. God gave women one body and they dressed it to seduce men. Women danced and pranced; they lisped, they ambled, they wanted equal pay as though they were equal, they had been corrupted by public schools and too close proximity to people of an inappropriate color.

When fundamentalists gained control of the Southern Baptist Convention, women lost their power, even those who had been pastors, university or seminary professors, or officers in the Convention. A woman was to have no authority over a man. In some churches there were arguments about women teaching teenage boys.

Women were supposed to be submissive to their husbands and that meant under the authority of all males, except juveniles. Every southern woman knew the mantra, "Keep them barefoot and pregnant." They wouldn't go to school barefooted, and hence would not discuss ideas, philosophy, or art with men—or with women if they had a bun in the oven, one trying to climb up her leg and another prone to falling off the front porch.

The Moral Majority, that turned out to be neither moral nor a majority, couldn't gain political traction but had some wishes in common with Catholics: private schools with public support, teaching six-day creation (maybe along with evolution) in public education, Christian statues, crosses and symbols in public places; Christian prayers and Bible reading at official events, Christian laws enforced by states and the federal government, male authority over women, and recognition of Christianity as the official religion of America.

Bonding fundamentalists and Catholics would give them a lot of votes, and when Reagan's first campaign speech was in the county where three civil rights workers had been tortured and murdered and he spoke of state's rights they knew Reagan was their man. States could roll back civil rights, voting rights, equal opportunity for women and minorities, and the war on hunger that allowed large black women flashing rings on every finger and driving shiny new Cadillacs to pick up welfare checks for half a dozen children by six different fathers. Such a woman was never found; rather, public subsidies went to those who flew shiny corporate jets to lobby Congress for government contracts. Reagan would make the federal government the problem for citizens, the solution for global corporations, and the states would be the defenders of the threatened white Christian majority.

Billy Graham, who would be disturbed by "a wedding between religious fundamentalists and the political right," was not disturbed enough to protest.

The Myths of Destruction:

In *Gilgamesh*, one of the earliest fully-realized works of literature that we know, Utnapishtim is told by the god Ea that the "great gods" are going to flood the earth. Utnapishtim is to build an ark and when people asked what he was doing, he was to say that another god had forced him to leave. Utnapishtim built a six-story house on a barge and took ravens, doves and swallows, animals, seed, gold and silver with him. The ravens would feed on dead bodies and not return. The swallows would build a nest of mud and not return. The doves would require vegetation for food and nesting.

When Utnapishtim found dry land he made a sacrifice and the gods smelled the sweet savor of burning flesh. The one who caused the flood was angry that someone survived but the other gods told him to punish the sinner not the guiltless, and thereafter to send lions, leopards and plagues to destroy people.

Gilgamesh was made into a film in 2009 and another is planned for 2019. That's the power and universality of some stories.

The biblical flood is believed to be borrowed from the Babylonians, who borrowed it from the Sumerians. In the Babylonian (Persian) account, humans were making so much noise that the gods couldn't sleep so they decided to drown the humans. One god, Cronus, appeared to the king and told him that the world would be destroyed and that the king was to write the story of the world from the beginning and save it by burying it. He was also to build a boat and with friends, family and animals set sail. The story gave the dimensions of the ark and called it an ark. After many days of sailing the king loosed birds and they returned. Again he released birds and they returned with mud on their feet. The third time he released birds they did not return.

The king grounded the boat, made a sacrifice and disappeared with his wife and daughter to live with the gods. When the other survivors sought them, the king spoke from heaven telling the remnant that they were in Armenia and they were to go to Babylon, recover the tablets and share the story with all mankind. One of the tablets, believed to be from the library of Assyrian king Ashurbanipal, 7th century BC, was found in the 19th century and pieced together from bits of broken clay and is now in the British Museum. Incidentally, the hero of the story was the tenth king of Babylon. Noah was the tenth male descendent from Adam.

In India, a man washing himself was asked by a small fish to save it. He kept the fish until it was grown and then returned it to the sea. The sea rose, the man got in a boat, tied the boat to the fish and the fish towed him to dry land. Karens, the tribal hill people of Burma and Thailand, far from the sea, have a story of two brothers who built a boat and the water rose so high that they could see into heaven. One of them plucked a mango from a tree in heaven and ate it.

In a Greek account there was a cleft in the ground where the water from the flood escaped and every year the Greeks threw soul-cakes into the cleft. At Hierapolis, founded by Alexander the Great, they brought water from the sea twice a year and poured it into a chasm where the waters disappeared.

In Phrygia, an ancient kingdom in what is now Turkey, there was a coin of an ark with a man and woman aboard, a raven, a dove with an olive branch and on the ark the Greek equivalent of the name Noah. Phrygia is remembered for its legendary kings— Gordias whose Gordian knot was untied by Alexander the Great, Midas who turned everything he touched to gold, and Mygdon who warred with the Amazons. Phrygians were among those on the day of Pentecost who heard speech in their own tongue. The Christian heresy of Montanism (aka the Phrygian heresy) originated in Phrygia and was characterized by ecstatic prophecy and women prophets.

During the reign of Caesar Augustus, the Greek historian, Nicolaus, a close friend of Herod the Great and tutor of the children of Anthony and Cleopatra, wrote: "There is a great mountain in Armenia, over Minyas, called Baris, upon which it is reported that many who fled at the time of the Deluge were saved; and that one who was carried in an ark came on shore upon the top of it; and that the remains of the timber were a great while preserved. This might be the man about whom Moses the legislator of the Jews wrote."

That's but a sampling of the many flood stories even among primitive tribes far from rivers, lakes and seas. Over the centuries, among diverse people and cultures a familiar thread runs through the story of destruction.

My Story of Destruction:

Paul Baker arranged for the Wurlitzer Foundation to provide houses and provisions for the Drama Department faculty for two weeks in Taos, New Mexico, so that we could plan for the next 10 years. McKinney and I, mostly McKinney, wrote a paper for the needs and goals of the playwriting program. Others wrote papers for acting, directing, scene and costume design, stagecraft and so forth regarding changes and improvements in curriculum, hardware, disposable equipment, props, production choices and schedule. Then the papers were read, studied and probed by everyone.

It was intense but we were hosted at a private club by Mrs. Wurlitzer one evening. We were also given a tour of her house. And yes, there was a Wurlitzer jukebox in the house. One of the resident psychologists of the foundation took us to the pueblo where he had been studying the Indians. The pueblo and its traditions appeared to be dying.

Jean called to say that I had received a check for publication of my first short story. Everyone celebrated with me but I had rather celebrated with Jean. A greater excitement was when Baker announced that we would be the first nonprofessional group to receive the right to produce Eugene O'Neill's Pulitzer winning play, "Long Day's Journey Into Night." That was a triumph for all of us. O'Neill's widow stipulated in the contract that the play could not be cut. It was a four-hour long production. President McCall, who had formerly been Dean of the Baylor Law School and had once served on the Texas Supreme Court, signed the contract.

I began my fourth year on the Baylor faculty and Jean began her first year of teaching with excitement anticipating a great year. Baylor publicized our production of "Long Day's Journey Into Night." It opened to a full house in the fall of 1962 and was one of our finest productions.

The following week Baker called me at home. He, McKinney and other members of the faculty were in Dallas at the Theater Center. McCall had ordered that "Long Day's Journey" be closed. I was to tell the cast that it would be their last performance. I was to prohibit news photographers from taking pictures of the play or of the audience or interviewing members of the audience in the building. I was also to stop any kind of student protest inside or outside the building.

The cast was stunned. I was unable to tell them why the play was closed because I didn't know. Later we would learn that a pastor from a small West Texas town had brought a group of boys to visit Baylor, to watch a Baylor football game and to see the play. The next morning the pastor was waiting in the president's office when McCall arrived. The practice of limiting sermons to the understanding of children had borne fruit.

Baker returned home to find a crowd of students outside his house. They wanted to do something to help. He asked them to return to their studies and to let the faculty handle it. Then he called a departmental meeting. We agreed to concentrate on our classes and our upcoming productions until we determined where we were in regard to the administration. We re-examined the plays that we had scheduled for production. We didn't want to give the president the power to decide what plays we could produce but we were forced into self-censorship, which was worse.

Part of our training program was that plays written by students were given to students in Directing classes. Each directing student selected one of the plays to direct, and cast students from acting classes for a public performance. McKinney and I were told that student writers were not permitted to ridicule ministerial students, football players or Baylor cheerleaders. McKinney sent one questionable student-written play to McCall and the president crossed out two forbidden words, virginity and unadulterated. McKinney kept the script and I believe it is now in the Southwest Writers Collection.

A former professor of mine who was president of the Baylor chapter of the American Association of University Professors, asked if the president had restricted my academic freedom. According to the AAUP's charter, "Protecting academic freedom is the AAUP's core mission. Academic freedom is the indispensable requisite for unfettered teaching and research in institutions of higher education." I told him of the restrictions on subjects that our students could write about, and the presidential censorship of a student play. He did not see these as a restrictions of academic freedom.

Some years later, the president of Trinity's AAUP asked me to speak to them about "sexual harassment." I agreed. When I returned from a conference I had a message that my speech was cancelled. When I asked why I was told that another professor had objected to me speaking on the subject. I pointed out that I hadn't chosen the subject; the subject had been assigned to me. I appealed to the national office but was told the local branch could invite and disinvite at their pleasure. That's my opinion of the AAUP.

The Christmas of my fourth year at Baylor was the bleakest Christmas we had celebrated. Santa had brought bicycles with training wheels for the girls but it was bitterly cold and windy with mist and freezing rain. The children knew that something was wrong but didn't understand that uncertainty hung in the air like the mist. The department's 10 year planning had vanished like waves on a sandy beach. We waited for the next wave which might be tidal.

Jean, the girls and I visited a former roommate of mine. He and his wife had kept our children when Jean and I went to Europe with my play. On Sunday morning we went to church with my roommate's family. On the back of the Order of Worship was printed a letter from McCall thanking the church for their support in his fight against faculty who believed that academic freedom gave them the right to stand on stage and shout obscenities at children. There are no words in the play that aren't found in the King James Version of the Bible. It was obviously a form letter that McCall sent to everyone who supported his decision to censor the play.

McKinney and I were ordained ministers. We were both veterans and knew all the words but didn't use them. When McKinney was First Sergeant in an armored unit an officer told him he was the only noncom he knew who could get soldiers to do what he ordered without cursing. McKinney later received a battlefield commission. I didn't have the rank to order anyone around so it was never a decision I had to make. That would come later in writing fiction. I told students that they would not be held accountable for what a character said. Bigots talked like bigots.

I showed the letter to Baker. He asked McKinney and me to go with him to meet the president. I didn't know then and don't know now why I was invited. Baker and McKinney were the body and soul of the department. I was a spare part but somehow I had been in the center of what I feared would become a tragedy. McCall said he had written the letter. McKinney asked if McCall could have said that he had confidence that the Drama Department could resolve the matter. McCall said he could have but didn't. McKinney asked if he would express confidence in the department. McCall said he would not.

McCall said the Baptist preachers didn't trust him because he was not a preacher but a lawyer and he saw closing the play as a way to get the preachers on his side. A few years later McCall was elected President of the Baptist General Convention of Texas.

On the way across the campus to the Theater, Baker asked, "It's all over isn't it?" McKinney said yes. I didn't want to believe it. I was not likely to get a job in a Baptist university or maybe even a Christian school. Teaching at a secular college seemed contrary to my vocation.

Baker was offered positions at several schools and at least one foreign opportunity but he refused to accept a job for himself and leave those like myself behind. James Laurie, President of Trinity University, a Presbyterian school, agreed to accept the Drama faculty, our curriculum and our graduate school at the Dallas Theater Center. When the entire department resigned, our woes escalated.

I was glad my brother Jim was pastoring outside of Texas. Likely he would have been dragged into the controversy where he would have had to choose one of his obligations, his brother's keeper or servant of the church he pastored.

The morning that the Waco newspaper reported our resignation, Jean was called to her principal's office. The photographs of the departing faculty along with the background of the issue behind our departure was spread on the principal's desk. The principal told Jean that if she turned in her resignation he would write a good recommendation for her. Jean refused and asked that the two of them meet with the Waco School Superintendent.

When the principal demurred, she said she would go by herself, and she did. Abner McCall was Chair of the Waco School Board, and the superintendent told Jean that if McCall wanted her dismissed it likely would happen. It didn't happen, so it was likely the principal was acting on his own.

Ironically I had been hired by the Southern Baptist Radio and TV Commission to write a two-part documentary on the religion of the cowboy. On two separate occasions I was in New York City for a week for the live productions, cutting and adding words or lines to keep the show on time. Both times during my absence, Jean received obscene and threatening telephone calls.

Church was no respite. Jean and I both taught Sunday School in the Youth Department of First Baptist Church. I taught college freshmen and Jean taught high school senior girls. We were sponsors of a youth retreat lead by the Youth Minister. One day Deirdre cried because her teacher told her we had to leave town because we were bad people and no one wanted us in Waco. Brigid spent church time in a guarded area that had a door that closed quickly and automatically to prevent children from escaping the room to look for their parents. When Jean retrieved Brigid after church, a mother leaving the room with her child momentarily held the door, then seeing who was behind her she let the door go. Brigid would have been knocked down by the door if Jean hadn't grabbed her.

The youth director's wife was expecting her first baby and Jean and the wife of a Waco architect who had children in the youth department planned a baby shower for her. The day of the shower we received telephone calls from those who had accepted the invitation but were not going to be able to come. Most of those who worked in the Youth Department were connected to Baylor. There were three couples at the shower: the couple being honored, the architect and his wife, and Jean and I. One woman explained to Jean that she had been told it would be better for her not to attend the shower. She would have a long and distinguished career at Baylor and I respect her for what she has accomplished.

Our pastor came to see us. He regretted that we were leaving Waco but McCall was a member of his church and the pastor had to support him. The pastor's daughter was in the Sunday School Class that Jean taught. That's not the exact equivalent of the Old Testament curse to "be cut off" but it's a Baptist approximation. The sharpest cuts are always those from the people with whom with you most closely identify.

Ironically, (religion is a great source of irony) the pastor resigned from the church to teach in Baylor's Religion Department. He came under the disapproval of the fundamentalists for a book he had written years earlier that had been published by a Baptist publisher. He was forced into resignation from the Baylor faculty.

In my usual demonstration of Christian charity, every Sunday I sat directly behind Abner McCall in the church balcony. I didn't say anything but "good morning" or do anything to disturb the president. He may have thought that I might push him off the balcony. The thought never entered my mind. Neither did the idea that I might accidentally trip and bump him over the balcony rail.

Despite the anguish and anger, leaving Baylor was confirmation of my call. I no longer long for the fleshpots of Baylor but I cheer their athletic teams. At Trinity I met James Laurie who was for me the ideal university president; he never believed that he was the institution or that the university was his to use to advance his own career. That caused some problems with other presidents.

That summer I began a play that became a novel, *North to Yesterday*. I would not have been able to write the books that I have written under my own name if I had remained at Baylor. Self-censorship would have been a betrayal of my vocation. Jean was hired as a teacher despite the ugly letter that her principal had written and signed. The principal who hired her said he knew the principal who wanted her to resign, and he knew the kind of person that principal was.

Jean was right. Baylor was not heaven and the good Lord had to shake me loose from idolatry.

The Myths of Redemption:

In a good story there should be redemption, restoration or enlightenment.

Hindus who die in Varanasi and are cremated on the banks of the Ganges receive instant salvation. For those who do not die in Varanasi, relatives throw balls of rice and sesame seeds into the Ganges reciting family names. Each sesame seed gives a thousand years in heaven for each relative.

In the Zoroastrian story, at death there is a bridge of judgment that each person must cross to face a spiritual judgment. Teh person is greeted by a beautiful maiden who will lead them to paradise or an old woman who leads to a bridge that narrows— until the person falls into hell where punishments fit crimes and those in hell are reformed. A savior born to a virgin impregnated by the seed of Zoroaster will raise the dead in both heaven and hell to a last judgment and the heavenly forces will triumph over evil in a final climactic battle similar to Armageddon in the book of Revelation.

The Buddhist story of redemption is a repetition of life on this planet until one learns discipline and grows upward through stages to a stillness of a mind no longer troubled by human desires including love, justice, truth. That peace is called Nirvana. In Hinduism, Nirvana is union with the Supreme Being that brings bliss.

In the Jewish Bible it is the story of Noah, the ark, the flood, a new creation evidenced by a green twig and a new covenant which promises a Messiah who will restore Israel to its rightful place.

The Islamic story is complete submission to God. Some Muslims believe Jesus will return to earth but not Muhammad.

The Christian story of salvation is both complex and a mystery. In Protestant denominations, we are saved by the grace of a loving and forgiving God through faith without the need for works or sacraments. Some believe an innocent Jesus volunteered to die on the cross because the loving and forgiving God required a blood sacrifice. Some believe that Jesus exemplified the kind of guiltless life and sacrificial love that is the way, the truth and the life.

Some believe that the Godhead placed part of itself on the cross to die in order to conquer death and to resurrect the image of God in human beings. Part of that image must be immortality because God is eternal. The destruction of this life as we know it is followed by happily ever after—sort of, since to be "immortal" one has to die—a new creation of a new heaven and a new earth and a new Jerusalem that comes down from heaven (Rev. 21: 1-4), with a new temple (Mark 14: 58), a perfect tabernacle (Hebrews 9:11), an eternal house not made by hands (2 Cor. 5: 1). This is the formula we use in baptism. Buried in his death and raised to walk in a new life with him.

When I hear of God's wrath, I remember Teresa Babe. For her twelfth birthday we gave Deirdre a just-weaned filly to train with the understanding that any mistakes she made with the filly she would have to live with as long as the mare lived. They trained each other and after Brigid's death, Teresa B did much of Deirdre's training.

Deirdre determined she would train Teresa B with a bosal so the mare would have a soft mouth. One day Jean and Deirdre were riding in a nearby pasture with a tree lined meadow. Something spooked Teresa B and she bolted into the trees showing her Joker B quarter horse bloodline with Deirdre fighting for control. Jean followed the sound of limbs and underbrush snapping and breaking afraid to get too close for fear of encouraging Teresa B to run.

Jean found Deirdre slumped on the ground beside Teresa B. Jean got off her horse and carefully approached Deirdre who was crying. "Where are you hurt?" Jean asked. "I'm not hurt," Deirdre said. "Why are you crying?" Jean asked. "I had to punish Teresa B," Deirdre said.

Baylor's Story of Reconciliation:

A Baylor chancellor invited the former members of the drama department and those students whose college experience had been interrupted or altered to a meeting of reconciliation on the Baylor campus. The chancellor recognized that a former official had censored a play written by the only American playwright to receive a Nobel Prize, damaging the reputation of Baylor. The play itself received a Pulitzer. The chancellor also acknowledged that the official had attacked those who were faithfully serving Baylor to promote himself.

It was fun reuniting with those who came. Actor Burgess Meredith returned. He had played Hamlet in a Baylor production and Charles Laughton assisted in the production and coached the actors. While I was in North Carolina, Meredith brought the cast of a play he was directing on Broadway to see a different production of Hamlet at Baylor. For the reconciliation Meredith and his son did a charming presentation and received a standing ovation.

McKinney and I, along with Baylor professor Robert Darden, had a session on writing with former students and some current Baylor students. There was standing-room only for a presentation by multitalented Robert Wilson, playwright, painter, sculptor, choreographer, performer who was famous for productions such as "Einstein on the Beach" with Philip Glass, "CIVIL warS" and "The Life and Times of Joseph Stalin," a 12-hour performance. Wilson also premiered nine theatrical works in Berlin and designed the set for Lady Gaga's MTV Video Music Awards performance. Wilson was never a Baylor student but he was in Baylor Children's Theater and credited Baker for much of his inspiration.

It was fun being at Baylor with old friends for a weekend, and Baylor was gracious. It may have been redemption for Baylor as well as for us but I was not homesick for Baylor.

CHAPTER FOUR

Stories Gone Wrong

Stories have a way of inventing themselves. If you create stories with realistic rather than stock characters—who respond like puppets filling stock roles such as simple heroine, brave hero and wretched villain—then you have the same problem, on a minor scale, as The Supreme Creator. The characters you have created have free will.

I attempted to write a story with the working title, "A Last Love," about an elderly man and woman who meet at a graveyard, each attending the grave of a former spouse. They stumble into conversation and in the conversation, in their loneliness, a romantic cord is tugged. However, the male character turned out to be as imposing, as unhearing, as insensitive as her first husband. The woman refused him, seeking instead a daring adventure, the first of her life. The story ended the right way regardless of the free will of the unsuitable suitor. I changed the title to "Living With the Hyenas," as she had been prey surrounded by male predators all her life.

Moses may not have been the first person God called to deliver the Hebrews from Egypt. He was the one who answered the call. GodStory ended the right way regardless of what his creatures did.

Stories come to this writer in different forms. *In the House of the Lord* began as a college student with many questions and few answers, but college students are supposed to have many questions and few certitudes. The protagonist became a Protestant pastor who was supposed to have answers but had more questions, who had little certitude but great faith.

Many years ago I met an elderly woman who lived alone

on a ranch in West Texas. She kept some exotic animals—zebras, camels, elks, something—that she liked to watch. But someone shot two of them through her fence just to kill them. In a nearby town I expressed sympathy for her to her neighbors. They said, "Don't worry about her. She's killed two men."

I knew someday I would write a story about a woman who killed two men, who they were, why she did it, and the consequences of her action. I didn't want to know any more about the woman I had met. That would constrict my imagination. For fifteen or more years I let the story work itself out in the unconscious part of my brain. It was published as *Tie-Fast Country*, not a good title because few people understand what tie-fast means, but the perfect title for those who do. A title should mean more after you have read the story.

Tie-fast ropers tie one end of the lariat fast to the saddle horn and so can't let go of whatever is on the other end. Some cowboys were known to have roped bears but that didn't always end well. The other method is to dally, wrap the rope around the horn and keep the end in your hand so you can let it go if necessary. Dally is a corruption for a Spanish phrase meaning "let it go." It was a fitting title because the story is about people who tie hard and fast to some things and never let them go regardless of consequences, and people who tie-fast to nothing, but dally and let go when the tie constrains them.

Stories Can be Interpreted in Different Ways:

The bane of writers is readers who don't read the story you wrote, but a story that they created based partly on the story you wrote. That's as true of sermons, letters and email messages as it is of novels and poems.

I thought *In the House of the Lord* was an inspirational story of an evangelical pastor who has questions, doubts, confusions and yet goes into the fiery furnace every day to do the best he can with failing people in a flawed world. A man who had received a Tony for his performance in a Broadway show told me it was the most depressing book he had ever read. Why? I asked. His father was a pastor and there was never closure. Pastors can rarely dust off their hands knowing the story is over. Funerals are the next story in the serial

One of the reasons people read stories is because most stories reach conclusions that amuse, edify or gratify, happily ever after. Ernest Hemingway and Margaret Atwood have pointed out there can be no happy ending to a love story unless both lovers die together. That ending rarely satisfies or gratifies the reader.

Whatever your intentions, the reader has his or her own understanding of the story. And the story goes wrong. I intended *The Last Klick* to deglamorize war. It failed to do so, as Dalton Trumbo had failed in *Johnny Got His Gun*, and Erich Remarque failed in *All Quiet on the Western Front.* As many writers will attest, you can't remove glamor from war any more than you can remove rape, pillage and atrocity.

I intended *North to Yesterday* to debunk the romanticized myth of the Wild West. I intended *Echoes of Glory* to demonstrate how our "reality" is created for us by politicians and the military/industrial/news and entertainment media that Marine Corps Commandant Gen. Smedley Butler and President Eisenhower warned us about.

Wanderer Springs was going to be about my paternal grandmother who died at the age of 90 the year I was born. I was told she once held me when I was a baby. I wanted to write the book to know her. I went to Vermont to meet some relatives who remembered her. There were two stories that they all knew: she traveled to California unchaperoned (gasp), to teach school when there was a school just down the road, and she was related to Abraham Lincoln.

Wanderer Springs was about a small town born beside the railroad track that died beside the interstate. I saw the story as a hand woven rug where threads crossed and the story was in the intersection of the strands. Grandmother's part in the story was little more than a footnote.

The Creation of Man and Woman:

Those who gave us the Bible included two creation stories. That has caused much disputation and the second story has gravely injured women. There is a Jewish tradition that neither man nor woman is in the image of God until they marry; it is the combination that makes them in the image of God. I like that tradition.

I prefer the first creation story with its its theme of man's relationship to a majestic God who created people in the image of the Divine. I believe Genesis 1 is necessary to explain Mozart, Bach, Picasso, Shakespeare, the mathematicians and scientists who have created the world we understand, those like Jonas Salk who rejected enormous riches to give the people of the world a vaccine against polio, those like Gandhi, Mandela, Martin Luther King, Jr. who defined love as the remedy for violence.

I believe the second story about man formed from clay and his relationship to woman are necessary to explain Hitler, Stalin, Mao, Pol Pot, and such horrors as the sexual abuse of women and children, and my own failures to be and do what I want to be and do. In the second story, God doesn't say the creation of man and woman is good. This is the world we live in rather than the earlier model and necessitates a fall from the ideal. Humans are created by both God's mind and Divine hands and are both breath and clay.

In the highly patriarchal times of the Jewish Bible, women identified as prophets included Miriam, sister of Moses and Aaron (Ex. 15: 20), Deborah (Judges 4: 4), the prophet Isaiah's wife (Isa. 8: 3), and Huldah, the interpreter of the Book of the Law discovered in the temple (2 Kings 22: 14; 2 Chron. 34: 22). They seem to be regarded as equals to Abraham, Isaac, Jacob, Moses, Elijah, Aaron, Samuel, Isaiah, Jeremiah and Amos.

Phoebe was a "deacon" and a "benefactor" of Paul (Rom. 16:1-2). Romans 16 names eight other women active in the Christian church including Junia ("prominent among the apostles"), Mary ("who has worked very hard among you"), and Julia. Chloe was an important member of the church in Corinth.

Baptism not Circumcision:

When Paul insisted that baptism, not circumcision, be the ritual of initiation into Christianity women should have become full members of the church with equal rights. For a while they did. However, that was too extreme for the patriarchal culture that viewed Christians as subversive and slowly women were relegated to their previous position.

Paul referred to the story of the Garden of Eden as the reason for male domination. Man was created "first, then" Eve. Was the first creation better than the one after the flood? If so, then why the flood? Paul followed that argument with the fact that the woman was deceived and sinned but the man willfully sinned. In the Genesis story God tells Adam he must not eat of the tree of the knowledge of good and evil before Eve is created. Who tells Eve? We don't know but if it was Adam we know what that was like.

"Babe, someone called while you were out."

"Who was it?"

"I didn't get the name."

"What was it about?"

"Uh...It may have had something to do with somebody you know and they needed you for a party or something like that. They'll call back." Yes, if the caller was another wife she will certainly call back.

Is being deceived into sin worse than willfully sinning? Paul wrote that sin entered the world through one man, and also death, perhaps because Adam willfully sinned (Romans 5: 12).

If Paul wrote the letter to Timothy, he contradicted himself (I Tim. 2:12-14). "But I permit not a woman to teach, nor to have dominion over a man, but to be in quietness. For Adam was first formed, then Eve; and Adam was not beguiled, but the woman being beguiled hath fallen into transgression."

If this passage in I Timothy applies to all women and all times, then braided hair, probably big hair, or hair that is artificially waved or curled would be disallowed. No jewelry, rings, earrings, bracelets, necklaces; watches would have to be practical, without decoration and useful only for telling time. No stylish clothes in church. There is no mention of women wearing pants in church but I think it would have been considered an abomination.

The rules for Christian men would also apply. "Everyone must submit himself to the governing authorities, for there is no authority except that which God has established. The authorities that exist have been established by God. Consequently, he who rebels against the authority is rebelling against what God has instituted, and those who do so will bring judgment on themselves." What? This nation began with the "founding fathers" rebelling against King George III who had been established by God? The Confederacy began with loyal soldiers attacking the United States that was established by God? There went my heroes. Gunmen! Militants! Insurgents! Terrorists!

That scripture was used to justify the "divine right of kings." I don't know of any American Christians who believe the American Revolutionaries were wrong or that it was sinful to rebel against King George. There are Christians in the South who don't believe Robert E. Lee, Stonewall Jackson, Nathan Bedford Forrest and their troops were traitors or sinners.

Paul writes the same message to the church in Rome.

"For rulers hold no terror for those who do right, but for those who do wrong. Do you want to be free from fear of the one in authority? Then do what is right and he will commend you. For he is God's servant to do you good. But if you do wrong, be afraid, for he does not bear the sword for nothing. He is God's servant, an agent of wrath to bring punishment on the wrongdoer. Therefore, it is necessary to submit to the authorities, not only because of possible punishment but also because of conscience. This is also why you pay taxes, for the authorities are God's servants, who give their full time to governing. Give everyone what you owe him: If you owe taxes, pay taxes; if revenue, then revenue; if respect, then respect; if honor, then honor" (Romans 13: 1-7).

Those who fear the government do so because they have done wrong? Men must submit to the government the way women submit to men? Pay your taxes? Those are sermons I have not heard. Pastor Hagee has a million dollar tax-free annual income. Does he know this scripture? This may have been the beginning of American exceptionalism. Everyone must do these things except certain American Christians.

But that's not all. "I want men everywhere to hold up holy hands in prayer, without anger or disputing" (I Tim. 2: 8). Has that ever happened? I have heard angry prayers from the pulpit, even imprecatory prayers. I'm a Baptist. At business meetings where every member of the church has a vote and a voice, few voices incline toward apathy. To quote myself, "Where you have two Baptists you have a Baptist church. Where you have three Baptists you have two Baptist churches." Winthrop Hudson, Professor of Church History, Colgate Rochester, identified Baptists as "Separating Separatists."

Genesis 2 and 3 still divide the church, and like the curse on Ham, are used as weapons by some on half the population of the world. The Apostle Paul also wrote that in Christ there was neither male nor female (Gal. 3: 28). There is a contradiction if in conversion a woman is forgiven of her personal sins but still must be punished for the sin of Eve.

Even some children ask if all female mammals experienced a change in anatomy after Eve tasted forbidden fruit? Or is the Garden of Eden a story explaining why birth is painful to all female mammals without knowing much about anatomy or the birth process?

Genesis 2 has done injury to women through the centuries, but Jesus supplied the remedy. Two sisters were hosting a meeting; one labored in the kitchen to provide for the visitors, the other wanted to sit at the feet of Jesus and join the conversation of the men. Martha asked Jesus to rebuke Mary and tell her to return to the kitchen where women belonged. Jesus said Mary had chosen a better duty and that it would not be taken from her (Luke 10: 38-42). That last part had to be foretelling because so far it has been taken from her.

CHAPTER FIVE

UNIVERSAL Love and PARTICULAR Law

Some believe the most important words in the Bible are not the words of love but the words of the law. The religious laws give us something by which to judge ourselves and they bring us comfort and satisfaction when we keep them. Some might say "self-righteousness" as they also give us means for believing we are holier than others. Jesus summarized the law and the prophets as "love God with all your heart and love your neighbor as you love yourself" (Matt. 22: 37-40).

The law must not contradict GodStory of epic love. Nevertheless, the religious laws are part of the framework, some would say the foundation, of Judaism, Christianity and Islam. For that reason we must differentiate between the particular and the universal in religious laws.

Every writer worthy of the trees that die for her words writes to please herself. If she is a religious writer she also hopes and prays to please God. But she is not writing to herself or, except for prayers and some poems, to God. Sometimes she writes to everyone who will read her words, a universal audience, and with today's technology her words can circle the globe. Sometimes she writes to a particular audience—anyone interested in fishing, better investments or how to lose weight without dieting or exercise. Jeremiah was writing for a particular audience that ignored him, but that audience has become universal through the inclusion of his words in the Bible.

If you read the Bible for yourself rather than having an authority tell you what it means, one of your tasks is to distinguish between what is universal for all people and all times, and what is particular for some people at a particular time. For example there are many scriptures about the sacrifice of animals and burnt offerings but not even Orthodox Jews do that any more. It's generally agreed by practice that those scriptures pertain only to a particular people and time.

Particular Rituals:

Rituals are important and most families, cultures, and religions have them. Over time some lose their relevance and are forgotten. Others continue, although no one remembers what they mean. Jean, Deirdre and I were invited to a celebration in Ireland. When we asked what we were celebrating, we were told that no one remembered. They just liked celebrating.

Because we were a farm family, many of the presents Santa was to deliver on Christmas morning were from mail-order catalogs and some didn't arrive until after Christmas. One of our family rituals was that on New Year's Day Santa stopped on his way back to the North Pole to leave those presents. I wanted to continue that ritual with my family but Deirdre was born on New Year's Day and that became the new ritual. Another new ritual was that a child's birthday was also the mother's "birth" day and she was also to be honored and recognized with a present.

Jean thought it unfair that everyone received a present except me, the one who started the whole thing. In the revised tradition, we parents gave everyone in the family a present. Every birth day was important.

I don't know of any religion or cult that practices the ritual prescribed in Numbers 5. It is generally accepted that the writer was writing for a particular audience at a particular time. Virginity tests are still used in parts of the world.

The Abrahamic religions accept the Bible as sacred literature but disagree with each other and among themselves regarding what is universal and what is particular and that pertains to stories, laws and commandments. Jesus told one man that to be saved he had to sell all that he had and give the money to the poor because the man was a materialist. It is generally agreed by American Christians, even Christians living in poverty, that Jesus's words applied only to that man at that time and perhaps to those who have a bigger income and more possessions than you.

Jesus told Nicodemus that he must be born again because Nicodemus was a literalist. Evangelicals generally agree that story is universal for all people and all times. Some believe it is less costly than giving money to the poor.

Did every statement by Jesus have universal application? Jesus warned of the wrath to come—the Roman destruction of Jerusalem, the Temple and the nation of Israel. "I say unto you, In that night there shall be two men on one bed; the one shall be taken, and the other shall be left. There shall be two women grinding together; the one shall be taken, and the other shall be left" (Luke 17: 34, 35). That's a specific time and place but the scripture is universal in that at the judgment there may be that kind of separation.

Universal Characters:

In describing an individual, real or fictional, universal characteristics help us to identify with that individual, even if it's a being from another planet or an animal like Br'er Rabbit, Peter Cottontail or Lassie in fables, folk tales and stories written for children. We feel empathy for anything that has emotions such as love, jealousy, fear, ambition, envy, and feel pity for anything that is in pain or hungry, or lonely, unless it is something that is repulsive to us, like a cockroach. We identify with the cowardly lion because we all fear failing when extreme courage is required. We are empathetic to the Scarecrow with his head of straw because we all would like to be smarter. If a character is too universal it becomes a type.

Christian, in *Pilgrim's Progress*, represents a typical Christian on the way from "this world to the world that is to come." Written by English Baptist preacher John Bunyan in 1678, it has been translated into more than 200 languages and has never been out of print. The protagonist, Christian, to escape the knowledge of his sinful self goes in search of the "shining light," falls into the Slough of Despond, is diverted by Worldly Wiseman until Evangelist turns him toward the "straight and narrow." Other characters are Lord of the Flies, Faithful, Pope and Pagan, Wanton, Envy, Superstition, etc.

We feel empathy with Christian in *Pilgrim's Progress* because we have experienced most of the same events. But Christian responds in a typical way that doesn't inspire us because it is a familiar experience. It doesn't teach us because we already know how to respond the way he does. The story is so familiar to many Christians, so universal that it tends to be not very interesting. Christian is so much a type that it is difficult for many readers to care much about him.

Jesus is unique but we can identify with him because he made himself vulnerable, tempted as we are, suffering emotional and physical pain as we do. Without that kryptonite and the helpless baby in the manger, he would be as difficult to know as God who is no longer confined to the Garden but is Creator of universes with a border beyond the detection of our most powerful telescopes in space and is expanding into...what? And that expansion into...nothing(?) is speeding up. Jesus is the Way to a personal relationship with that unsearchable Creator.

Particular Characters:

Particular characteristics are those that make us unique, distinctive and real through details such as name, physical description, particular ways of behaving or responding. John the Baptizer had raiment of camel's hair, and a leathern girdle about his loins, and his meat was locusts and wild honey (Matt. 3: 4). That's particular. I'm familiar with camel's hair, and hair was the garment of the prophet (Zech. 13: 4). I've eaten honey and the Bible gave John, and you, permission to eat locusts (Lev. 11: 22.) It's hard for me to identify with the John who sent two of his disciples to follow Jesus and stepped aside for Jesus. That is so unAmerican. It's hard for me not to step in front of Jesus. I have to remind myself that what I do is not always about me.

You know people who are types—jocks, lawyers, preachers, physicians, Big Mama—but you don't have any close friends who are types. You love them despite and because of their contradictions.

A Character can be so Particular
that we have no Empathy for him:

Consider the biblical folktale of Balaam and his donkey found in Numbers Chapters 22-24. The Hebrews were killing and destroying their way to the Promised Land. Balak, son of the king of Moab, saw the Israelites coming and sent Moabite and Midianite elders with money to persuade Balaam to come and curse Israel. When God asked who Balaam's visitors were and Balaam told him, God commanded Balaam not to go with them and not to curse Israel. Balak sent them again with promises of more money. This time God told Balaam to go with them but to say only what God gave him to say. Balaam went, but God was angry, perhaps because Balaam like a naughty child kept asking after God had said no. God set an angel with a flaming sword before Balaam to kill him if he persisted. Balaam's donkey saw the angel and ran into a field.

The next time the angel with the flaming sword positioned itself in the narrow space between two vineyards with walls on either side. The donkey tried to slip by on one side crushing Balaam's foot against the wall. When God moved the angel to a narrower space where there was no room to pass, the donkey lay down. The donkey was more perceptive than Balaam but Balaam beat the donkey each time the donkey saved his life.

God opened the donkey's mouth and it asked why it was being beaten. Balaam replied that if he had a sword he would kill it. Then Balaam's eyes were opened and he saw the angel. God told Balaam that if the donkey hadn't stopped, God would have killed Balaam. Balaam said he would return home, but God told him again to go with the elders but to say only what God gave him to say.

I think it is hard for modern Bible-readers to become emotionally or theologically involved with the story. I know evangelical pastors, all of them male, who say that when they retire the title of their last sermon will be, "When God Spoke Through Balaam's Ass" (Num. 22:28). It's not only in the Bible, it's in the Bible authorized by King James.

My sympathy is with the donkey. The only emotion I have reading the story is humor. The story does reveal something of the culture of the Hebrews and their neighbors. There seemed to be a set price for divination. Balaam had a reputation for pronouncing blessings and curses somewhat like an early day Oprah.

The story of Balaam also reveals how the image of God was evolving. The God who had to ask Balaam who his guests were and couldn't judge the width of a narrow passage is not the God of Genesis 1, who thinks or speaks the universe into existence. This is the primitive God who has to go looking for Adam and Eve who have gone into hiding. The God who tells Balaam to go, then prevents Balaam from going, then tells Balaam to go is somewhat familiar to most of us. We've had go, no go, go experiences usually because of our faulty understanding of what God desires. Or because we kept praying that our desires be granted after God has said no.

That may be what Jesus' prayer, "lead us not into temptation" (or testing) is about. The things for which we pray most earnestly may be the wishes that would cause us the greatest temptation or most painful testing.

Genesis 1 with its sweeping vision of God the Creator of ALL is not the oldest story we have in the biblical canon. It's the first that we read.

When the Israelites killed the Midianites (Num. 31: 8, 16) they also killed Balaam. I find that sad.

The Universal and Particular in stories:

In Franz Kafka's story, usually translated as "Metamorphosis" or "Transformation," Gregor Samsa awakens one morning to discover that he has become an odious insect, sometimes translated as giant cockroach, that disgusts his family. Samsa is unique, too different to arouse empathy in some readers. I have known college students who think the story is science fiction, fantasy or magical realism. When you were a child you probably feared that if your family knew who you were or what you did or what you thought, you would be repugnant to them. If as an elderly parent you fear that your children will find you loathsome or disgusting you will understand the story. Although Gregor is a particular character, the story is universal.

The story of King Saul is generally regarded as a particular story. Saul didn't nominate himself; he didn't compete for the office. Saul was appointed the first king of Israel and given a task beyond his capability. He battled for his people and won victories but never the destruction of his and their enemies. And, like the older brother, King Saul saw a younger man receive the honor and glory that he had been denied despite his best efforts. His own son betrayed him to favor David. Samuel, who anointed him as king, turned against him and Saul turned to a witch to learn his fate. He seemed doomed from the moment he accepted the crown. It's hard to find a moral in the story that is really about David and how he replaced the first born of Saul like a Roman emperor.

Even in death King Saul is not a popular subject. Perhaps that's because the scars of our Civil War are still raw. Most Americans don't recognize the Confederate flag but everyone recognizes the Confederate battle flag and that's the flag that some Americans want to wave, the flag of defiance.

Some politicians and some citizens can't honestly pledge allegiance to "one nation indivisible" because they want the nation to be white and black, rich and poor, Christian and other. Perhaps it's because we have been given a task that is or seems to be beyond our capability and we never fulfill our own or God's expectation. Some of us give up and some soldier on, all of us hoping that what we have done will be acceptable in God's sight and will by God's grace accomplish the Almighty's purpose for us (Psa. 138: 8).

The parable of the Prodigal Son or Forgiving Father or Elder Brother is easily identified as universal. It applies to people everywhere, even primordial ones and as far into the future as we can imagine. A certain man had two sons. There is not even a name because the author of the parable wants universal identification with each of the characters at every stage of life. I still identify with each of them, but when I was younger I mostly identified with the prodigal. However, there has always been a bit of the older brother in me, although I was the youngest of three children. When I became a father I understood better the forgiving father and what forgiveness costs, both to the one who gives and to the one who receives. (Read Isak Dinesen's "Sorrow Acre".)

A certain man went down from Jerusalem to Jericho, and fell among thieves. Many of Jesus' parables begin, "A certain man." That declares the story is universal and applies to all humans. This story is easily recognized as universal and is the definition of "neighbor." Most of us have been injured by some and ignored by others. And most of us have pulled our clothes around us, ducked our heads and pretended not to notice those who needed a friend but whose friendship could mar our reputation or our chances for upward mobility. You are judged by the company you keep.

When I was in high school the pastor asked me why I spent time with the son of a deacon. The son wasn't a bad kid but he had a pickup and three or four friends and when they were together they did dumb things like riding in the back of the pickup roping yard signs and dragging them down the street until one of the boys roped a sign that was rooted in concrete and yanked him out of the pickup. Not exactly illegal but annoying to neighbors with no sense of humor.

I told the pastor that the deacon father thanked me for spending time with his son because when I was with him the son didn't do really dumb things that caused neighbors and sometimes the police to warn him of retribution. But people noticed. The neighbors viewed me with suspicion.

When the "certain man" falls among thieves and is beaten and robbed, he is ignored by those who should care for him. But a despised Samaritan sees him and has pity on him. There is not an exact equivalent of a Samaritan today, but perhaps a Will Campbell story published in the *Wittenburg Door* will suffice. One of Will's friends drove his wife to an Episcopal Church for a meeting. While he waited for his wife, the friend picked up trash on the church's parking lot. He stooped to pick up a half-eaten candy bar when someone said, "Don't eat that." He looked up to see a homeless man. "Here, eat this," the homeless man said, handing Will's friend a bag containing a soft drink and a hamburger, probably the reward for a day of begging.

The half-breed Samaritan is the hero of the parable. Jesus tells the righteous lawyer, "Go thou and do as the Samaritan." What a slap in the face to all of us. Exemplify the best qualities of those you despise.

Does it matter whether Jonah was a real person? Or Job?

One of my friends had an elderly mother who could no longer see or hear well enough to read, listen to music, watch TV or take part in conversations. She had also lost the sense of taste, didn't sleep well and arthritis limited her movement. "Why won't the Lord let me die?" she complained to her pastor who had none of her problems.

"Perhaps there is something the Lord still wants you to do," the pastor wrote on a large pad while mouthing the words.

"Well, I'm not going to do it," she said. Perhaps sometimes we should keep easy answers for ourselves.

There is more than one Jonah.

Particularizing the story of Jonah or Job makes them less powerful and condemnatory than they are. If Jonah is a particular Jew at a particular time with a mission to save Nineveh, that was built by Nimrod the mighty hunter (Gen. 10: 8-11), then that is history and we can argue over when that happened and what kind of fish. If it is universal, it applies to the Abrahamic religions—all Jews, all Christians and all Muslims, who were given a mission to make God known to the world. Instead, each religion claims God as its own and attempts to deny the one true God to everyone else.

I attended a "unity" meeting at a Christian church where a rabbi, an imam, and a Christian pastor were to discuss ways the three Abrahamic religions could peacefully coexist. What they said was good and full of hope. I, impolitely, asked if they all three worshiped the same God. The rabbi talked about Jewish traditions, the pastor said Christians believed in the God revealed by Jesus Christ. Only the imam said yes without reservation. The three religions worshipped the God of Abraham.

I think Jonah was a jerk. I'm better than Jonah. I try to do what I believe God tells me to do. Is that the point of the story? To make me feel good about myself? The point of the story is that I am not better than Jonah. I am Jonah. I have refused to love my enemies. I am disappointed that God has not destroyed them. I hate it when God does good things to my enemies. Like, give them oil. Which they use to buy our respect.

Universal or particular words:

Words can also be particular or universal, for example when a day is not a calendar day. A day can be 24 hours, or less as in a day's work, or from dawn to dusk. Or more, as in "the day of the Lord" (Joel 2: 11); "I know that my redeemer liveth, and he shall stand at the latter day upon the earth" (Job 19: 25). How long is the "day of the small things" (Zech. 4: 10), or "that day" (Eze. 4:9), or "the day of the Jezreel" (Hos. 1: 11), or "the day of prosperity and the day of adversity" (Ecc. 7: 14), or "the day when I went to Mahanaim" (I Kings 2: 8), or "the day of his coming" (Mal. 3: 2, Joel 2: 2; Eze. 30: 2), or "the son of man in his day" (Luke 17: 24), or "the day of his wrath" (Rev. 6:17)?

When Jesus revised the Ten Commandments, he said, "...whosoever is angry with his brother without a cause shall be in danger of the judgment...." Is "brother" universal like "neighbor" or particular like sibling?

And how universal is "neighbor?" Thanks to technology, print and electronic media and 24-hour news networks, an American sees a minimum of hundreds of thousands of people in need every day. Are they all my neighbor? It's easy to be stunned into indifference because there are so many needy that I can't help them all. It's easy to be stunned into inaction by having to choose which to help: those in my church? those in my congressional district? those in my country? I try to assuage guilt by throwing coins at Heifer, American Friends, OxFam, Mercy Corps, Habitat, Doctors Without Borders, etc. but is it enough? I have an empty bedroom in my house. I have enough food to last for more than a week in my house. Jesus doesn't make it easy for us to define words, and neither did he intend to.

God said to Abraham, "I will bless them who bless you,

and whoever curses you I will curse; and all peoples on earth will be blessed through you" (Gen. 12: 3). Is that blessing, curse and promise particular to Abraham alone and to a particular time, the years of Abraham on earth? Or is it universal, to all the children of Abraham and to all time? All the children of Abraham would include Ishmael father of twelve tribes, and the children of Keturah, Abraham's wife after Sarah died (Gen. 25: 1-16).

All the children of Abraham would also include Christians as Paul wrote, "Even as Abraham believed God, and it was accounted to him as righteousness, know you therefore that they which are of faith, the same are the children of Abraham" (Gal. 3: 6,7). When the Pharisees and Sadducees said they needed no repentance because they were children of Abraham, John the Baptizer replied that God could turn stones into children of Abraham (Matt. 3: 9).

When the Pharisees tried the same argument with Jesus, he said they were the children of Satan (John 8: 34-44). That is a particular condemnation of self-righteous people. It does not mean all Jewish people, although it has been interpreted that way, causing much pain and suffering. You may be good, but only God can make you righteous. That's why self-righteousness is universally condemned.

Ham, a son of Noah, saw his father naked and Noah cursed Ham's son, Canaan: "the lowest of slaves shall he be to his brothers" (Gen. 9: 25). Was the curse particular, only to Canaan? Or, was the curse universal, a curse on dark-skinned people to forever be slaves?

That scripture was used to justify slavery in America, "the land of the free." I heard a lot about "the curse of Ham" when I was young; there was a particular church that taught that people with dark skins were inferior and were intended to be a servant class. That theology still exists in America. If you check with the Southern Poverty Law Center you will discover there are militant white supremacy groups in the U.S. who declare themselves to be Christian. That's why distinguishing between the universal and the particular is important.

Universal and Particular Commandments:

"Do not mate different kinds of animals. Do not plant your field with two kinds of seed. Do not wear clothing woven of two kinds of material" (Lev. 19: 19). I'm sure that scripture was never preached in the South where mules, a cross between horses and donkeys, were the most powerful thing on a farm. Dad regularly planted watermelon seeds in cotton fields and a rare joy of chopping or picking cotton was finding a ripe melon that we broke open and ate with our hands. Forbidding the blending of two kinds of material would wipe out the garment industry and empty the closets of a lot of Christians. Some Christians have ignored these. Some Christians have made Lev. 20: 13 a secular law.

Other Laws From Leviticus We Have Ignored:

Don't reap the edges of your field or gather the leftovers of the field; do not harvest grapes a second time or pick up grapes that have fallen (19: 9,10). That was for the poor and undocumented workers. My father and some other farmers followed that rule for crops like corn but factory farms do not. Do not deceive one another (v. 11). That would eliminate advertising and public relations industries, lobbyists and politicians. Do not hold the wages of a worker overnight (v. 13). Don't gossip or do anything that endangers your neighbor's life (v. 16). Do not seek revenge or bear a grudge but love your neighbor as yourself (v. 18). Do not cut the hair on the side of your head (the Marines never read that scripture) or clip the edges of your beard (v. 27). Do not put tattoo marks on yourself (v. 28). Do not go to fortune tellers (v. 31). Love an undocumented worker as yourself (v. 33).

How did you score on that check list? Few have been excluded because of gossip, hair, tattoos or astrology. In a past administration some decisions by the White House were made by an astrologer. Some things forbidden in that list are embedded in our culture. Deceiving others is legitimate in business, war and politics. If we loved our undocumented neighbors then immigration wouldn't be headline news or a divisive issue in Congress and churches. One Baptist preacher gained a few minutes of notoriety by asking what would Jesus do with undocumented children? He answered that Jesus would send them back home because they had violated the law. In what Bible is that law found? Jesus violated God's law by healing on the Sabbath. Jesus also identified his followers—"I was a stranger and you took me in" (Matt. 25: 35).

What's surprising in that list are the unimportant laws that we know but ignore like gossip, hair, tattoos, astrology, and the important ones forbidding things that are embedded in our culture: deceiving others, revenge, grudges, not loving your neighbor as yourself and not expanding the meaning of neighbor to include residents without papers. Without revenge and grudges there would be almost no TV or film dramas, and in most of them exacting vengeance is the "feel good" part of the drama.

Leviticus 19 also forbids making your daughter a prostitute lest the land fall to whoredom (v. 29). Some Jewish writers believe that meant delaying marrying her to another until the perfect deal was sealed or the right man became eligible, perhaps through divorce. Others believe it was a reference to the fertility religions that dedicated young girls at their temple by introducing them to sexual relations as worship. That would turn the land to the Islamic, Jewish and Christian definition of prostitution.

I think it might be a reference to the ease with which a man could divorce his wife without cause. Where could she go, what could she do unless the father who arranged her marriage permitted her to return to his house? If fathers didn't, that would also turn the land to prostitution. This was centuries before the spinning wheel that allowed a woman to support herself, perhaps her children. In modern day India you can see houses that have the palm print of a widow who dipped her hand in paint and pressed it on the outside wall of her house. Those are houses of widows who immolated themselves on their husband's pyre because they had no place to go. Some of them carried their children into the fire with them.

I know no examples in the Bible where a father welcomed the return of a divorced daughter. In Judges 19 a married woman returned to her father's house and he welcomed her and wanted her to stay. The writer or compiler of the book said she was unfaithful, but leaving her husband and returning to her father's house would have been considered unfaithful. If she committed adultery there are no indications of blame or punishment for it.

I remember in weddings when pastors asked, Who gives this woman in marriage? The notion that a woman was the property of her father until she became the property of her husband has largely passed in this country but the notion that her uterus is the property of a male-dominated institution such as the church or the state prevails. In 1707, English Lord Chief Justice John Holt described "the highest invasion of property," meaning a husband's property, as a man having sexual relations with another man's wife.

As you should know from reading the novels of Jane Austen, in England when a woman married her property went to her husband. If a woman writer had copyright when she married the copyright passed to her husband until 1882 when the English Parliament allowed married women to own and control property in their own right, except in Scotland. If there was no will, the real property of the father went to the oldest son until 1925.

I don't know what we can do about Leviticus except to determine which laws are universal and which are particular and no longer relevant. It is generally agreed among Christians that the food restrictions in Leviticus 11 are particular to orthodox Jews and Muslims and have little importance to Christians, although shellfish are an abomination (Lev. 11:10). What we should not do is to select one law and make it dogma while ignoring the others.

When I was a freshman at Baylor, I tried to find a position that would permit me to be somebody and not just a face in a crowd of beautiful people. There was a lot of competition, All-American athletes, athletes in a popular sport like football, former gang leaders whom Jesus had saved from prison or worse, those who had cars, beauty queens, flamboyant student evangelists, those popular for being popular, war heroes. I tried to be identified with the "aginners" who attempted to be known for the things we were against. Eschewing dancing wasn't enough; you had to cast a condemnatory eye on those who danced, had danced or went to places where dancing occurred. I never went to a "function" because there would be dancing. Baylor didn't allow dancing on campus so publicity about off-campus dancing advertised "functions." I also saved a lot of money. An aginner friend did ask for a date, bought a corsage, paid for two tickets to the dance but he and his date sat outside in his car to keep their garments clean by shunning those who danced inside.

I and a couple of friends rented a house off campus because it was cheaper. One day while they were gone I found two beers in the back of the refrigerator. Horrified, I opened the bottles and poured the contents in the sink. When they returned, horror of horrors, they asked if I had drunk their beer. How could two "friends" believe I had taken what belonged to them to enjoy myself? That would be stealing. I did enjoy the rightness of pouring their beer down the sink. I think they believed they were properly chastised.

Being an aginner was difficult because the contenders were serious about limiting the freedom that Jesus had given his followers. If you were opposed to choirs that sang hymns in a foreign language because it couldn't be religious music if you didn't understand the words, someone else was opposed to all music that didn't have words. Who knew what it meant? "This old house," sung by a country/western singer was a campus hit. "Ain't gonna need this old house no longer; I'm getting ready to meet the saints." Everyone knew what it meant.

If you gave up soft drinks into which you had dropped peanuts, someone else gave up cream and sugar in coffee. I never made the top of the list; closing your Bible during worship meant the spirit had left the room.

I dropped out of Baylor to enlist in the the Marines and discovered there were big things to oppose like bigotry, oppression, single mothers, love of country that required me to hate the enemies of my country, certitude of my country's righteousness that required me to hate fellow Americans who thought my country was capable of error, greed, bigotry and lust for the resources of other nations.

I also discovered a secret passage, at least secret to me. Paul wrote that you should let no one criticize you for what you eat or what you drink, how you observe a religious festival or keep the Sabbath (Col. 2:16).

Jesus's Commandments:

Jesus told his followers not to pray in public to be seen. Is that a universal commandment? I was aware of that scripture, of course, but ignored it's meaning for years, hoping that others would notice the piety of my family with our heads bowed and eyes closed. Surely silence and respect would ensue in the diner. Silence did not occur as everyone assumed we were part of the decor and respect fell on us like dove dung.

Jesus told his followers to do charitable deeds in secret. Well dang. What reward is there if you can't require gratitude? It wasn't until after I married that I discovered the high price of gratitude. Jean was willing to go to graduate school while teaching high school English so I could pursue my dream of being a writer, that

I believed was also my religious vocation. Gratitude required me to be more humble than I wanted to be. It was a debt that could be repaid only by acknowledging my need. That is a high price to pay.

Jean and I went with a church group to take staples and toys to a young couple with three small children. They had been devastated by medical bills and were facing eviction from their crowded apartment. There was barely enough room for us and the gifts, so I and a couple of other men stood in the open door. The father was at work, holding two jobs trying to save his family. The mother picked up the broken crayons and toys, hid dirty clothes and dishes, and tried to settle the children that hung to her skirt, cried in a corner and screamed in excitement at our visit while our leader gave a little homily, prayed and we sang joyful songs of Christmas.

The flustered mother thanked us while trying to put away the toys before the children saw them. The ladies looked in her cabinets and refrigerator telling her how to clean them, where the staples could go and what she should toss in the garbage. They also told her recipes she could make from the staples we brought, tricks to help her manage the children and how to arrange her tiny closet while the poor woman cried in embarrassment.

On the way home Jean and I vowed we would never again deliver goods looking for gratitude. People who need help are grateful but not all of them need an audience to witness their gratitude.

Many churches request government funds so they can do good deeds in the name of their church.

CHAPTER SIX

Why Definitions Matter

Late 1970 and early 1971, I went to Vietnam on special assignment for a "men's magazine." I had wondered how Jesus learned his purpose and how he held on to that belief when no one else comprehended his purpose or desired it. They wanted a different kind of messiah. They wanted a messiah who would restore the Kingdom of David—a messiah who would rescue them the way John the Baptist wanted Jesus to rescue him from prison and almost certain death (Luke 7: 18-23).

I thought I could explore Jesus' unique vision of himself in the story of a "sole survivor" who was the only person to have experienced a disaster that quickly became a media and a political event with each trying to shape the event for their purposes. Could the sole survivor hold on to his unique reality when everyone else understood it in a different way? Eventually, that book became *Echoes of Glory*, published 28 years later. Part of that delay was because I didn't believe the government would fabricate stories or that the media would parrot them without fact checking them until 9/11, Jessica Lynch and Pat Tallman.

As home work for that book I rode a guntruck from Da Nang over the Hai Van Pass to Phu Bai, a road the French called "The Street Without Joy." The crew had painted "The Wild Bunch" on the guntruck that had armor plating on the sides. One crew member counted more than 200 bullet scars on the plating. They had been ambushed the previous day and their driver had been killed. Another crew member talked of RPGs that had missed the truck. An RPG would have turned the truck wrongside out. They had spent the previous night mounting a second .50 calibre machine gun on the truck and were surly, believing that I was there to photograph and report their deaths.

The second day our trip through Hue, Quang Tri, Dong Ha to a firebase on the DMZ was delayed by a crew member who refused to go to the DMZ. He was a short-timer who had too few days left in Vietnam to go to the DMZ. Others in the crew said they weren't going without him. Their appeals failed to move him.

At Dong Ha we were joined by an armored car and a second gun truck. A previous convoy had turned back because the trucks loaded with gun powder, artillery shells, food and bullets for those who lived in rocket range of the North Vietnamese Army were too heavy to pull the muddy mountain roads. Our trip to the DMZ was uneventful but I wrote a story about the crew called "Up the Street Without Joy With the Wild Bunch."

For a time I embedded myself with Golf Company (CUPP), Second Battalion, Fifth Marines, led by Captain Robert Tilley and Gunny Steve Shivers. When I returned home the world had changed. At least my definition of the world had changed.

America had changed. The confident, optimistic nation of hope and freedom had become suspicious, hateful, and filled with resentment. The university where I taught had changed. We were no longer a community of scholars but competitors fighting over minor issues trying to prevent others from climbing the narrow ladder of success and standing on the heads of others to gain the favors dispensed by the royalty at the top. Students had changed. One wanted me to give him a second chance for missing an assignment and a class because he had a hangover. Some students in class appeared stoned.

Home had changed. My wife was diagnosed with Multiple Sclerosis. Her health insurance company knew before we did and dropped her from coverage. Her doctor told me she would be restricted to a wheelchair, go blind and die. I would be a single parent with two young daughters. Less than six weeks after I returned, Brigid died before we celebrated her twelfth birthday.

Brigid died alone. We had taken her to the doctor and when

we came home she was feeling better. My last conversation with her was when I put her to bed. She asked why I was laughing at her. I explained that I wasn't laughing at her. I smiled because I was so happy she was getting better. Jean and I exchanged bed rooms with Deirdre so that we would be closer to Brigid if she became ill during the night.

Jean was awakened by Brigid who was having rigors. While I dressed, Jean called our family doctor and he met us at the hospital. There was a feeding frenzy of "specialists" who examined, tested, studied the tests, conferred with or advised other "specialists" and so on until she died. We never saw them, they never conferred with us, one "specialist" had just graduated from med school and therefore was an expert on everything new that was being taught. As far as we know he was never in the hospital while Brigid was there but he billed us $500 for every day that Brigid was there.

What parent will ask the cost when a "specialist" believes he can help your child? We surrendered Brigid to them as a hostage. Brigid was diagnosed with encephalitis and quarantined. We watched her die through a glass screen. Jean had to avoid being close to Brigid because of MS. One of my regrets is that I did not kick in the glass and hold Brigid while she was dying.

Later, a mother, Jean and other women from the church took turns holding a young boy who had liver disease and waited for a transplant. They held him 24 hours a day for weeks so that he knew he was not alone. I don't care if I got encephalitis. I don't care if I was sent to jail. I was Brigid's father and I should have kicked the door down so that she did not die alone.

Brigid died in the morning after Deirdre had gone to school. Jean and I came home and sat in desolation waiting for Deirdre to come home on the school bus. In an act of thoughtful charity a friend sat in his car across the street to be certain than no sympathizers came before Deirdre arrived home and that we had time alone with Deirdre.

Jean and I sat with our arms around Deirdre and told her that her sister had died. That night Deirdre slept in our bedroom instead of her own, the only time she has ever done so. I think she did it to comfort us and to try to close the breach in the family.

While I was dealing with Jean's illness, Brigid's dying, and teaching my classes, the magazine that sent me to Vietnam wanted my stories. They rejected the first two, liked the third but it was too late. Unable to find a niche among *Esquire*, *Playboy* and *Sports Illustrated*, the magazine failed.

I sent the stories to my editor at Knopf, Harold Strauss. Harold was a fine editor and we had worked together on my first three novels. Harold compared the book favorably to Harry Brown's *A Walk in the Sun* but begged me not to publish it. Everyone was sick of Vietnam. No one wanted to read about it and all that would be remembered by booksellers was that the book didn't sell. The book was later published by Texas A&M University Press as *A Personal War in Vietnam*.

Publishing had changed. In the 1960s and early '70s, publishers had "stables" of writers whose careers they promoted and publishers relied on sales of warehoused books. Writers like F. Scott Fitzgerald sold better after they died than when they were alive, but the Supreme Court limited the way publishers, and others, could "write down" the value of inventory. Publishers "remaindered" books for as little as $1 a book or shredded them to cut warehouse expenses. Publishers were no longer interested in stables of writers but in bestseller books that sold for three months and then disappeared. Midlist authors such as I were dropped.

Harold Strauss retired and died shortly afterwards. Knopf had an option on my next novel so I sent them *Wanderer Springs*. An editor I did not know rejected the book without comment, the fate of midlist writers everywhere

I have Marine buddies who still suffer PTSD. It's a terrible condition that infects everyone around them. They lived with death and struggle to return to a life that no longer exists. I didn't live with death but Vietnam, the shock of a different America, Jean's illness, Brigid's death, and rejection by my publisher gave me symptoms similar to PTSD, something that I have only recently understood. I doubted my mission. I doubted my marriage. I doubted myself.

One reason many marriages fail after the death of a child is because, unhinged by grief, you turn for comfort to your spouse, the one you have always turned to but she is overwhelmed with grief. Rather than sharing part of your load she mirrors your pain. I failed Jean. I couldn't share her pain. I could barely endure it.

We both failed Deirdre. Deirdre had always been a little daredevil. She climbed trees that boys her age wouldn't climb. She jumped off a twenty-foot-board into a pool before she could swim. I had to wait in the pool for her to jump, then drag her to the side. And then she would climb up to the board again.

One evening while a babysitter was bathing Brigid, Deirdre walked out the front door and disappeared. In panic the babysitter alerted the neighborhood and the neighbors called Deirdre, mispronouncing her name in interesting ways. The babysitter's boyfriend was son of the chief of police so she called the chief and the chief alerted those on duty. A patrolman spotted Deirdre walking purposefully down the street. He stopped the car and asked where she was going. She was going to the theater to see her daddy. The policeman brought her to the theater where I was watching a rehearsal. I was surprised to see both of them. He said he would take her home and I advised her to stay there.

A bit later a neighbor kept most of the children on the block while their parents worked or were in school. When the woman went inside to check the younger kids who were taking a nap, Deirdre pried a loose board out of the backyard fence and led the other children on a freedom march to our backyard and another kind of captivity that she liked better.

Brigid took part in Deirdre's antics but she didn't take solo risks. If things went wrong it was always Brigid who was injured. Once they raced their horses down the gravel drive, something they were forbidden to do. I was trimming the hoofs on Teresa B and had her foot between my knees. Startled by the other horses the filly jerked her leg free kicking me in the face. It wasn't a bad kick but it could have been. Jean came out and ordered them into their rooms for timeout. Brigid went quietly. She preferred timeout to scolding. Deirdre said, "Can't you just spank me and let me play?" She had no time for timeout.

We feared Deirdre was trying to comfort us by being less spontaneous like Brigid, but Deirdre was being cautious to protect us. We wavered between being overly protective and letting her be the daredevil she was at heart. Once I told her, "Deirdre, we haven't been parents any longer than you have been a child. We make mistakes too."

Deirdre saved our marriage. I believe she also saved my life. I wanted to run as far and as fast as I could, as though you could ever outrun death and pain. I wanted to drive aimlessly until I found comfort or danger or physical pain to distract me. I wanted to escape the life in which I was trapped any way that I could and yet still be close to Jean and Deirdre. I didn't lose faith but I was in a valley shadowed by death and I found little comfort in God's rod and staff.

Yet, I didn't want to be immune, to be exempt from such pain. I knew people who seemed to have never troubled over tomorrow, never feared they wouldn't survive the night, never touched a sleeping child to be certain their flesh was warm, never questioned God's ways. Their lives seemed unbearably shallow.

Unable to find comfort in each other we sought refuge separately. Deirdre found escape in training her own horse and in a close friend who brought laughter to our house. Jean went to night school while teaching and earned a degree in library science.

Disappointed to find that there were no biographies of heroic women for young girls, she asked a publisher why. The publisher suggested that if she wanted a biography for young women she should write one. To Jean that was like weighing anchor. Once the ship started moving it wasn't going to stop. The publisher wanted her to write biographies of Texas heroes. Male heroes. She published five biographies of male heroes before the publisher would accept a biography of a female hero.

Writing was also my escape and my salvation. For part of every day I was in a different world, a world of my own making, a world without NOW and its new definition of father, husband, family. Returning to the prison of NOW was always unpleasant with no happy ending.

Jean's physical symptoms didn't return but the false diagnosis of MS was still in her records as a preexisting condition, affecting her health care for years. Eventually, what I worked on became three books, *Seasonal Rain,* *The Last Klick* and *Wanderer Springs.* Vietnam is a presence in each of those books and in each a young girl dies. I had to redefine myself, my faith, my world. Moses, Miriam and Aaron had the same problem.

The Pentateuch or Torah:

Moses, Miriam and Aaron had a bigger job than leading the Hebrews out of Egypt. They had to organize clans that knew how to be Egyptian slaves by the laws and regulations of Egypt but did not know how to be a distinct people capable of becoming a nation with a land of their own.

In the Torah, Jewish leaders tried to define what it meant to be Jewish and a Jewish nation with laws that attempted to standardize and regulate human desires and impulses— greed, lust, jealousy, aggression, revenge, domination, etc. Were they to be like everyone else or were they to live by a higher standard? Despite their leaders' wishes and their declaration that their laws were given by God and written by Moses, they were tempted by foreign gods and foreign practices.

The Psalms, Proverbs and other books of wisdom, chronicles of the kings and words of the prophets, all clarified what it meant to be Jewish. Together the library called The Jewish Bible created a distinct people, a remnant, who clung to their definition of themselves and to each other, through wars, captivity, disintegration, dispersion. Until they returned to the Holy Land.

Whose Holy Land Is It?

The deed to Palestine is more complicated than most Jews, Arabs and Christians wish to admit. God promised the Holy Land to the seed of Abraham (Gen. 12: 7, 13: 14-15). That story and that promise is in the Jewish Bible, the Christian Bible and the Koran. Abraham was the father of Ishmael and Isaac, and others (Gen. 25: 1-6).

The Hebrews had a problem because according to the Jewish Bible the first born son had the birthright and the royal succession was through the first born son. Ishmael was Abraham's first born son. Some claim that Ishmael doesn't count because his mother was a sex slave but the birthright belonged to the father and not the mother. The firstborn son was the first sign of the father's reproductive strength (Deut. 21: 15-17). That son received a double portion of all the father had.

However, the Jewish claim to God's promise was through Abraham, Isaac and Jacob—but Isaac was Abraham's second son, and Jacob, whose name was changed to Israel, was Isaac's second son. Jacob's birthright did not go to his firstborn, Reuben, but to Judah. The two best known kings of Israel, David and Solomon were not firstborn sons and did not follow the succession.

In the covenant with Abraham, God promised Abraham that he would be the father of many nations. The land of

Canaan would belong to his descendants, Ishmael, Isaac and the others (Gen. 17: 4-8), and they would inherit the earth (Ps. 37: 11, Matt. 5: 5). Whoever blessed Abraham would be blessed and whoever cursed him would be cursed and through him all families of the earth would be blessed (Gen. 12: 1-3). That covenant was repeated with Isaac (26: 2-4), Jacob (28: 13-15), and Moses (Ex. 3: 6-8).

However, in the Jewish Bible not all of Abraham's children are included in that covenant, or all of Isaac's children, or all of Jacob's children. Rather than becoming many nations, the children of Abraham were contracting until there were the tribes of Judah and Israel, and the Jewish Bible discouraged marriage outside the tribe (Ex. 34: 15, Num. 36: 6, Ezra 9: 1-3,12, 10: 16-44; Neh. 13:23-27).

The Covenant Was Conditional:

Literally, covenant means "coming together," as in agreement to terms. The word is most often used in marriage, an agreement between two people that can be broken, but with consequences. "Now if you obey me fully and keep my covenant, then out of all nations you will be my treasured possession. Although the whole earth is mine, you will be for me a kingdom of priests and a holy nation. These are the words you are to speak to the Israelites" (Ex. 19: 5, 6).

"But if they confess their iniquity and the iniquity of their fathers in their treachery that they committed against me, and also in walking contrary to me, so that I walked contrary to them and brought them into the land of their enemies—if then their uncircumcised heart is humbled and they make amends for their iniquity, then I will remember my covenant with Jacob, and I will remember my covenant with Isaac and my covenant with Abraham, and I will remember the land" (Lev. 26: 40-43). See also Deut. 7: 12; I Kings 9: 6-9; Josh 23: 15,16; II Chron. 7: 19-22.

The Hebrew prophets tried to call Israel back to faithfulness to the covenant. "This is what the Lord Almighty, the God of Israel, says: Reform your ways and your actions, and I will let you live in this place" (Jer. 7: 3). "Come, let us return to the Lord. He has torn us to pieces but he will heal us; he has injured us but he will bind up our wounds. After two days he will revive us; on the third day he will restore us, that we may live in his presence" (Hosea 6: 1, 2).

The prophets looked for a new covenant based not on Levitical laws but with the law written in the heart. "The days are coming," declares the Lord, "when I will make a new covenant with the people of Israel and with the people of Judah. It will not be like the covenant I made with their ancestors when I took them by the hand to lead them out of Egypt because they broke my covenant, though I was a husband to them," declares the Lord. "This is the covenant I will make with the people of Israel after that time," declares the Lord. "I will put my law in their minds and write it on their hearts. I will be their God, and they will be my people. No longer will they teach their neighbor, or say to one another, 'Know the Lord,' because they will all know me, from the least of them to the greatest," declares the Lord. "For I will forgive their wickedness and will remember their sins no more." (Jer. 31: 31-34).

The Christian Claim to the Promised Land:

In the Christian Bible Jesus was a direct descendent of David who was a descendent of Abraham (Matt. 1: 1). Matthew's genealogy mentions Rahab, Bathsheba, and Ruth who were gentiles. Luke's genealogy traces Jesus' ancestors back to Adam, making him a descendent of every tribe and nation.

John the Baptist told the Pharisees, who were morally upright and spiritually secure because they were children of Abraham, that God could turn stones into children of Abraham (Matt. 3: 9). When some Jews said they were children of Abraham, had never been slaves and needed no one to set them free, Jesus told them they were children of the devil (John 8: 39-45). This was a particular reference to particular self-righteous individuals and not a universal statement about all Jews or all self-righteous people.

When God sent Moses to deliver his people from Egypt, Moses asked what name he should give to the Hebrews. God gave him a to-be verb similar to "is." Who is. What is. The active force in the universe. All life, all creative power is what God is. And is beyond. Jesus applied the name to himself (John 8: 58-59) and barely escaped stoning.

Jesus read from the first two verses of Isa. 61 and said that this scripture was fulfilled in him (Luke 4: 18-21). At supper the night before his crucifixion Jesus took a cup of wine and said, "This is the cup of the new covenant in my blood" (1 Cor. 11: 5).

In Acts 3: 24-26, Peter claimed that covenant for Jewish Christians. In his letter to the Galatians, Paul claimed that covenant for Abraham's spiritual descendants (3: 6-9). The writer of Hebrews argued that the new covenant was superior to the first covenant (Heb. 8: 6-13).

When the resurrected Christ met with his disciples they asked, "Are you going to restore the kingdom to Israel?" (Acts 1: 6) They had already forgotten that Jesus had said his kingdom was not of this world (John 18: 36). Jesus replied that it was not for them to know but that they would be his witnesses in Jerusalem, Judea, Samaria, and to the ends of the earth. That would be the restoration of Israel.

The apostle Paul wrote that a Jew was one who was circumcised not of the body but of the heart (Rom. 2: 29), echoing Deut. 30: 6. In Rom. 4: 13-17, Paul wrote that Abraham was father of all those of faith and therefore father of many nations. Luke wrote that the law of Moses could not justify but that in the new covenant, through faith, Jesus could (Acts 13: 38, 39). In heaven there would be a multitude from every nation, tribe, people and language (Rev. 7: 9).

The New Testament or New Covenant writers regarded Jesus, descendent of Abraham, as the one through whom all nations would be blessed and the church as the new Israel (Gal. 6: 15, 16). Whoever blessed the church would be blessed and whoever cursed the church would be cursed.

The Christian claim to the Promised Land is not to present-day Palestine but to the new heaven and new earth where God will dwell with believers in the new Jerusalem that is above (Gal. 4: 26), whose architect and maker is God (Heb. 11: 10), with walls of jasper and city of gold. There will be no temple because God doesn't live in a house made by men (Acts 7: 48-50). Jesus identified himself with the temple (Matt.12: 6; John 2: 19-22). In the new Jerusalem God and the Lamb are the temple, and there will be no tears, no night and its gates will never be shut (Rev. 21).

There are Christian citizens of Israel who lack the same political preference as Muslim citizens do. There are Christians in Palestine who suffer the same occupation as Muslim Palestinians. Christians in America are hardly aware of them and many believe they have no right to their homes, their property, their lives because of the false teaching of Christian Zionism. Although Jesus told his disciples it was not theirs to know the time of the restoration of Israel (Acts 1: 7), Christian Zionists believe God can't do it alone and seek an Israeli empire with a temple in Jerusalem that will cause the return of Christ to earth. Christians will inherit the Promised Land and Jews can convert to Christianity or be killed. Christian Zionism is a profitable enterprise and most of its prophets show no sign of wishing an immediate return of Jesus as they lay up treasures on earth.

The Christian leaders of the Latin Patriarchate, Jerusalem; the Syrian Orthodox Patriarchate, Jerusalem; the Episcopal Church of Jerusalem and the Middle East, and the Evangelical Lutheran Church in Jordan and the Holy Land wrote "The Jerusalem Declaration on Christian Zionism," stating among other things:

"Christian Zionism is a modern theological and political movement that embraces the most extreme ideological positions of Zionism, thereby becoming detrimental to a just peace within Palestine and Israel.

"The Christian Zionist program provides a worldview where the Gospel is identified with the ideology of empire, colonialism and militarism. In its extreme form, it places an emphasis on apocalyptic events leading to the end of history rather than living Christ's love and justice today.

"We reject the teachings of Christian Zionism that facilitate and support these policies as they advance racial exclusivity and perpetual war rather than the gospel of universal love, redemption and reconciliation taught by Jesus Christ."

(For the complete statement go to http://www.zenit.org/article-16848?l=english.)

I don't understand what makes one part of the earth more sacred than any other part of the earth but I own my father's share of my grandfather's farm that was founded in 1888, a year before the Oklahoma land rush, 19 years before Oklahoma became a state. The farm in northwest Texas is 400 miles from where I live but it's where I was born, where my ashes will be left, and I still have to go and walk on it. My land.

Laws Regarding the Holy Land:

According to the Jewish Bible, God did not want the accumulation of property in a few hands. Every seven years the land was to lie fallow, no sowing or reaping and people were to hunt and gather and trust God to provide. Every 50th year, the Year of the Jubilee, the land and other property must be returned to the original owner and slaves must be set free (Lev. 25). According to II Chron. 36: 21, the Israelites did not keep the Year of the Jubilee and consequently God delivered them to Babylon, allowing the land to lie fallow for 70 years.

Laws Regarding the Accumulation of Wealth:

According to the Jewish Bible, God also did not want wealth to accumulate in a few hands, and required just treatment of the poor. At the end of seven years debt must be cancelled (Deut. 15: 1). That law must be for a particular people at a particular time. I don't think anyone believes God requires that today, although the majority wish it were so.

When those laws were ignored or forgotten, Solomon became the "pharaoh" of Israel, counting his money and his wives that had become symbols of his wealth and power. Every day his palace required 100 sheep or goats, 10 oxen from the fattening pens and 20 pasture-fed cattle (1 Kings 4: 23). His kingdom crumbled but he, his wives and his cronies lived well.

"If you lend money to one of my people among you who is needy, do not be like a money-lender; charge him no interest" (Ex. 22: 25). "Do not take interest of any kind from him, but fear your God so that your countryman can continue to live among you" (Lev. 25: 36). "Do not charge your brother interest, whether of money, food or anything else that can earn interest" (Deut. 23: 19). Money-lenders are no longer pariahs as they were when the Bible was written and Jesus lived on earth. In America some are too big to fail or to be charged with fraud.

The Jews learned about banking in Babylon and ignored the prohibition regarding interest as thoroughly as Christians have, although the early Christians believed it was "contrary to mercy and humanity to demand interest from a poor and needy man." Today the exploitation of misfortune is the greatest abuse of the poor by the powerful but Christian lawmakers are unwilling to stop it. In the Middle Ages, the Catholic Church forbade Christians from charging interest. The Council of Vienne (1311) declared that if a person claimed there was no sin in demanding interest, he should be punished as a heretic.

Jews could collect interest from Christians and Jews became the money-lenders of Europe.

Defining a Jewish Family:

The Jewish Leaders believed The Torah was a template for standardizing lust and establishing the norm for family life.

I wish the Bible had stories of family life so that we could see the definition of a godly family, but family was very different then. Women were naturally unclean, wives were chattel and their worth was determined by the number of sons they gave their husbands, marriages were arranged, wives and children could be killed for the sin of the husband/father (Josh. 7: 1-26), children could be stoned for disobedience. I suspect some of the children executed for disobedience, if any, were killed because they refused to marry the person chosen for them.

Abraham is not a good role model for a husband or father. Abraham feared the king would kill him and take Sarah as a concubine. He told the king she was his sister (Gen. 20). The king accused him of lying, but Sarah was his half-sister. That story is not in the Koran because Muslims don't believe Abraham would have deceived the king about his wife. There is the love story of Jacob and Rachel, for whom Jacob worked seven years, but then is deceived into marrying Leah. He worked seven more years for Rachel (Gen. 29: 16-30). Jacob loved Rachel more than Leah and that brought strife to the house and Jacob came to have four wives, somewhat diluting the love story.

The Torah Gave Parents Authority
Over Their Children and Men Over Women:

"If someone has a stubborn and rebellious son who does not obey his father and mother and will not listen to them when they discipline him, his father and mother shall take hold of him and bring him to the elders at the gate of his town. They shall say to the elders, 'This son of ours is stubborn and rebellious. He will not obey us. He is a glutton and a drunkard.' Then all the men of his town are to stone him to death. You must purge the evil from among you. All Israel will hear of it and be afraid" (Deut. 21: 18-21).

The punishment must be a warning and an object lesson. A father could punish his son harshly but not kill him. That must be left to the community elders (Prov. 19: 18).

"Anyone who curses their father or mother is to be put to death" (Prov. 20: 20). This is an example of a wife being *almost* equal to her husband. Children were to obey their mothers as well as their fathers. "Whoever spares the rod hates their children, but the one who loves their children is careful to discipline them" (Prov. 13: 24).

Then, as now, the only way to control men's lust was to control women. The Israelites adopted the customs of the other nations, meaning patriarchalism. The Jewish leaders did create some rules improving the condition of women.

Rules Regarding Wives:

If the father had a wife he loved and a wife he hated he still must give the birthright to the first born even if it is a child of the wife he hates (Deut. 21: 15-17). That did not happen with Ishmael or Esau.

A husband could divorce his wife by saying three times, "I divorce you." A wife could not divorce her husband. May 22, 2014, the *New York Times* reported an Orthodox Jewish wedding where protestors chanted "Bigamist" and "Shame on you." The groom had been divorced for seven years and had taken a new wife but refused to give his former wife a "get," without which she cannot marry. The story mentioned that federal prosecutors had filed charges against a New Jersey Rabbi accused of taking "tens of thousands of dollars to kidnap and torture" reluctant husbands who refused to give their wives a get (*New York Times,* 10/10/13).

If a man married a woman, divorced her and married another woman, he could not divorce the second and remarry his first wife. (Deut. 14:1-4) Some believe that was to prevent wife swapping. Did you believe your generation was the first to think of it?

A woman captured in war (usually a prepubescent girl) must be given 30 days to mourn her dead parents, siblings and other relatives. After that the captor could take her as his wife but he could not sell her or treat her as a slave. He could let her go when she no longer delighted him (Deut. 21: 10-14).

A woman was forbidden to be alone with a man to whom she was not married. Some of that was to protect girls and women who had little protection except that of a father, brother, husband or other male relative. That law is still obeyed by many Orthodox Jews and Muslims. Boys and girls go to separate schools; men and women are separated in the synagogue or mosque.

Rabbis determined the earliest age at which a girl could be at risk alone with a male. Some believed she could be at risk as early as three years old (http://www.torah.org). Some people are horrified by the brutality in the Jewish Bible, especially regarding females, but similar stories can be found in almost any national newspaper. Recently the media reported that a three-year-old Florida girl had died after being raped and beaten by her stepfather. A 3-year-old Arizona girl was found malnourished and serially raped. A 3-year-old girl in New Jersey died of rape and other injuries. Polling shows that such events are much more common than public reporting would indicate.

Some Muslims forbid a woman to be in close proximity to a man who is not a close relative. That is a problem in air travel where seats are assigned, especially a problem during Ramadan when many Muslims are going to or returning from Mecca. Our flight from Nepal to New Delhi was delayed for several minutes by Muslim men who, despite orders from the air crew, moved passengers around so that their wives would be sitting between them and a woman or between two women.

In a study of Jews living in Yemen, girls were procured and raised in the boy's father's house until the groom was sexually mature. Between one-third to one half of marriages in the study "took place between a sexually mature male and a just-pubertal female." This was justified by God's command to "be fruitful and multiply" (Gen. 9: 1). (See http://www.utoronto.ca/wjudaism/journal/vol2n1/ article1_d.html.)

Jean and I saw a parade following the betrothal of a nine-year-old boy and a six-year-old girl in Katmandu. She would return to her home or go to the home of her betrothed as prearranged but bride and groom would live separately until she reached puberty. That was likely similar to the betrothal of Jewish couples such as Joseph and Mary and is still common in much of the world.

Lev. 18 covers what must be every variety of incest. If it hadn't happened, it's unlikely that there would be a law against it. Those laws are universal to most Jews, Muslims and Christians. Laws regarding divorce and remarriage are not universal in those religions.

If a man had sex with a female slave who was promised to another man but who had not yet been given her freedom, they were not to be stoned because she had no choice. The man, however, had to give a ram as a guilt offering (Lev. 19: 20, 21).

If a man raped a virgin who was not betrothed to another, the rapist had to pay her father what he would pay to marry her, and he had to marry her. He could never divorce her (Deut. 22: 28-29). The law was later revised because some men chose this method for obtaining a wife they wanted rather than a wife chosen for them. Read the book of Judges from Chapter 19 through the rest of the book that ends with the kidnapping and rape of brides. The Talmudic justification for acquiring women at almost any cost is the Deity's command to Noah and his sons: "be fruitful and multiply" (Gen. 9: 1). The Talmud interpreted this injunction as requiring men to procreate, but not women"

Marriage between a Jew and a foreigner was forbidden because foreign daughters would prostitute themselves to their fertility gods and lead Hebrew sons to do the same (Ex. 34: 16). Jesus also seemed suspicious of gentiles. When a gentile woman asked him to heal her daughter who was demon-possessed, Jesus said he was sent only to the lost sheep of Israel. At the woman's persistence he said that it was not right to give the bread for children to dogs. That seems uncharacteristically harsh of Jesus but it is a magical moment when Jesus realizes he is not to be the Messiah of only the Jews but the Savior of the world and heals her daughter (Matt. 15: 21-28).

Until the decoding of DNA, no man could be certain that his children carried his genes. Perhaps more than any other culture the Jews were determined to maintain tribal identity. Marriages were arranged in order to maintain that purity. For that reason girls were sequestered until they were betrothed and, after marriage, women were secluded from non-relative males.

In Hebraic law a groom could require virginity testing of his prospective bride (Deut. 22: 13- 21). Since it was unlikely that her parents could have taken the bed clothes from her husband's house the virginity testing must have been at home by her parents. If there were proof of her virginity the groom had to pay a price to her father. However, if there were no proof then she was stoned to death. According to the *Midrash Hagadol* to Genesis 24: 67, Isaac tested Rebecca's virginity before he married her. In the apocryphal Book of James is a story of Salome testing Mary's virginity to assure Joseph that his pregnant wife was a virgin.

The Jews, and later Christians, struggled against Hellenism, the Greek culture borrowed and promoted by the Roman Empire. Hellenism considered humans as the apex of creation, the ultimate in physical beauty. The pleasure of humans, including intellectual and creative pleasure, was the greatest good and the human mind was the gateway to truth (http://www.followther-abbi.com/guide/detail/a-far-country-decapolis).

In foreign cities Jews lived together because they could travel only a short distance to worship on the Sabbath and because they required a kosher butcher. Some believe that "kosher" was intended by God to make it difficult to socialize with those of foreign religions. You can see how powerful those laws were by reading the dispute between Peter and Paul regarding unclean foods that were restricting the Gospel to Jews (Acts 10: 24 to 11: 18; Gal. 2: 11-16).

Jesus met a young man who had been circumcised who had kept the Jewish laws and believed he lacked something (Luke 18: 18-22).

A Pilgrim for Jesus

CHAPTER SEVEN

Jesus: the Definition

The writers of the Christian Bible defined "Christian" as being like Jesus. It is an impossible ideal but ideals are supposed to be impossible for what is ordinary. There is no ideal painter, no ideal composer, no ideal writer, no ideal computer or automobile. The Gospels and the book of Acts present a more achievable definition of a Christian man or woman.

There were also cautionary tales of Peter, Judas, Ananias and his wife Sapphira who kept some of their money for themselves, not trusting their fellow Christians, and a woman in the church in Thyatira who called herself a prophetess and encouraged fertility rites. Her children were struck dead and she was condemned to a bed of suffering, along with those who worshipped with her. Perhaps venereal disease?

The Christian Bible has fewer laws than the Jewish Bible that defined Jews, but some Jewish laws were also used to define a Christian or a Muslim.

Jesus Also Condemned the Accumulation of Wealth:

Jesus said, "I tell you the truth, it is hard for a rich man to enter the kingdom of heaven. Again I tell you, it is easier for a camel to go through the eye of a needle than for a rich man to enter the kingdom of God" (Matt. 19: 23-26). Some claim that Jesus was referring to a "needle gate" that was so small that a camel had to be unloaded before it could pass through. That's a good use of metaphor and an example of how fundamentalists use figurative language. However, there's no evidence that such a gate ever existed.

Some have tried to balance the parable of the barn builder who built bigger barns to secure his future with the parable of the Ten Minas. A man was going to a far country to become king and gave ten minas to ten servants and told them to put the money to work. Instead of using the money for good, one servant hid his money so as not to lose it and was chastised for not—at least—putting it in the bank and drawing interest (Luke 19: 11-27). But some sent a message that they did not want the king-to-be to rule over them and the story concludes with the king calling for those who did not want to serve him to be brought before him and executed.

The parable is not about money. Jesus tells it because they are close to Jerusalem where he will be welcomed, betrayed and crucified. It's about Jesus going away for a while and, when he returns, his followers will be asked what they have done in his absence.

The modern day parallel to the parable of the barn builder is the saver who says, I'll rent another storage bin. Or, I'll open another bank account.

Don't push a parable, as my friend and colleague Eugene McKinney taught. The king calling for those who opposed him to be killed does not authorize any person or any power to execute those who disagree with them about who Jesus was or what Jesus said. Sadly, that still happens.

This is the occasion for a scripture often taken out of context. "I tell you that to everyone who has, more will be given, but as for the one who has nothing, even what they have will be taken away" (Luke 19: 26). It's not about money; it's about faith put to work in positive ways.

Jesus had a lot to say about riches. Do not store treasures on earth (Matt. 6: 19). Jesus defined his followers. "Then Jesus said to his disciples, 'Whoever wants to be my disciple must deny themselves and take up their cross and follow me'" (Matt.16: 24). These days, I don't hear much about denying oneself to follow Jesus, but I hear a lot about denying oneself to look good in a bikini.

To one would-be follower who had kept the commandments Jesus said, "You still lack one thing. Sell everything you have and give to the poor, and you will have treasure in heaven. Then come, follow me" (Luke 18: 22).

To a larger audience he said, "If anyone wants to sue you and take your shirt, hand over your coat as well" (Matt. 5: 40). Neither lawyers nor corporate CEOs are likely to have memorized that scripture. Jesus also said that his followers were to pay their taxes. Does that apply to TV preachers and prosperity gospel pastors? Or the rich who open an offshore bank account?

The next time you need a loan, quote Matt. 5: 42, "Give to the one who asks you, and do not turn away from the one who wants to borrow from you," and ask the lender if he or she is a Christian. I think you will be surprised by how irrelevant the Bible is to economics.

Pie in the Sky Religion:

During the Depression when many people had little, there was a lot of preaching about rewards in heaven. "Pie in the sky bye and bye" detractors called it. It was about all some people had to hope for. That's true today in pockets of poverty where young people see no hope on the horizon and the elderly live in despair. But for most of us, life is pretty good and we don't yearn for heaven as much as we yearn for a raise.

The Bible has far more to say about the dangers of accumulated wealth than it does about homosexuality or abortion, except as punishment, but it's not a popular subject because many TV preachers, even church leaders, are busy themselves laying up treasures on earth. The early Christians could not image the kind of wealth that today's "prophets" and "evangelists" possess, or the kind of food security I have. If they could imagine it, it's unlikely that they would approve of it, or the use that is made of abundance.

Pope Francis, who may be the greatest evangelist of our time, has rejected the trappings of emperors, caliphs, earlier popes and TV evangelists. He has also denounced the accumulation of wealth. Incidentally, so did the Founding Fathers of the United States.

Thomas Jefferson, credited with writing the Declaration of Independence, wrote: "I hope we shall...crush in its birth the aristocracy of our moneyed corporations which dare already to challenge our government in a trial of strength, and bid defiance to the laws of our country." Those early corporations weren't global corporations and had a small fraction of the wealth and power of such corporations that today challenge the health, wealth and general welfare of citizens in many nations. Jefferson also wrote, "The end of democracy and the defeat of the American Revolution will occur when government falls into the hands of lending institutions and moneyed corporations."

James Madison, credited with writing much of the U.S. Constitution, said, "There is an evil which ought to be guarded against in the indefinite accumulation of property from the capacity of holding it in perpetuity by corporations. The power of all corporations ought to be limited in this respect. The growing wealth acquired by them never fails to be a source of abuses."

Although some fundamentalists and evangelicals proclaim capitalism as God's economic plan for America, it has not always been so. Charles Finney, a major evangelical in the 19th century, declared capitalism was detrimental to Christianity and that "the business aims and practices of business men are almost universally an abomination in the sight of God." What was so bad about capitalism? "Seeking their own ends; doing something not for others, but for self."

Charles Finney would be a heretic today in an America that believes we are a "Christian" nation and that we prosper because of it.

I don't think politicians who want to rule America under biblical laws mean laws against acquisition of wealth. Clearly neither the prosperity preachers nor America's richest families obey those laws. I believe the politicians mean the laws that restrict the definition of women and punish citizens with minority sexual or gender orientations.

As an aside, some groups profess to be frightened by the religious laws (Sharia) of some Muslims becoming the law in America, although much of Sharia is derived from or comparable to the laws of the Jewish Bible. Religious laws have long been a part of the laws of the U.S. Consider the "blue" laws that are still enforced, the laws regarding what you can and can't do on Sunday. The right of women to decide whether they will or will not have children was once the concern of only the Catholic church, but has now expanded to some fundamentalist churches and some fundamentalist politicians. Opposition to same-gender marriage, bigotry toward LGBT citizens and laws that permit employers to deny religious freedom to employees are "Christian" sharia laws.

Is Genesis 9:1 Universal or Particular?

The Jewish interpretation that "be fruitful and multiply" was binding on men but not on women was a huge advancement for women. For most of human existence sex, was at the demand of a man. The Gospel of John makes an oblique reference to this—"born not of blood, nor of the will of the flesh, nor of the will of man..." (John 1: 13). The NIV softened it to "will of the husband" but the Greek text is clearly "man." According to a government survey nearly one in five American women have been raped or have suffered attempted rape (*New York Times*, 12/15/11).

It has been in my lifetime (1971) that it became possible for a husband to rape his wife. Most rape laws defined rape as forced sexual intercourse by a male with a female not his wife. It was a monumental act of courage by a wife who charged her husband with rape and a district attorney who filed charges against the husband. It has made a huge impact on wives' legal standing. In 1984, a New York court ruled: "A married woman has the same right to control her own body as does an unmarried woman." However, that is still not universally true in the U.S., and in many countries the husband/father has control of the bodies of his wife and daughters.

Because men are physically stronger, birth on demand has been the rule of the jungle from the beginning and it is still the plight of women in much of the world. In times of social disorder or war or occupation, any man can require any fertile woman to give birth to his child. In some countries a woman forcibly impregnated is killed to prevent the impurity of foreign genes in the family or nation.

For most of human existence if a wife did not produce a son for her husband he could take another wife. Contraception has been known for centuries. However, it has been in my lifetime that contraceptives have been effective. Releasing women from the requirement to procreate is another advance in women's freedom and self-realization.

Romantic love was not worshipped as it is today. Generally it was discouraged because it occurred outside of arranged marriage and usually brought dishonor and death to the woman (except for Bathsheba). Marriages were arranged by fathers who knew what was best for his family, not necessarily what was best for the bride and groom. I believe that's why the Song of Songs is in the Bible—to define romantic love. All love is not agape. There is also eros and "Song of Songs" is a poem about it. This is what romantic love looks like.

"Sacred" and "sex" rarely share the same bed. At least in church. That's why Song of Songs is shocking to some Bible readers. But there should be more talk in church about the sacredness of sex and not only to the unmarried. I've never heard Song of Songs read in a wedding. Christians prefer I Corinthians 13, a practical guide to a loving relationship.

Christianity and Lust:

Early Christian leaders attempted to standardize lust and set the norm for family life, but the Gospels offer no examples. We know little about the family of Jesus except that he had brothers and sisters (Mark 6: 3). All was not well in Mary's house as she and Jesus' brothers tried to take Jesus home as he was risking his life and showing signs of madness (Mark: 3: 20, 21). Jesus declared that his followers were his mother and his brothers, suggesting that they were not believers (Matt. 12: 46-50). Peter was the only one of the twelve who was married and he was either a widower or left his wife to follow Jesus (Mark 10: 28-31). If the latter, then his statement of having left all is even more poignant. And even more provocative.

Early Christians had a bigger problem with sex than the Jews did because early Christians were far more diverse than the Jewish tribes and the new Greek and Roman converts came with different traditions and mores. Without understanding the confusion of new converts one might think that the Apostle Paul was obsessed with sex. One might not appreciate the rage of the religious leaders of Jesus' day when Jesus said that prostitutes, some of them male priests to fertility gods, would enter the kingdom before they would (Matt. 21: 31). That was the mother of all insults.

Dionysus, the god of wine, agriculture and fertility, was worshipped in the Decapolis (ten pagan cities near the Sea of Galilee where Jesus did much of his preaching), which explains why there were pigs at Gadara (Mark 5: 1-20). The Jewish Talmud and writings of the church fathers believed those who lived in the Decapolis were descendants of the Canaanites that the Israelites drove out of the Promised land (Josh. 3: 10, Acts 13: 19-21). Historians believe they were Greeks who settled the cities under the reign of Alexander the Great's successors.

Rome was the center of fertility religions. Paul and the other apostles were surrounded by fertility gods and goddesses. Much of the Bible was written to thwart the worship of fertility gods and to expose the apostasy of King Ahab and Queen Jezebel.

Peter addressed the problem. "But Israel had false prophets as well as true; and you likewise will have false teachers among you.... Having eyes full of adultery, that cannot cease from sin; beguiling unstable souls, an heart they have exercised with covetous practices; cursed children which have forsaken the right way ... following the way of Balaam.... They utter big empty words, and make of sensual lusts and debauchery a bait to catch those who have barely begun to escape from their heathen environment" (II Peter 2). That sounds like converts from fertility religions.

The church at Pergamum, "the city where Satan lives," is criticized, although they had not renounced their faith. However, some members followed the teaching of Balaam to eat food offered to idols and to commit sexual immorality (II Peter 2: 15; Jude 11; Rev. 2: 14).

The church at Thyatira had not lost its faith, but the Book of Revelations comes down hard on that church: "But I have this complaint against you. You are permitting that woman—that Jezebel who calls herself a prophet—to lead my servants astray. She teaches them to commit sexual sin and to eat food offered to idols. I gave her time to repent, but she does not want to turn away from her immorality. Therefore, I will throw her on a bed of suffering, and those who commit adultery with her will suffer greatly unless they repent and turn away from her evil deeds. I will strike her children dead. Then all the churches will know that I am the one who searches out the thoughts and intentions of every person. And I will give to each of you whatever you deserve" (Rev. 2: 19-23).

Diana (Artemis) had a temple in Ephesus. Her temple is still the most striking feature in the ruins of Ephesus. Paul's preaching in Ephesus had provoked a riot to defend the cult of the goddess Diana, "the many breasted one" (Acts 19: 23-41). Women speaking out in public or teaching men would likely have provoked another riot.

Aphrodite, the goddess of love, had replaced Asherah and her temple was in Corinth. A Roman writer reported that Aphrodite's temple had 1,000 prostitutes/priests and priestesses. There was immorality in the church in Corinth, and confusion (I Cor. 6). The cultural environment must have been part of that. Converts from fertility religions had been taught that sexual intercourse was worship. Converts who were Jewish knew that polygamy was part of their history as were sex slaves. Women were unclean, and brides had to pass a virginity test or be stoned. Greek converts likely knew about Greek Love.

In 385 BC, Plato published the *Symposium*, in which Greek intellectuals argued that love between males was the highest form, while sex with women was lustful and utilitarian. In Greek love, an older male was mentor to a younger male. Sometimes the younger was a boy but usually there was not a great difference in ages. Greek love was not always sexual but sometimes was. Some scriptures are wrongly applied to homosexuals when they were intended for male prostitutes. Their greatest sin was not adultery or being treated by another man as an inferior, a woman, but idolatry, worship at a fertility temple.

Was sex worship or was it evil? In Corinth, some husbands and wives who were recent converts seemed to believe they should be celibate (I Cor. 7: 3-5). "A man should fulfill his duty as a husband and a woman should fulfill her duty as a wife, and each should satisfy the other's need." It's possible that Paul's preaching that he was free from the law might have encouraged some converts to believe they were free from the restrictions of marriage. Ephesians 5: 21, "Submit yourselves to one another out of reverence to Christ." Not Diana. This was Christian sex. One husband, one wife.

If you're married stay married, if not married remain single if you can. That "if you can" was written to men. Women had little choice in the matter.

Those scriptures still cause confusion. When Jean and I were newlyweds, in our circle of newlywed Baylor students was one wife who boasted that she permitted only one "tonight's the night" a month "to keep it special." I don't know what happened to them. They weren't a good fit in our circle.

Fundamentalists who want to read the Bible literally often interpret "submit" as washing and filling dishes and caring for the kids but I believe submitting to your spouses's sexual desire is the true meaning. Paul comes close to saying that the purpose of marriage is to prevent fornication. "Now concerning the things whereof ye wrote: It is good for a man not to touch a woman. But, because of fornications, let each man have his own wife, and let each woman have her own husband" (I Cor. 7: 1 & 2).

I don't think Paul meant preventing fornication was the only or foremost purpose of marriage. Christians were not concerned with bloodlines or the furtherance of their ethnicity because they believed that Jesus would come again in a few years. Sex, marriage and children were an unnecessary distraction; therefore remaining single was an excellent thing.

Christian women had good reasons for not wanting to be pregnant. They were poor, a minority, under suspicion and surveillance; a husband could easily abandon them, especially one who was not a convert, and Jesus had warned of the wrath to come— the Roman destruction of Jerusalem, the temple and the nation of Israel (Luke 17: 34, 35).

Paul also wrote that prohibiting marriage was false teaching. "Now the Spirit explicitly says that in the later times some will desert the faith and occupy themselves with deceiving spirits and demonic teachings, influenced by the hypocrisy of liars whose consciences are seared. They will prohibit marriage and require abstinence from foods that God created to be received with thanksgiving by those who believe and know the truth" (I Tim. 4: 1-3).

Despite my formal training in religion and the Bible, I never heard of the fertility gods and how confused gentile converts must have been regarding sexual matters. My training was from the chin up and the only stories regarding sexual relations were written by men about women causing men to sin—Eve and Adam, Potiphar's wife and Joseph, Delilah and Samson, Cozbi and Zimri, Moabite women and Hebrew men, Bathsheba and David. Potiphar was a eunuch. Delilah was a patriot helping her people. Bathsheba could not refuse the king. Let's allow them a bit of grace.

To avoid the time-consuming frustrations and confusions of sex, the early American Christians called Shakers lived celibate lives in communes and dwindled, as there were no children to replace them but only new converts.

How would you define adultery today? Abstinence made sense when it was important to keep tribal and royal bloodlines pure, girls were sequestered until they reached puberty and were betrothed to males selected for them. After virginity tests. Popular magazines today report that young women prefer oral sex in order to preserve their "virginity" until marriage. As always, women are held responsible for sexual morality.

When Jean and I were in school, many girls married immediately after graduation. The other choices were college or a job with the telephone company, the only employer that paid women a decent wage. Jean and I married three days after she graduated from high school. Today that is no longer popular or in many cases even possible. Two people cannot support a family on minimum wages meaning that marriage has to be postponed. We were both chaste but she was 18 and I was an immature 21. Would we have been chaste when she was 28 and I was an immature 31? I doubt it. Many couples cohabit for a few months or years before they marry, yet they marry in church and the church accepts them.

There are many single women and some single men who cannot remarry because they will lose benefits that they cannot afford to lose. Many churches turn a blind eye to their situation and accept their relationship as holy. A couple of generations earlier they would have been rejected, isolated, greeted with stony silence.

The Household Code: Eph. 5: 22-6: 2 and Col. 3: 18-4: 1

"Wives, submit to your husbands as to the Lord." I believe these rules or guidelines were written to a particular church at a particular time. Christians were regarded as subversive to both Judaism and Rome. The apostles were preaching, "We must obey God rather than men" (Acts 4: 19-20; 5: 29). That sounds subversive, particularly to an autocratic government with Caesars who were gods. Further, Paul was preaching that believers were no longer under the law. "All things are lawful unto me" (I Cor. 6: 12). In addition to being subversive, that must have excited women and slaves. How were they to express their freedom?

Like the proverbial forest, the message was lost in memorization of a proof-text tree. All those in a relationship have a duty to each other, husbands-wives, parents-children, employers-employees. Many churches opposed labor unions because the Bible said servants were to obey their masters even if wages were so low a man could not support his family, even if working conditions were unhealthy and shortened lives, even if unnecessarily dangerous jobs cost lives.

Some Christians opposed "painless" childbirth because the Bible said women should bear children in pain. The same curse was applied to all female mammals. I have never heard a preacher condemn air-conditioned offices for employers, air-conditioned cars for salesmen or air-conditioned tractors for farmers who no longer earn their bread by the sweat of their brow.

Many Christians opposed the criminalization of marital rape because rape is an abuse of power by one spouse to gain dominance over the other, and it was their belief that the Bible gave dominance to husbands over their wives. So that couldn't be a crime.

Women's Place in the Church: I Tim. 2: 11, 12

Some scholars believe this letter was not written by Paul but by another writing in Paul's name and style. That was common in the manner of "this is the sword of Genghis Khan." Painters often signed their paintings with the name of their teacher meaning "from the school of" Michelangelo, et al. If it is Paul's writing, it is not his best writing—but it's in the Bible and must be dealt with.

Few, if any, of the writers of the Christian Bible knew or believed that they were writing for a universal audience centuries after they died. They were addressing a particular audience regarding particular issues and problems. Much of that has meaning for us today, especially the moral and ethical messages of the prophets, the history of God's relationship to Israel, the hope and inspiration of the Psalms, the wisdom of the Book of Job that is written like a Greek drama. But not all of it is efficacious for us. We have already mentioned blood sacrifice, food restrictions, genocide.

One of the most beautiful Psalms, 137, begins, "By the rivers of Babylon we sat and wept when we remembered Zion." It summons universal nostalgia and homesickness, but the end of the poem is rarely read in church. "Daughter Babylon, doomed to destruction, happy (blessed) is the one who repays you according to what you have done to us. Happy (blessed) is the one who seizes your infants and dashes them against the rocks."

"Let a woman learn in quietness with all subjection. But I permit not a woman to teach, nor to have dominion over a man, but to be in quietness" (I Tim. 2: 11).

The writer was pointing out the need for order in the church. Those churches usually met in homes—and the ruins of those homes are unbelievably small to my eyes. The houses were also close together, often having common walls. A church in a cave near Antioch could have held no more than a dozen standing adults and children. A church in Cappadocia was carved into a hillside that had a bench on each side carved from stone and in the middle a table that had been cut from the stone. I loved the symbolism of sitting around a table for church services but most Sunday School rooms are larger. Again, no more than a dozen could have pressed around the table.

In most houses the windows were open for cooling. No householder wanted trouble with neighbors because of noisy services or trouble from the law because of disorder.

I don't believe Paul was backing down from his statement that in Christ there is neither male nor female, neither slave nor free. (Gal. 3:8) In I Cor. 11:5, Paul pointed out a wife's right to prophesy. There is a problem here, but I don't believe it was Paul's problem or that he was as misogynistic as some believe.

First, everyone should learn in quietness with all subjection. The bane of teaching is a student asking a question that has already been asked and answered.

Scholars have pointed out that silence *(hesuchios/hesuchia)* is usually translated as "peaceable," "quietness," "undisturbing," "keeping one's seat." Few women in Greek and Roman communities could read or write, and educating women was subversive to the Roman government and repugnant to many Christian converts from cultures that did not permit women to be educated or allowed them to be educated only by their father or their husband. Imagine the shock when women's voices were heard in neighboring houses. That sounded more like a fertility religion.

"Nor to have authority over the man."

Exousia is commonly used for "authority" to execute official duties and it is used more than a hundred times in the New Testament. Here the writer uses *authentein* and it is the only time the word appears in the New Testament. Other uses of *authentein* from the same time period refer to violent sexual actions known today as sexual domination that includes bondage and physical punishment and is often delivered by prostitutes. Chrysostom, an early church father, used *authentia* for "sexual license" or perverse sexual practices. Another church father, Clement, used the word for women involved in sexual orgies. In fertility religions worship looked and sounded like orgies to outsiders.

It isn't until the 3rd and 4th centuries that *authentein* was used for other purposes, and then it was translated as "dominating men" or "domineer over men." It wasn't until centuries later that the KJV changed the meaning to "usurp authority over a man." I think most male and female Christians would be opposed to anyone usurping legitimate authority from another. Part of the cause of the Reformation was the usurpation of authority by the Bishop of Rome. It wasn't until after World War II that the translation was changed to "have authority." That change occurred in my lifetime and it has hobbled women.

CHAPTER EIGHT

Literary Techniques

"If your foot causes you to stumble, cut it off; it is better for you to enter life lame, than, having your two feet, to be cast into hell, where their worm does not die, and the fire is not quenched." Is that universal or particular?

It's hyperbole or exaggeration, a legitimate literary device often used in humor to soften a criticism or complaint. I've told you that a hundred times. Perhaps you've even said "a hundred times" or more to a spouse, or maybe you told a teenager, "Your room is so cluttered you could hide a Chinese army in the closet." Sometimes it's used for emphasis as in this occasion when Jesus wanted to accentuate that it was better to be physically handicapped than to be spiritually handicapped and that it was better to remove whatever led you into sin than to be cast into "Gehenna," the Valley of Ben Hinnom.

Gehenna was the landfill or trash dump for the refuse of Jerusalem. It was once a place of worship of fertility gods and human sacrifice to Molek, aka Molech (Jer. 32: 35). King Josiah made it into a horrible place where trash burned and worms made their way through garbage and human waste so that it would not again be used for worship.

Jesus probably got a laugh of recognition when he said, "Why do you look at the speck of sawdust in your brother's eye and pay no attention to the plank in your own eye? How can you say to your brother, 'Brother, let me take the speck out of your eye,' when you yourself fail to see the plank in your own eye? You hypocrite, first take the plank out of your eye, and then you will see clearly to remove the speck from your brother's eye" (Luke 6: 41, 42).

Some early Christians mutilated themselves after reading the scripture literally. According to legend, Origen castrated himself because of Jesus' statement about eunuchs: "For there are eunuchs who were born that way from their mother's womb; and there are eunuchs who were made eunuchs by men; and there are also eunuchs who made themselves eunuchs for the sake of the kingdom of heaven. He who is able to accept this, let him accept it" (Matt. 19: 12).

Paul wished that those who required gentile Christians to first be circumcised would castrate themselves (Gal. 5: 12). That is sarcasm, derived from a Greek word meaning "to tear flesh or bite." It's a legitimate literary technique and sometimes produces humor among those who are not bitten. It is best used with family members and others who know you love them, not with fellow church members. Sarcasm.

Origen believed it was a hard task but urgent for those who could accept it, like taking up the cross to follow Jesus. Origen may have done so that he be permitted to teach young women. Only fathers, husbands and eunuchs could teach women. Others may have done the same—and let's regard them and many public school teachers as martyrs. Humor.

There were men who castrated themselves to honor the Phrygian fertility goddess Cybele, also called Kubala, Mother of the Gods (Mater Deum), Great Mother (Magna Mater), Heavenly One (Caelestis), Inanna, Aphrodite and Isis. Perhaps that influenced some early Christians to read the passage literally and castrate themselves because they believed it was a radical but urgent imperative.

The earliest reference to self-castration by Christians is by Justin Martyr in the second century who mentioned an Alexandrian Christian who sought government permission to have himself castrated. Castration was illegal within the Roman Empire. At the Council of Nicaea in 325, men who had castrated themselves were removed from clerical office, but castration was not forbidden to Christians who were not priests.

Augustine of Hippo named the Valesians, a Christian sect that practiced self-castration, in his list of Christian heresies. The church fathers who mentioned self-castration condemned it. Male priests/prostitutes are called "dog priests" in Deut. 23: 18. Some believe that "beware of dogs" (Phil. 3: 2) is a reference to those who mutilate themselves, and that "dogs" will be outside the city of God (Rev. 22: 20). Some Christians still practice self-punishment.

"Let the dead bury their dead", "do not worry about tomorrow," "call no man father" are not to be taken literally. However, when I was on an advisory board with a Catholic priest I had a hard time calling him "father." For a time Jean taught at a Catholic school. She claimed I called Monsignor Murray Señor Murray. I believe that's an exaggeration.

Other Literary Techniques:

I believe Jesus used humorous voice techniques, including hyperbole and irony, when emphasizing some condemnations of common people so that they would remember his instruction. It wasn't the fishers, farmers and shepherds who angered Jesus. An angry voice was used by Jesus and the prophets and usually toward the same people—the self-content. "Woe unto you," they preached. I counted 88 "woes" in the KJV Bible.

Jesus used an angry voice with evil spirits (Mark 1: 25) and with the self-righteous. Matthew Chapter 23 is a sermon denouncing hypocrites who demand much of others but not of themselves, calling them "blind guides that strain at a gnat but swallow a camel" and "whitewashed sepulchers that look good on the outside but inside are full of dead men's bones and everything unclean, snakes and brood of vipers, on them will fall the righteous blood beginning with Abel."

Some literary tools don't make it through translation.

Alliteration is a passage using words that begin with the same sound: of the people, by the people and for the people. Since neither Hebrew nor Greek uses the Roman alphabet that English does, the effect is often lost in translation or transliteration. That's also true of assonance, onomatopoeia, and cacophony.

Happily the Beatitudes keep the Greek form in the repetition of "Blessed are," although blessed doesn't entirely catch the meaning of the Greek. Happily, in Psalms 1: "like the chaff which the wind driveth away" the KJV captured the breath that driveth the chaff away. Do you suppose Jesus used the same "voice" in the Beatitudes as he did in cleansing the temple? Do you suppose that if the writers of the Bible were alive today they would want their stories read the same way? Samson killing Philistines the same as the Good Shepherd and the Lost Sheep? (Luke 15: 1-7)

During World War II, the actor Charles Laughton wanted to read poetry to the troops fighting in Europe. The proposal was laughed at by some who believed soldiers wanted to hear off-color jokes and see young starlets showing a lot of skin, but Laughton's performance was a hit with the troops.

After the war Laughton made a one-person tour presenting the reading to others. I was privileged to hear Laughton when he read Shakespeare at Baylor, but he also read Genesis 1, Psalms 1, and the story of Shadrach, Meschack, and Abednego. I had never before heard the Bible read as poetry or story. It was hypnotizing and inspiring.

Did you memorize the Ten Commandments? Did you memorize the Beatitudes? They are not written in the same voice or with the same purpose. The Commandments give me a way of pointing a finger at you. The Sermon on the Mount points a finger at me. Genesis 1 is poetry. Genesis 2 is prose.

There is also inspirational voice in the Bible. "but those who hope in the Lord will renew their strength. They will soar on wings like eagles; they will run and not grow weary, they will walk and not be faint" (Isa. 40: 31). It's hard to read that scripture without being inspired. There is comforting voice. "Comfort ye, comfort ye my people, saith your God" (Isa. 40: 1). "Come to Me, all who are weary and heavy-laden, and I will give you rest" (Matt. 11: 28).

The story I told earlier about questions for which I had assumed easy answers occurred—but over a period of time and more than one bull session. That's compression. You do the same when telling about a favorite vacation—toured the White House, went to the Lincoln Monument, Arlington Cemetery, the Vietnam Memorial, the statue of Marines raising the flag on Iwo Jima, the Smithsonian. But not in one day and not necessarily in the order of occurrence, but beginning with the favorites or maybe saving that for the last when the audience's interest seems to flag.

Hebrews 1, Hebrews 11, the Sermon on the Mount, are examples of compression. Peter did the same on the day of Pentecost, revealing a bit of history, quoting some scriptures, and concluding, "God has made this Jesus, whom you crucified, both Lord and Christ." Acts 2:14-41)

Another literary tool is deliberate ambiguity. It's hard to get tone of voice in writing. Frequently writers use a character's body language to put the emphasis on the correct word. What a character does when saying it may be as important as what is said. "Good lawyer" can be interpreted in more than one way, depending where the emphasis is. The same is true of "Bravery has always run in my family." "Cheap at any price." "Head and shoulders above the others" can be both literal and figurative. I hope the writer intended both meanings, physically taller than the others but also above them in other ways (I Sam. 9: 2).

An example of ambiguity in the Jewish Bible is the commandment forbidding graven images; however, God tells Moses to make graven images of two cherubim and place one at each end of the Mercy Seat (Ex. 25: 18, 19). Solomon had two cherubim placed in the Temple. When the Hebrews were attacked by poisonous snakes in the wilderness God commanded Moses to make a graven image of a snake and when the victims of snake-bite looked upon the image they would not die (Num. 21: 8, 9). Looking upon the image implies faith in the image to save them. Jesus referred to that story saying, "And as Moses lifted up the serpent in the wilderness, even so must the Son of man be lifted up." Those who heard Jesus didn't understand that any better than I understand the bronze serpent.

John the Baptizer said, "He that cometh after me is preferred before me: for he was before me." Sure, you understand that but can you imagine what John's audience thought? That's like the old railroad joke, "Conductor, why is the train slowing down?" "Because the train ahead is behind."

"For my yoke is easy and my burden is light" (Matt. 11: 30). Yokes are heavy. The burden may seem light today for those who live in the luxury of a majority religion in a nation with freedom of religion generally determined by the dominant religion. That was not the condition of those who heard those words from Jesus who also told his followers that they must leave their fathers and mothers and give up all that they have to follow him. What did they make of "my yoke is easy and my burden is light?"

Stories need elements of mystery and suspense, and part of that is not knowing the exact meaning of an ambiguous line until the right time. Jesus told the money changers in the temple, "Destroy this temple, and in three days I will raise it up" (John 2: 19). Even his disciples didn't understand that until after the resurrection.

Human beings leave unanswered questions behind them, especially Jesus. Many things about Jesus are described as mysteries by the Church. This life is not easily tied up, all questions answered and put in an attractive box. Perhaps you already know that I like questions better than answers because questions excite your mind, keep you awake at night, inspire the search for greater meaning. Answers give you comfort that you may not wish to surrender when the question outgrows the answer.

I remember Mother appearing as if by magic in the school room for the lower four grades. I was in first grade, Jim in fourth. Bettye, who was in the upper room, was with Mother. Mother had been crying, Bettye was crying. Sometime in the long drive to Grampa's house I understood that Uncle Boyd was dead and my parents didn't want us asking about it. Uncle Boyd wasn't in the parlor as my great grandfather Connor, a Confederate veteran, had been. Uncle Boyd was at a Funeral Home. I remember Jim boosting me up to see Great-Grandfather Connor in his coffin in the parlor and the dead smell of the flowers around him.

Mostly I slept where I was, in a chair, a bed, the floor, at the table, in the church. I remember the low voices when I was awake, the bits of conversation I overheard. Uncle Boyd had been shot by his best friend. The friend said, "Slim, you're too good to live," and shot him in the back. I wondered how I could be so good that Edward, my best friend, would shoot me in the back. For years I tried to imagine a scenario in which that would work.

Questions remain about Jesus' life and words. Centuries later scholars debate the exact meaning of some of Jesus's parables. There is a depth and dimension to his stories and statements that are deliberately ambiguous so that we ponder them and so that our understanding of them grows as we mature as believers, for example, the parable of the forgiving father, the prodigal son and the envious brother.

A parable that I struggle with is the parable of the unjust manager or steward, that leads to the statement that you can't serve God and riches and ends with the proclamation that what men value most, in this example money, is an abomination to God (Luke 16: 1-15). Others may value power or glory or reputation most but whatever it is means nothing to God who knows where your heart and your treasure is.

In GodStory some will have a footnote, some will be a footnote, some will fail to make the index. I have long thought that if

I could be a skilled football player, if I could be a daring war hero, if I could be a great writer, *then* I could really serve God. God had better people for that.

Another parable is that of the workers, some of whom work all day and others who work only the last hour but all get the same wage (Matt. 20: 1-16). When one of the first workers complains about the last workers getting the same pay, Jesus concludes by asking, "Are you envious that I am generous?" I think many of us would say "Yes. This man lived selfishly while I denied myself pleasure in order to follow your way." And Jesus responded, "The last shall be first and the first shall be last."

Jesus said that more than once—when the disciples argued over which would sit on the right hand of Jesus when he established his kingdom (Mark 9: 33-35), when Peter said they had left everything to follow him (Mark 10: 28-31), when Jesus preached that followers should enter by the narrow door and those who believed they were friends of the householder would stand outside unrecognized and that people will come from the North, South, East and West and those who were last would be first (Luke 13: 22-30).

Some believe that the Jews who had long been toiling in the Lord's vineyard would be last and the Christians who were latecomers would be first. Others believe that the Roman Catholic and Eastern Orthodox came first but that Protestants came last and would be first. You could make the same argument that it was the Muslims who came last or the Mormons (Latter Day Saints), or the Christian Scientists, Jehovah's Witness, Scientologists who were late comers.

And, of course, Adam who was first would be last.

I find the same ambiguity in the parable of the sheep and the goats (Matt. 25: 31-46). That's the scariest scripture in the Bible to me because I think I am a sheep, which may be a sign that I am a goat. I think Jesus didn't like "know-it-alls." His disputes weren't with the ignorant publicans and tax collectors but the learned Scribes and Pharisees. I don't believe Jesus wanted his followers to be comfortable in their faith. He wanted us always to seek his will, his presence, to always ask whether we are the sheep or the goats. Salvation is a process. It may begin in a flash-of-light-epiphany or a slow progression through doubts, questions, even denials and desertion. That was the progression of the twelve with their final affirmation coming with their death.

Is it possible that the citizens of Nineveh were sheep and Jonah a goat?

Sometimes a writer wants something to mean more than one thing, a word to be understood two ways. Poets do this more often than writers of prose because prose goes from margin to margin but in a poem a line can break anywhere. In the poem below, the sun is a metaphor for God.

> *Sometimes (the sun) flares in fury we are told*
> *that love can burn every sin away*

The writer intended "we are told" to refer back to "flares in fury" and forward to "love can burn every sin away."

The Cult of Comfort demands certitude, especially in the resurrection. Jesus spoke positively of the resurrection, that there would be no marriage in heaven (Mark 12: 25), that a host should invite the poor and unloved to a banquet and would be rewarded at the resurrection (Luke 14: 13, 14), and that he was the resurrection (John 11: 25). Paul spoke less positively, referring instead to "the hope of the resurrection."

"If only for this life we have hope in Christ, we are of all people most to be pitied" (I Cor. 15: 19). Paul was imprisoned, he was beaten, he had to escape from those who wanted to kill him and he was executed. Some of those who first read the letter suffered the same. If they suffered all that and were wrong, then they were to be pitied.

That scripture is particular. I can't say that of myself. If there is no resurrection, am I to be pitied more than unbelievers? I don't think so. I have been favored because I am a Christian. I have been given preference because I am a white Christian. I haven't lived in great luxury but there were only a few times when I worried that I might lose the little that I owned and have to depend on the charity of others. I have lived about the way I wished to live.

I wish I had more wisdom, more knowledge, more time with my family but that wouldn't have changed if there is no resurrection. Still, I have faith in the hope of resurrection.

CHAPTER NINE

Why Jesus had to Redefine the Ten Commandments

A man tells a woman that he loves her. She replies that she loves him. Do they mean the same thing? No. God loves us and we love God. Is it the same love? No.

Abstractions such as love, hope, faith have to be defined because those words don't mean the same to everyone. In stories, abstractions are defined by the way a character in the story thinks and acts more than by what the character says. God's love is shown on the cross, not God's punishment. Man's love for God is exemplified by doing God's will. Redemptive love is exemplified by Jesus on the cross.

In theology, as in philosophy, arguments usually end up in definitions:

There is neither time nor space to define all the abstractions in the Bible, but let me define words in the Ten Commandments that some wish to place in every public space in America. Any church, mosque, synagogue, or temple can place monuments bearing the Ten Commandments on their property, but public property belongs to all citizens. Jesus reduced the Commandments to two, "Love the Lord your God with all your heart and with all your soul and with all your mind. This is the first and greatest commandment. And the second is like it: Love your neighbor as yourself. All the Law and the Prophets hang on these two commandments" (Matt. 22: 37-40). The Jewish Bible says the same (Deut. 6: 5; Lev. 19: 18).

Wouldn't you think that if we Christians want to assert our dominance in America that we would want Jesus's summation of the law and ethics in public places rather than the Ten? I think we don't because of the "love your neighbor" problem. Some of those who want the Ten Commandments placed in public places believe that being poor is a sin and unpatriotic, and that those whom Jesus called "the least" are unworthy to be neighbors.

I have two good Christian friends who have three large storage bins in the backyard because they own more than they can use. Is that loving your neighbor as yourself? I have Christian friends who live in gated communities for security. Can you love your neighbor as yourself if you lock your neighbors out of the neighborhood? I have neighbors with security fences on three sides of me. What if there's an accident at my house or theirs and I need help or to render aid? How do I get through the gate?

For honest disclosure, the reason I don't have a security fence is not out of concern for my neighbors. Deer, sometimes coyotes, pass through my property and I occasionally see a fox. Possums and raccoons are common and armadillos dig up my yard. My neighbors don't want wildlife in their yards or gardens and those with cats or small dogs fear the coyotes will eat their pets. Perhaps I am being unneighborly by allowing the animals to pass through my yard to get to the street and find other houses without fences.

Which Ten Commandments?

There are two accounts of Moses coming down from the mountain with the Commandments but they are not exactly the same. Moreover, when Moses saw his people worshipping a graven image he was so distraught he threw down the tablets and broke them. He had to go back up the mountain for an unbroken copy. God told Moses, "Hew thee two tables of stone like unto the first: and I will write upon these tables the words that were in the first tables, which thou brakest" (Ex. 34: 1). "And he wrote on the tables, according to the first writing, the ten commandments, which the Lord spake unto you in the mount out of the midst of the fire in the day of the assembly: and the LORD gave them unto me" (Deut. 10: 4).

However, they are not the same. These are priestly or ceremonial commandments. It is these tablets that contain "the words of the covenant, the ten commandments" (Exodus 34: 28). One of them is: "Thou shalt not seethe (boil) a kid in its mother's milk" (Deut. 14: 21; Ex. 23: 19, 34: 26). That's why Orthodox Jews use separate dishes for milk and meat. A colleague who was not a religious Jew and whose parents did not keep Kosher told me that the thought of a cheeseburger made him sick to his stomach. That's the power of that particular commandment—one that is largely unknown among Christians.

Whose Ten Commandments?

Catholics believe "graven image" is part of the first commandment, and that "thou shalt not covet thy neighbor's wife is the ninth, a separate commandment from coveting other things. Catholics do have three-dimensional images and sometimes bow before them, even pray for intercession to the persons the statues represent, but do not worship them.

Most Muslims and Orthodox Jews do not make images of anything. "Do not raise up a stone idol or a sacred pillar for yourselves. Do not place a kneeling stone in your land so that you can prostrate yourselves on it. I am God your Lord" (Lev. 26: 1). Their art is abstract design. Jean and I saw a metal sculpture that looked like an image of the outline of a butterfly in a garden pond at a private residence in Morocco and marveled at it.

Generally Protestants and Eastern Orthodox permit only two-dimensional images in churches, and Protestant images are rarely of any person other than Jesus. Lambs and fish are symbolic images of Jesus and Christianity.

Why Jesus had to revise or redefine the commandments:

The commandments are not as simple or as absolute as some claim. Much depends on the definition.

Thou Shalt Not Commit Adultery:

"Under Jewish law the first purpose of marriage is for companionship, not reproduction. Even the primary purpose of sexual relations is not to procreate, but to maintain the happiness of the marriage and ensure the couple's mutual physical pleasure.... As a result of this exemption from the duty to procreate, women are permitted to use contraception. In making such decisions, women are expected to consider the well-being of themselves, the family, and the born children" (*Kosher Sex,* www.mechon-mamre.org/jewfaq/sex.htm).

This was one reason Hitler used to justify his hatred of the Jews: "The increase and preservation of the species and of the race...alone is marriage's meaning and its task." The religious freedom of Jews to reject birth on demand was denied in America as late as mid-twentieth century.

However, for Christians and Muslims, that commandment led to much trouble. In a well-publicized story, in an Islamic country a woman was caught sitting in a car with a man who was not a relative. She was charged with violating the law and sentenced to lashing. There were no charges against the man. Remember that story when reading John 8: 3-11 where a woman was caught in the act of adultery. That act might not have been as erotic as many commonly believe. They may have only been discovered alone in a private room. The story is really a test of Jesus. Would he obey Moses' law, or would he obey the Roman law that did not permit Jews to execute anyone? Even Jesus' command that she go and sin no more may not have been as radical as commonly believed.

Some ask what happened to the man. If the sin was being together in a private room it was not a sin for him. Even if they were caught in sexual intercourse it was not adultery for him if he were not married or if he was married and she was not. For him it would have been fornication, a lesser sin; for her, married or not, it was adultery. King David had several wives and concubines and female slaves, but did not commit adultery until his relationship with Bathsheba who was married to Uriah.

Jesus defined adultery differently, putting the responsibility on the man. "You have heard that it was said, 'You shall not commit adultery.' But I tell you that anyone who looks at a woman lustfully has already committed adultery with her in his heart" (Matt. 5:27, 28). No man could ever again casually check off Number Seven, "Never done that."

Is that definition particular and applicable to men only? Does it also apply to women who lust after men? When I first read the story of Joseph and Potiphar's wife I didn't believe it. I accepted it because it was in the Bible but I didn't believe women lusted after men. I had never heard that in church. Women had never lusted after me. At Trinity I had a younger colleague who said he went through the sexual revolution without firing a shot.

However, it was the sexual revolution and the Pill that made it possible for women to be as lusty as men. The waves of the tsunami of sexual freedom for women have not yet receded despite opposition from male-dominated organizations like the church and the state that have never been able to restrain sexual freedom for men except by sequestration and severe laws and punishment of women.

Jesus said divorce and remarriage was adultery (Matt. 5: 22) yet divorce and remarriage is common in America and in American churches and it doesn't seem to be a great concern.

Women are not returning to the back of the bus. Churches should light the way to equal rights, equal pay, equal opportunity rather than support politicians who want the world to return to some 1920s version of the Garden of Eden. Politicians are notorious for denying equality to their mothers, wives and daughters. Autocrats in the home are unlikely to be democratic in the halls of power.

The church and state must defend women, especially young girls, from trafficking and sexual violence.

No Other God:

Thou shall have no other God before me was simple enough when written. There was Yahweh and there were the gods represented by graven images. America has more gods than Athens did when Paul preached about an "unknown god." I'll begin with self-love and confess that other than my wife and children I've never loved anyone as I love myself.

When Deirdre was born I discovered wives were wives until they became mothers and then they were mothers. Good mothers loved their children more than they loved themselves. Mother was their vocation. Whatever else they were doing, one part of their mind focused on the children—too quiet or too loud whether they were babies, children or teenagers. Both were danger signs.

One day when I was keeping Deirdre, Jean came home from work and couldn't find her. That unnerved both of us; I felt guilt more than fear. I knew she couldn't get out the door but hours and months of practice had allowed me to focus on what I was writing to the exclusion of all else. I had forgotten Deirdre. I discovered her asleep in a closet. She had somehow gotten inside and closed the door.

I loved our children as fiercely as Jean but sometimes I was in a world without them. I told our daughters that when I wore a hat I was writing and they were not to speak to me unless they were bleeding or the house was on fire. They broke that rule only once and before I turned away from my desk, I knew why. They had found a baby skunk. I persuaded them to return it to its mother.

Jean wrote also, but she explained to others that she wrote after the dishes were clean and put away, after clothes were washed, ironed, folded, the bills were paid and dinner was ready.

Nationalism as an Extension:

America first and the world be damned is an extension of self-worship. You must indulge your country's every wrong, suffer defeat in your country's every slight, accept impotence with every failure, lose immortality with the death of every soldier who died in vain and every baron whose kingdom crumbled. And face the inevitability of decline.

You can't Serve God and Riches:

In the last quarter of the 20th century some fundamentalists and some evangelicals preached that the acquisition of wealth was a sign of God's favor. By the 21st century many Christians believed living in poverty was a sin and the poor were unworthy of aid. The political myth of a large black woman with many children and several husbands driving a Cadillac to pick up her multiple welfare checks trumped Jesus's "least of these."

Recently Pastor Joel Osteen's church was in the news because someone had stolen several hundred thousand dollars from the church's Sunday offering. A well publicized safecracker stole from banks because "that's where the money is." I can understand that. What I can't understand is the church being "where the money is." I can't separate Christian greed from capitalist greed. How can any church be rich when there are hungry children in the same city?

What incentive is greater than money?

What earthly reward is greater than money? For many serving others is a greater incentive. For public school teachers, public nurses, Doctors Without Borders, serving in the military, law enforcement or fire control, etc, knowing they have made a difference to someone is a greater reward.

Robert Darden wrote a book about twenty Christian CEOs. I was surprised that there were twenty CEOs who were also Christians. The printing process of the book was stopped because one of the twenty was Kenneth Lay, CEO of Enron, that had just collapsed costing 20,000 Americans their jobs, many their life savings, and investors billions of dollars. Lay was found guilty of conspiracy and fraud. He was also described as a devout Christian.

Today's gods are in monumental buildings on Wall Street, in Hollywood and television sets that deify luxury and lust, and worship sex, drugs and violence; in the halls of Legislatures and Congress that worship power and control; in gated communities that venerate security; in middle America where guns are gods that save men from cowardice; in fervent nationalism and in loving oneself to the exclusion of all others. Even false gods are a demanding lot. They require your soul.

At what shrine do you worship and what graven image do you serve? If you work for a corporation you may want to give that some thought. Theoretically corporations serve profit for the good of the public; by law corporations are required to make a profit and that profit comes with graven images on it. Would Shadrach, Meshach and Abednego work for a corporation? Corporations are essential in America but some presidents didn't trust them.

Abraham Lincoln said, "We may congratulate ourselves that this cruel war is nearing its end. It has cost a vast amount of treasure and blood.... It has indeed been a trying hour for the Republic; but I see in the near future a crisis approaching that unnerves me and causes me to tremble for the safety of my country. As a result of the war, corporations have been enthroned and an era of corruption in high places will follow, and the money power of the country will endeavor to prolong its reign by working upon the prejudices of the people until all wealth is aggregated in a few hands and the Republic is destroyed. I feel at this moment more anxiety for the safety of my country than ever before, even in the midst of war. God grant that my suspicions may prove groundless."

Grover Cleveland wrote: "As we view the achievements of aggregated capital, we discover the existence of trusts, combinations, and monopolies, while the citizen is struggling far in the rear or is trampled to death beneath an iron heel. Corporations, which should be the carefully restrained creatures of the law and the servants of the people, are fast becoming the people's masters."

Theodore Roosevelt wrote: "We stand for the rights of property, but we stand even more for the rights of man. We will protect the rights of the wealthy man, but we maintain that he holds his wealth subject to the general right of the community to regulate its business use as the public welfare requires."

Franklin Roosevelt stated, "A small group had concentrated into their own hands an almost complete control over other people's property, other people's money, other people's labor—other people's lives. For too many of us life was no longer free; liberty no longer real; men could no longer follow the pursuit of happiness." He also said, "The real truth of the matter is that a financial element in the large centers has owned the government since the days of Andrew Jackson."

Dwight D. Eisenhower, who had spent his career in the military said, "In the councils of government, we must guard against the acquisition of unwarranted influence, whether sought or unsought, by the military-industrial complex. The potential for the disastrous rise of misplaced power exists and will persist. We must never let the weight of this combination endanger our liberties or democratic processes. We should take nothing for granted."

Do We Even Consider Covetousness a Sin?

I don't remember ever hearing a sermon about covetousness, not even during the Depression. When my parents visited friends, at least one of whom had dirt floors in their two-room house, we children had to decline any food they offered, even pie. Custom required them to offer what they had, even if it was all they had. Christianity required us to decline. Only if they asked Mother, "Is it all right for the children to have a piece of pie?" were we allowed to eat someone else's food. They were sharecroppers; we lived on our own property and raised or grew our own food.

Covetousness is the American Way of Life, it's the American Dream, it's Keeping up With the Joneses, it's a consumer economy. If citizens didn't covet, the American financial system would collapse. You can never have "enough" money, "enough" power, "enough" security, "enough" luxury, "enough" stuff. When I was a child, country people could scarcely say "banker" without it sounding like a curse.

I don't think Jesus would approve of any economic system that I know of, not because they are all evil but because they are all organized and operated by people more like me than I wish.

Thou Shalt Not Bear False Witness:

Jean was in a Distributive Education program her senior year in high school. Students in the DE program took core classes in the morning and worked outside the school learning a trade in the afternoon. Jean worked in the shoe department of the most fashionable women's store in Vernon, Texas. Her boss, that I will call Fred, was a fundamentalist but told her that women always wanted a shoe size smaller than their feet. When they asked, "Is this a size seven?" Jean was supposed to say, it "fits a size seven."

Being the judgmental person I am, I asked her if she ever told that fib to sell a shoe. Instead she told me how Fred got his recompense. He was sitting on the fitting stool with a woman's foot in his lap trying to get a size seven foot in an expensive size six shoe when his hands slipped and his customer shoved the shoe into his groin. Jean saw it and quickly stepped into a small closet big enough for one person, hoping her laughter couldn't be heard outside the closet. The door opened, and Fred, doubled over, tried to get in the closet with her.

Jean, who is still the most honest person I have known, told consumers what they wanted to hear. That's the dilemma isn't it? Not just in commerce but in religion and politics as well. Sometimes it seems that scientists are the only true prophets we have telling us of the wrath to come.

In Jewish law, a man who gave false testimony suffered the penalty of the accused. If he gave false testimony regarding a murder, then he would suffer the penalty for murder. Failing to come forward or speak up when one had evidence was also a sin. That's difficult in postmodern America because citizens would be flooding the mail of news outlets and government officials with evidence. Perception is important in a capitalistic society and/or a democracy because deception is built into the system. Positive information is stressed, negative information is concealed or reduced to brain-boring small print legalese.

The Hurrah:

On the farm the work week ended at noon on Saturday. After lunch that we called dinner, we bathed, dressed and went to town for groceries, business and visiting. My brother and sister and I went to the picture show and stayed there until a parent came and got us. After grocery shopping and business, Mother and her friends sat in cars on Main Street to comment on the dress, posture, age, quality and reputation of the women who walked by. Dad and other men gathered on Snuff Street to enjoy tobacco, scratching and spitting. And attempt to hurrah others. The hurrah was a story that was plausible enough in the beginning but was stretched until the last person realized he had been hurrahed. It was a favorite male activity and if it was a good hurrah it was told and retold around the county for weeks afterwards.

A hurrah that passed around the county and maybe beyond was about a farmer who fed his family on a ham until what could easily be cut from it was gone. He passed it to a neighbor whose wife made soup of it and his children gnawed on the bone until all the meat was gone and that man passed the bone to a neighbor who cracked the bone and made a broth of the marrow. That good man passed a bag of bones to the storyteller who threw them in a pot of beans. All the storyteller had to give to his neighbor was the unwashed pot.

The hurrah was also educational. Don't believe everything you see, hear or read. America was at war and the news media and entertainment media—they were separate then—were the propaganda arm of the government. Pearl Harbor was a shock and it was followed by a drumroll of defeat: The air and naval defenses of the Philippines were destroyed a few hours after Pearl Harbor; Wake Island fell to the Japanese; the impregnable defenses of Singapore collapsed; Bataan fell; Corregidor, the Gibraltar of the East, surrendered. It's understandable that the news media tried to bolster civilian morale and military spirit.

Some young men, usually accompanied by their fathers, tried to brush aside the propaganda and heroic movies to get the facts by talking to Dad. Enlisting or waiting to be drafted? Whether to drive tanks and trucks as many had driven heavy farm equipment or sign up for the infantry? Army or Navy, Air Corps or Marines? Dad set them straight on the few options they would have once they had taken the oath, how easily a bullet passed through a steel helmet—and how a wounded German soldier had made a Masonic sign seeking mercy. Being a Christian wasn't enough for mercy on either side. It was a sign Dad didn't understand until he became a Mason.

Dad repeated that story like the Ancient Mariner. As though it were a weight on his mind. I suspect that Dad killed the wounded Mason. Probably with a bayonet as they had bolt action rifles and there might be more Germans in the trench.

I enjoy hurrahing people, hooking them with a premise that is peculiar but plausible and seeing how far I can take them until they recognize they have been gulled. Jean said, "You always take things too far," and I explained that I have to push the story until others recognize it's not true. Otherwise it's a lie. I rationalize that I am teaching them to be more wary and that I am learning how to get others to suspend disbelief since that it is essential in writing fiction.

If you read the news, hear the news or watch the news you are likely to be dumbfounded by the triviality but also by the variance. It can't all be true since much of it is contradictory. Some people ask for truth in advertising; revealing the facts would be sufficient. It is difficult for a consumer to get information in order to be a careful consumer. We are so accustomed to deception that we plan to be deceived. It takes the federal government to force those who provide our foods and medicines to reveal the ingredients, the harmful side effects and the nutritional value in their consumption.

It's important to remember that the Supreme Court has always ruled that only the publisher has freedom of the press. Reporters, columnists and other writers do not. Presently six corporations control 90 percent of the news outlets. Ultimately that means that six CEOs control the information you receive since the CEO can hire and fire the publisher. Newspapers get approximately 70 percent of their income from advertising, with magazines it's approximately 50 percent, for TV networks it's 100 percent. He who pays the piano player decides the modulation. That's why there is little news about workers and much news about corporations and consumers. Yes, workers are also consumers but the news isn't about their work but their consumption, their unnecessary desire to organize, or the reliability and skill of a corporation's employees.

Typically when someone tells me something that sounds questionable I ask the source of their information. That's important because the *International New York Times* that is owned by the *New York Times* reports abroad important stories regarding America that are not reported by the U.S. *New York Times* and usually not by any other U.S. media outlet.

Jean worried about a community college student in her Sunday School class who could not distinguish between the news and TV entertainment that mimicked the news. Other students pointed out to him that the story he was talking about had not actually happened but was the invention of humans for entertainment, not enlightenment. Their efforts were in vain; he had seen it on television. He was the only one I know who was so easily confused but I wonder if there are others who can't tell televised stories "based on actual events" from televised news and staged events.

After our accident, when Jean was released from ICU Colin brought us home. I was unable to stay awake for an extended period of time. I was sore from the wreck and the pain in my neck and shoulders was a constant ache so I awoke every time the car hit a bump. I asked Jean how she was and she said she was okay. When we were back home I went immediately to bed. Deirdre was there to assist her mother and Jean said she wanted to watch game seven between the Spurs and the Heat. Deirdre said Jean couldn't stay awake but she couldn't stay asleep either as pain kept waking her up. Each time she asked the score.

Colin woke me to say that Jean had trouble breathing and that he had called an ambulance. He told me to get dressed because we needed to follow the ambulance to the hospital. I looked out the window and saw an ambulance in the street but not the driveway. I don't remember anything after that. A few days later, when we exited through the emergency waiting room that was crowded with people and at least four cops in uniform, I asked Colin what it was. He said it was the emergency room and that's where we waited until Jean was in a room.

The hospital was next door to a med school and every day three doctor/professors led students to the room and described the patient's condition and what was being done for her. I found it reassuring. Her vital signs were good and her brain function was normal. Colin was more cautious. He had worked two years as an emergency room technician in a government hospital for Yupik Indians in Alaska. He knew what the doctors were not saying.

Jean had been intubated from from the time of the wreck except for the 10 or 12 hours she spent between the trauma center in Temple and the teaching hospital in San Antonio. Friends took me to the hospital and brought me home. I thought I could drive myself, but the first time I did I became lost in the parking garage. I had to go outside, check the street intersection and then walk the way I had driven into the garage. Friends brought flowers, food, other gifts to Jean's room. Some of the visitors I didn't recognize until other friends reminded me who they were.

The doctors told Colin and me that they were going to drill a hole in Jean's skull and drain the blood off her brain. Normally the body absorbed the blood as my body was doing but this would speed up the process. Once that was done Jean would become responsive. Colin and I watched the slow drain and I expected almost immediate results. Colin pointed out that the drain was not dark and was probably brain fluid. I insisted that it would help but Colin asked what if it was the last remedy they had.

Jean remained unresponsive. A few years earlier Jean had a craniotomy to remove a cyst from her brain. At one point in her recovery the nurses said that the left side of her body was paralyzed. Jean tried to scratch the site of the incision or perhaps to feel the staples that ran from ear to ear. When she was in rehab Colin called her his "zipperhead grandmother" and she laughed, but in the hospital they tied her right hand down so she couldn't reach the site of the incision. While I was sitting with her, she raised her left arm to feel her head. I held her hand and when the nurses returned I told them she could use her left side. She was annoyed at them for restraining her and wouldn't do what they asked.

I was certain that was what was happening after the accident. She stubbornly resisted doing what they asked. I reminded Jean that she had always been strong and she needed to be strong now, that she was the magnet that kept the family in orbit. I begged her to squeeze my hand and she did. It was light and quick and it could have been a tremor or a spasm but I believe she squeezed my hand. Colin was not convinced. I asked Jean to move her toe. If she could move her toe everything would be okay. I begged her to move her toe. Her toe didn't move. I believe she tried to move her toe but was exhausted. The whole weight of the hospital was closing in on me.

A number of chaplains came by, mostly to see me rather than Jean. They all asked if they could pray for Jean and I said yes. One asked me to stand beside him and hold his hand while he placed his other hand on Jean's head. One paused in his prayer to ask Jean's name as though God didn't know who she was.

One of the chaplains, Janet Deitiker, was a young woman who had introduced herself as a Methodist when I first met her. I teased her about being a Methodist; it's a Baptist-Methodist thing. The room was grimmer than I could bear and when Janet came to the room I tried to joke with her. She would not have it. She made me sit down in a chair facing her. She asked me to look in her eyes but I didn't want to look in her eyes. She told me I needed to tell Jean how I felt about her. Jean knew how I felt about her. She told me to tell Jean that I would be okay without her but I wouldn't be okay without her. She said I needed to tell Jean that it was okay for her to go if she needed to go. But it wasn't okay for Jean to go.

The next day the first two doctors sounded promising. They were going to do another drill and drain more blood. The third doctor was a neurosurgeon. He had canceled the drain. He pinched Jean's skin that was loose from being fed by a tube and twisted it. Jean grimaced. It was one of the cruelest things I have ever seen. He already regarded her as a cadaver. He said they could keep her alive indefinitely but she would never respond to anything but pain. I told him that fifteen years earlier Jean and I had both signed a medical power of attorney that we did not want to be kept "alive" artificially. He asked that we bring it to the hospital.

Colin and I got the papers and went to tell Deirdre to be certain she agreed with our decision. Colin said there was more bad news. When Deirdre awoke that morning she discovered that her service dog was dead. As the result of an earlier car wreck, Deirdre has grand mal seizures in which she has broken bones and teeth. The service dog warned Deirdre of a seizure so that she could get to a safe place and the dog protected her by preventing her from banging her head on hard objects. While Colin buried the dog Deirdre and I talked. She agreed that the tubes should be removed. She recognized that she would be terribly vulnerable without the dog but preferred staying alone than coming to my house or one of us staying with her.

There was no room in hospice care so Colin and I spent one night in straight-backed wooden chairs. After breakfast I told Colin I was going home to shower, change clothes and maybe take a nap. I slept four hours and returned to the hospital but Colin refused to leave. Late afternoon they moved Jean to hospice. Friends brought homemade ice cream that Colin shared with the nurses. I would have eaten it all myself. The nurses brought a cot with springs but no padding, not even a sheet. I spent the night mostly lying on the springs. Colin lay on the floor although I offered to split time with him on the springs.

The next morning Colin said he was going to shower, change clothes and come back. A few minutes later Jean began gasping for breath. I have told this to only two or three people who were close to Jean. I haven't written this before because it reads like a romance novel. I was alone with Jean and I lay down beside her, putting no weight on her because she had trouble breathing. I told her that I would always love her, that I would never forget her, that we would miss her terribly but, if she needed to go, we would cling to each other and we would be okay. With my last words Jean released her last breath.

Jean needed to go. She was hanging on because I begged her to be strong. Because she thought we needed her. Wherever she was in her consciousness she thought of us.

For a short while, too short, I would hear a noise in the house and account it as Jean in another room before I remembered. It was hope followed by disappointment but I was sorry when I no longer thought it was Jean. I hoped to see her in dreams. We both dreamed of Brigid and it was joy seeing her again, followed by sorrow and waking up depressed. We always shared the dreams with each other and hoped the dreams would continue. Once I was filled with bliss being with Brigid but I told her she would have to go back. "You're the one who keeps bringing me here," she said. I haven't dreamed of Jean but one night I was awakened by someone holding my hand. I was so startled I turned on the light. There was no one there but I knew who had been there.

Once when alone in the house I was brushing my teeth and felt a sharp tug on the tail of my tee shirt. It was something Jean often did when I was in my private world and she wanted to remind me of her presence. It left me with the quandary of the road commissioner of Donegal County with whom we had been guests in an Irish farmhouse. On a major road in the county a large tree grew in the middle of the roadway and in both directions the road swerved around the tree. Back home the tree would have been cut down if it had been planted by George Washington.

We knew the tree must be important and asked its significance. The commissioner said the road builders would not cut the tree down because it was a fairy tree. We asked what a fairy tree was. Sure and begorrah it was a tree around which the fairies danced at night. You don't believe in fairies do you? we asked the commissioner. No, he said. But they're there.

Shaping Information:

There is a huge industry shaping the information that we receive in a free nation. There are battles over public school textbooks and who and what should be included, and how slavery and the Civil War and Jim Crow and segregation and genocide against the Indians and wars of aggression should be treated and what emphasis each should receive. It should not be necessary to state that we have more access to the facts than citizens of other nations, but the British press publishes news about the U.S. that American media do not. We stayed in a hotel in Moscow that had free English language news sheets that reported information regarding the Russian government that was not in Russian language media reports. Sometimes you have to turn to comedy to get the facts.

Jesus said, "I am the truth" but the church is not free of false witness. According to some Christians, the Supreme Court expelled God from public schools. So, when Christian administrators, teachers, janitors, students, parents go into public schools God doesn't go with them? Does anyone really believe that?

Some say that prayer isn't permitted in public places. I have prayed in courtrooms, government buildings, public schools, mosques, temples, synagogues, anywhere I have ever been. I don't require a covering or a kneeling rug or closed eyes or bowed head or clasped hands. It is not Christians who suffer discrimination in public places but Muslims, Jews, Buddhists, Sikhs and others who do require obvious signs that they are praying.

"Equal protection under the law" is part of the Constitution yet some Christians want to deny that equality to gays, the poor or people of color. That is false witness. Attempts to defeat the

Equal Rights Amendment included a scary warnings that men and women would be forced to use the same toilets. The amendment didn't pass, unisex toilets are ubiquitous and we still don't have equal rights.

On a personal level, I am acquainted with grief. I know the emptiness, bitterness, the everlasting and futile steps to rise above it; the unbearable lightness of words, the valley of the shadow that you must walk alone. I know enough to want to assuage the grief of others, enough to know I can't. Enough to know that "God needed another angel in heaven" is false witness. Enough to know that "God won't give you more than you can bear" really means until you can't bear it any more.

The only thing I remember about Uncle Boyd's funeral is that Gramma fainted several times and her older son, Frelon, used smelling salts to revive her. I hated him for that. Why couldn't he leave her alone? She didn't want to bear it for a while.

"The gunny won't order you to do something you aren't able to do." Of course he will. That's why he's a gunny.

Sometimes you can't bear it until you die. You may not die of grief, but death may be willed or hastened.

Nothing on earth is truth without possibility of error, and we must be certain that false witness is not another sin that has become a virtue. Believers have an obligation to bear witness in words and deeds to God who is the truth. Perhaps it's truer in false witness than elsewhere that sin is contagious. Getting away with the sin encourages others to commit the sin.

Thou Shalt Not Take The Lord's Name in Vain:

You may have learned in Sunday School that taking God's name in vain meant swearing. That's a school boy sin and OMG has become as common as goodbye, which once meant "God be with you." You see and hear "God" and "Jesus" everywhere, even by Christians, and not in a religious context.

The adult version of blasphemy is the superstition that God's name is magic, that using God's name gives import to impotent words and covers a multitude of sins. "In God we trust" is an abstraction and may be false witness. What does it mean? Nationally we trust in nuclear weapons, Star Wars, Full Spectrum Dominance, huge defense budgets and military hardware like tanks, planes, drones. Privately we trust in automatic weapons, 50-round magazines and cop-killer bullets. Yet we cower before TV's real and fictitious threats and wait for the commercials that promise security from harmful bacteria, lingering illness, financial ruin and unpleasant people.

The phrase "...under God" was inserted in the Pledge of Allegiance as a talisman and the mindless repetition of "under God" is a holy rabbit's foot to protect us from nuclear annihilation or hijackers with box-cutters. It also causes non-believing children and patriots to take God's name in vain. We can use God's name in our motto and on the graven images of our money because the Supreme Court ruled that it was for a secular purpose. Isn't using God's name for a secular purpose the definition of blasphemy? The magic of God's name can cause a multitude of sins.

Remember the Sabbath:

All three Abrahamic religions recognize a Sabbath but remember it on different days and in different ways. When I was a child it was okay to eat out for Sunday "dinner," but going to a movie was a serious and visible sin. For true-believers, Sunday was for worship all day. Until professional football on Sunday afternoon. When men watched TV football on Sunday their wives and children asked why it wasn't okay to watch TV entertainment or go to a movie. In a few years watching TV on Sunday was common among fundamentalists. Today, after a church service most Christians can spend the rest of the day as though it were Saturday or a work day. Disclosure: After church I write on most Sundays.

Honor Your Father and Your Mother:

When I was a child I heard sermons and lessons declaring that this was "the Commandment with a promise"—that if you honored your parents then you would have a long life. That's not what the scripture says. Those who want to put the Commandments in public places usually use only the first six words. The full Commandment is: "Honor your father and your mother that your days may be long in the land that the Lord your God is giving you" (Ex. 20: 12).

The Jews see it as a promise that the Jewish people will long be in the land the Lord gave them. Past tense, "has given you," might suggest "forever" but present tense does not.

Honoring one's parents was simpler for the Hebrews, early Christians, and much of Islam. Households included children, parents, grandparents and sometimes great-grandparents. Seeing that they were fed, clothed, sheltered and cared for when old or sick honored them. How do you honor your parents when they live in another country, state or city?

You should honor your parents the way you honor others you love—tell them about your joys and fears, make certain their grandchildren know them, not just by sight but by touch; gather family history and, when practical, preserve family traditions so that your father and mother are never forgotten. As long as they are alive you listen when they tell you about their failing health, their failing resources, their fears of inadequacy. You don't have to offer advice. You have to hold them and listen. And preserve their stories.

Thou Shalt Not Steal:

We all understand stealing a loaf of bread. That's a sin and a crime. A few powerful people gained millions of dollars from the Savings and Loan collapse, leaving investors the losses and taxpayers half a trillion dollars in debt—but it wasn't a crime for most. When CEOs of corporations receive millions of dollars in salary, bonuses, benefits, stock options and perks such as private airplanes, luxury apartments and conferences at exotic resorts, that is money taken from workers and investors but it's not a crime. And neither is secreting money in offshore banks. Is it a sin?

On a smaller scale, Jean, who should be the patron saint of bookkeepers, discovered an unnamed 50 cents charge on one of our bills. She called the corporation to discover what we were paying for. The woman she reached was unable to say what the charge bought. Jean escalated the complaint until she got a supervisor who didn't know what the charge was for either. "It's just 50¢," the supervisor said. Jean pointed out that the corporation had more than 10 million customers. That would be a profit of more than $5 million a month for which the corporation provided nothing. When Jean said she wasn't going to pay it the charge was erased. How many times does that happen to how many citizens? How many citizens have the time to prevent such chiseling?

Forty million Americans owe student loan debts of more than $1.2 trillion, "caused by the deceptive practices of loan providers and servicers." The Senate Banking Subcommittee on Financial Institutions and Consumer Protections are examining more than 2,300 complaints of "crucial information not being available, changes in loan terms without consent and without apparent reason, and blatant lying by loan providers and servicers." Student borrowers have nowhere to turn and no one to advocate for them. "Nancy Hoover, Director of Financial Aid at Denison University, said that graduates are increasingly seeking the help of their alma mater's financial aid office, a department typically ill-equipped to handle their cases" (Campaign for America's Future, Emily Divito, 6/8/14).

In 2005, taxpayers in Arkansas paid $4 million in public welfare to employees of Walmart, one of the richest corporations in the country. According to the *New York Times,* taxpayers in

California pay $84 million a year for Walmart welfare. According to TaxFairness, nationally Walmart employees need $6.2 billion in food stamps and other public assistance while Walmart receives $1 billion in federal tax breaks. It's not a crime and I've heard no religious figure charge that the owners of Walmart, a Christian family, were stealing from employees and taxpayers. The fast food industry likely costs taxpayers even more but no one has dared publish the cost.

The Hebrew prophets were not so timid toward those who profited from the misery of the poor. "The Lord enters into judgment with the elders and princes of His people, 'It is you who have devoured the vineyard; The plunder of the poor is in your houses. What do you mean by crushing my people And grinding the face of the poor?' declares the Lord GOD of hosts" (Isa. 3: 14-15).

"You levy a straw tax on the poor and impose a tax on their grain. Therefore, though you have built stone mansions, you will not live in them; though you have planted lush vineyards, you will not drink their wine" (Amos 5: 11).

"Do not take advantage of the widow or the fatherless. If you do and they cry out to me, I will certainly hear their cry. My anger will be aroused, and I will kill you with the sword; your wives will become widows and your children fatherless" (Ex. 22: 22-24).

Those scriptures don't scare anyone any more. The fear of God has been replaced by fear of the poor. Money rules whether it is in business, elections, courts, sports, the arts, religion; the rich win, the poor lose.

There are few level fields for competition in America, not even in religion and politics.

Thou Shalt Not Kill:

Thou shalt not kill is often translated as thou shalt not murder. That does not make it simpler or more absolute. Jesus redefined the commandment thus: "Ye have heard that it was said to them of old time, Thou shalt not kill; and whosoever shall kill shall be in danger of the judgment: but I say unto you, that every one who is angry with his brother shall be in danger of the judgment; and whosoever shall say to his brother, Raca, shall be in danger of the council; and whosoever shall say, Thou fool, shall be in danger of the hell of fire (*Gehenna*)" (Matt. 5: 21, 22).

Is "brother" universal or particular here? I think it was intended to be both. Don't be angry with your siblings or fellow church members or fellow citizens or foreigners who are also our brothers and sisters. My older brother and I loved each other but we couldn't be together for long without getting into an argument that might be over something trivial but that often led to anger in both of us. We haven't physically fought each other since we were in high school but the rivalry was there.

And in America competition is encouraged. Rivalry is not bad but it can become bad. Dividing a nation, a religion or a family into winners and losers is bad. Following Jesus' summation of the law and the prophets is better than memorizing commandments.

Government Policies That Kill:

War is governmentally sanctioned murder. There are many murders in war beyond that of combatants. Who is responsible for the deaths of children and civilians? I have heard no one express concern over zygotes, embryos, fetuses destroyed in our wars on Afghanistan and Iraq. Civilians are not always innocent, not even children. They may be messengers, they may be informants, they may set mines and booby-traps or make weapons for the enemy. There were civilians in German and Japanese armament factories and they were repeatedly bombed by the allies. Tokyo and Dresden, nonmilitary targets, were firebombed to destroy civilian morale.

After the horror of Dresden, Churchill said the Allies should stop terror bombing and England did. The U.S. did not. Was that murder?

The Marines landed in Nicaragua like a biblical curse. From 1912 to 1924 U.S. Marines occupied Nicaragua. In 1925 they were sent back to Nicaragua, 1927-1934 the Marines fought Sandino and his guerrillas. In 1972, the Marines were again sent to Nicaragua.

Major General Smedley Butler, Commandant of the Marine Corps, was one of 19 Americans to receive two Medals of Honor and one of three to be awarded both the Medal of Honor and the Marine Corps Brevet Medal for valor. He fought in the Philippines against guerrillas protesting American occupation, was wounded in the Boxer Rebellion in China, and fought in the banana wars enforcing the financial interests of American corporations, especially the United Fruit Company, now called Chiquita. He received his first Medal of Honor in Mexico in 1914. He received the second in Haiti in 1915.

After he retired from the Marines, Butler lectured against war profiteering, military adventurism and fascism in the U.S. Years earlier than Eisenhower, Butler warned of the military/industrial complex that has become the military/industrial/media complex. General Electric, a major military contractor, owns whole or in part NBC, NBC Universal TV, NBC International TV, NBC Universal Cable, A&E, the Biography, History, Military History Channels, Bravo, Chiller, Lifetime, Crime & Investigation Network, CNBC, CNBC World, MSNBC, SyFy, Sleuth, USA Network, The Weather Channel, NBCUniversal Global Networks, Telemundo, Universal Studios, Universal Studios Home Entertainment, United International Pictures, and at least a dozen major TV stations.

General Butler wrote of his 33 years of Marine service "as a high class muscle man for Big Business, for Wall Street and the bankers...I was a racketeer, a gangster for capitalism." Butler claimed that he and his Marines made Honduras safe for U.S. fruit companies in 1903, Mexico safe for U.S. oil interests in 1914, Haiti and Cuba places for the National City Bank and International Banking House of Brown Brothers to collect revenues in 1902–1912, the Dominican Republic for the American sugar interests in 1916, China in 1927 for Standard Oil.

Gen. Butler said, "I might have given Al Capone a few hints. The best he could do was to operate his racket in three districts. I operated on three continents." After he retired from the Marines he wrote, "War is a racket. It always has been. It is possibly the oldest, easily the most profitable, surely the most vicious. It is the only one international in scope. It is the only one in which the profits are reckoned in dollars and the losses in lives." Wall Street never loses money when Marines die.

In the "peaceful" years between the World Wars humorist Will Rogers said, "I had an unusual experience the other day—I seen a Marine in America."

That's not the history I learned in school or heard and read in the news. How do you form your notion of reality? Your picture of America? Your view of the world? What sources inform your opinion? Much of what I learned in school was biased. Much of what I believed in the '50s, '60s and '70s I now know was not true, although I considered myself informed. I read newspapers, magazines and books regarding history and current events.

In 1981, the U.S. began funding Nicaraguan Contras with money from weapons sold to Hezbollah and other terrorist organizations supported by Iran. At least 50 Contra entities smuggled drugs into the U.S. according to declassified government documents, especially the third report by the Inspector General of the CIA in the National Security Archive. Smugglers who were caught were defended by the U.S. Department of Justice (nsarchive.org). In 1985, Daniel Ortega was democratically elected President of Nicaragua. In defiance of Congress and the law, the Reagan White House flooded Nicaragua with money and guns.

Nicaragua appealed to the International Criminal Court and the United States was found guilty of international terrorism. In 1990, Ortega lost his bid for reelection. He has since been reelected twice and is presently serving his third term as president of Nicaragua. No one in the news media seems to have noticed or to care that Ortega, once a "major threat" to U.S. security, is no longer feared by anyone.

In 1999, almost 50 years after the Korean War ended in stalemate, the Associated Press reported that U.S. soldiers killed from dozens to hundreds of Korean civilians trying to escape the fighting by passing through U.S. defensive lines. The AP reported the story as an atrocity. The U.S. and South Korean soldiers were in danger of being pushed into the sea by the North Korean army. Soldiers will suffer mental and moral anguish, but no army in the world is going to permit people wearing civilian clothing to pass into their rear without first being checked for weapons and explosives. That's a reality of war. If it's murder, who are the murderers?

The embargo on Iraq included chlorine useful in making poison gas but also needed to purify water and thousands of Iraqi children died from water borne diseases. Was that justifiable homicide? Many more will die because of depleted uranium used in bombs and artillery shells. The half-life of depleted uranium is more than 4 billion years.

Mammon trumps life:

Feb. 2, 2008. For more than seven months, the Center for Disease Control and Prevention blocked the publication of an exhaustive federal study of environmental hazards in the eight Great Lakes states because it found "low birth weights, elevated rates of infant mortality and premature births, and elevated death rates from breast cancer, colon cancer, and lung cancer." (See http://freegovinfo.info/node/1615.)

Unborn U.S. babies are soaking in a stew of chemicals, including mercury, according to a report by the Environmental Working Group based on tests of umbilical cord blood that reflects what the mother passes to the baby through the placenta: "Of the 287 chemicals we detected in umbilical cord blood, we know that 180 cause cancer in humans or animals, 217 are toxic to the brain and nervous system, and 208 cause birth defects or abnormal development in animal tests," the report said. A Government Accountability Office report said the Environmental Protection Agency does not have the powers it needs to fully regulate toxic chemicals (Reuters, 7/14/05).

In 2012, "pro-life" candidates running for the presidential nomination vowed to eliminate the EPA or reduce its power. Also in 2012, a federal appeals court overturned the EPA's effort to reduce emissions of dangerous chemicals—sulfur dioxide and nitrogen oxide—from coal-burning power plants in 28 states. The EPA estimated the rules could save up to 34,000 lives per year and result in tens of billions of dollars in health benefits. After a major campaign by utilities and corporate groups, the appeals court ruled 2 to 1 that the regulations exceed the EPA's authority.

"A new study has revealed that the chemicals replacing BPA in most of our plastics are just as bad or worse for us than BPA itself—and all of them are especially dangerous for children." The 1976 Toxic Substances Control Act presumes that chemicals are safe until proven otherwise. More than 80,000 chemicals approved for use have never been tested for their effects on adult health or child development (http://www.naturalnews.com/044551).

Before Obamacare 45,000 Americans died every year from lack of health insurance, 120 every day. Already Obamacare has saved lives.

Those living in poverty have a 19 perccent greater chance of early death. There is much concern about keeping people alive as long as possible regardless of the quality of their life, but little concern about the effect of poverty on length and quality of life, or health or brain development in children. Keeping people in poverty not only affects their health and education and chance for upward mobility but inclines them to escapism through recreational drugs, truancy, absenteeism, predatory sex, adventurism through risky behavior and potentially dangerous pranks (http://www.theguardian.com/science/2014/feb/16).

Corporations That Kill:

When I was a child, Mother went to the doctor complaining of fatigue and "nerves," probably from being the mother of three young children on a cotton farm in a house with no electricity. The doctor "prescribed" that Mother buy a carton of cigarettes and every hour sit down and smoke a cigarette. The doctor believed what he was told by those who advertised tobacco products. Mother followed directions but luckily did not become addicted and soon quit smoking.

For two years I taught at a Baptist college in North Carolina, a tobacco state. A lot of Baptist money came from tobacco producers. A lot of Methodist money came from tobacco producers. Preachers stepped lightly when it came to the morality of nicotine. Students sometimes argued whether or not it was a sin to smoke. I never heard anyone discuss whether it was a sin to work in an industry that caused harm to others. Will D. Campbell, my Baptist hero and a tobacco chewer, is believed to have said that it was a sin to burn something that tasted as good as tobacco.

Good Americans, some of them Christians, most of them believed to be ethical, knowingly produced a product that could injure and kill. They knowingly committed perjury when telling a congressional panel that tobacco was harmless and that they had no information that indicated otherwise. They obstructed justice by concealing studies that showed that nicotine was harmful, even dangerous, and that they had deliberately kicked up the nicotine punch to addict people.

Hundreds of thousands of deaths are blamed on tobacco every year. Tobacco products are still being sold, people are still dying, and advertising is still aimed at young people.

When your national god is Mammon, then a clean, healthy, beautiful world is as remote as Eden. You must destroy your country—plow mountain tops, poison the air, pollute rivers and lakes, sacrifice your children—to save it.

An American chemical plant in India killed thousands of people because of improper maintenance. Is that murder? If so, who are the murderers? Seven former employees were found guilty of negligence and sentenced to two years in prison. The combination of a car and a certain tire resulted in rollovers, injuries and deaths if a tire blew out. The companies settled out of court, had the records sealed and more than 80 people died before the deaths became public.

A woman testified to a congressional committee that she had saved her corporation half a million dollars by delaying a health procedure to a client until he died. Was that murder? Was it stealing? Who was the criminal? The woman who did her job? Her superiors who required and/or rewarded such action? The investors who coveted more profit and gained it from a man's death? Apparently, death by corporate decision isn't a crime. Is it a sin? I've heard no preachers or priests condemn such acts although many of the actors sit in pews. Some imams have denounced such practices and many Muslims believe the America lifestyle is evil. Where is the Christian condemnation?

The executives of an auto company knew that one of their products would explode in flames if hit from the rear but decided it would be cheaper to pay for the deaths of the occupants than to fix the car. Ignition problems could have been fixed for 57 cents per car but it reduced profits. Thirteen people died.

"Do not do anything that endangers your neighbor's life. I am the Lord" (Lev. 19:16). Many ethical, moral and religious people work for corporations that do endanger lives but because there is no accountability at the top neither is there accountability at the bottom.

Jobs That Kill:

2010, Twenty-nine miners died at a Massey Energy mine. A state-funded independent investigation found Massey Energy directly responsible for the coal dust explosion because of flagrant safety violations and multiple failures to meet basic safety standards, including failure to properly maintain its ventilation systems. Investigators had to wait more than two months to enter the mine because of the concentration of toxic gases. The independent investigators also faulted the Mine Safety and Health Administration for failing to act although Massey was issued 515 citations for safety violations in 2009 and MSHA could have fined the company up to $220,000. According to the report, Massey intentionally neglected safety precautions to increase profits. One superintendent confessed to conspiring to impede enforcement.

The evidence accumulated during the investigation demonstrates that PCC/Massey promoted and enforced a workplace culture that valued production over safety, including practices calculated to allow it to conduct mining operations in violation of the law.... Witness testimony revealed that miners were intimidated by management and were told that raising safety concerns would jeopardize their jobs (www.msha.gov/.../ExecutiveSummary).

In 2010, a BP oil rig in the Gulf of Mexico blew out when the cement capping the well failed, incinerating 11 workers. BP had ignored regulations although the same blowout had happened in the Caspian Sea but without the loss of life. Mixing the cement with nitrogen sped up the drying process saving BP a half million dollars a day in rig rental. Five months before the blowout the BP Vice-President for Gulf Exploration testified to the U.S.

Congress that the company had drilled offshore "for the last 50 years in a manner both safe and protective of the environment." That was more than a year after the Caspian Sea blowout. The chiefs of Exxon and Chevron also testified that the drilling methods were safe although they knew of the Caspian Sea blowout (*Vultures and Vote Rustlers,* Greg Palast).

Corporations are necessary in today's world, perhaps even global corporations, but they must be controlled by the people, meaning a federal government of the people, by the people and for the people. We the people and the state and federal governments must not be controlled by global corporations that have no loyalty to any government but their corporate government. And if collectivization and public welfare are good for employers, then they should also be good for employees.

Speech That Kills:

Some Christians, and other believers, are so upset about the Constitutional equal protection of the law and a literal reading of Leviticus 20:13 that they have unintentionally encouraged some people and some governments to make homosexuality a crime punishable by death. This is a glaring example of poison-picking the Bible.

A Christian minister announced that he was going to burn a Koran. The federal government asked him not to do it. That's the kind of glory he brought on himself, but he brought death to some Christians in Islamic countries. Jesus and James warned about the dangers and sins that could be caused by the tongue (James 1: 26, 3: 5-8). Jesus said that it was not what goes into the mouth that defiles but what comes out of it (Matt. 15:11).

What Christian could say to Jesus, "I have kept all the commandments; what more do I lack?"

Do the Ten Commandments have any relevance in the world's most materialistic nation where greed, celebrity and conspicuous consumption are virtues? Murder, stealing, false witness, covetousness have become meaningless in a survival-of-the-fittest predatory capitalism backed by military might and subsidized by taxpayers. And the shortest way to profits is exploitation of those Jesus called the "least of these".

Do we need a new council to decide a biblical canon acceptable to Americans? Presently, in fundamentalist Christian churches, one can hear preachers declaring that Christians should rebel, usually without violence, against a government providing health care for citizens, although Jesus clearly stated that those who do not feed the hungry and care for the sick are doomed to the same eternity as Satan and his angels (Matt. 25: 41).

Some Christians believe they are sovereign and what is best for them is more important than what is best for another or even of all others.

Perhaps, the Commandments can be redefined by prophets of the Hebrew kind who suffered rejection, persecution, slander and death. None of them are remembered for their success.

Laws, rules, commandments can condemn but they can't redeem. Loving God with all our heart and loving our neighbors almost as much as ourselves doesn't need redefining and doesn't scrutinize others but only ourselves. And love and grace can redeem.

That's what we are called to do. It would be an heroic achievement but you would have to be humble about it. You can't be humble if you've never done anything. You're just someone who has nothing to brag about.

CHAPTER TEN

Two Confessions, Three Myths, a Heresy and the Fleshpots of Egypt

The American Heresy of Redemptive Violence:

Americans were not the first to think of or resort to redemptive violence but we are its apostles. Newspapers and magazines christened "westerns" morality plays because the good guys always won. They killed the bad guys by being more violent and quicker to kill than the bad guys. That's the moral of hundreds of stories, thousands if you include TV westerns.

In a popular western, Shane stops at a farmhouse. He is wearing buckskin and has a pistol on his hip, the marks of a gunman. The farmer and his family take Shane in and outfit him in clothes befitting a farm hand. Shane lays the buckskin and six-shooter aside and takes up farming. He seems to enjoy being part of the family, but the farmers are threatened by greedy rancher brothers and their cowhands who seem to have no women or need of family. The ranchers hire a gun to balance power since Shane has aligned with the farmers.

After the hired gun kills a farmer, Shane puts on his buck-skins and six-shooter and rides into town alone to take on the hired gun and anyone who backs him. Shane kills the gunman and the two rancher brothers because he is deadlier. Despite the pleas of the kid and Shane's previous enjoyment of family life, Shane rides off alone, leaving the farmers with no leaders to guide them, no structures to protect them from the next ambitious predator to come along. Mission accomplished.

The plots of most westerns are paradigms of American military incursions. Ride in, kill the bad guys, ride out leaving the country no better off, sometimes leaving the country in chaos. Consider Nicaragua that is largely forgotten by the media but was a major concern of the U.S. in the 20th century.

The Hymn will continue until each Crusader has selected a target to destroy. Suggested targets are: L.A., D.C., New Orleans, N.Y.C., Dallas, your hometown.

Myths Define a Country:

I'm not talking about Paul Bunyan, Pecos Bill or John Henry the steel driving man.

There was a brief time in America when a strong, healthy man could chop or plow a farm in the woods or on the plains, plant a crop, get a wife, make some kids and be self-reliant if he had enough guns and ammo and if the Indians had been killed or driven off their land. If bad men didn't come to kill him while he was working in the field or asleep in his bed. If he could find and kill enough game for food and shoes. If predators didn't kill his livestock. If he wasn't injured in a farm accident. If the wife and kids didn't need friends and never got sick. If the kids didn't need an education and no one needed a church even for burying. If the kids never grew up and wanted to start their own families. Even at its best self-reliance was a dream filled with ifs.

Herbert Hoover believed every person should be able to provide for himself and protect himself and his family from giant corporations. The market would take of itself with contracts, tax cuts, tax loopholes and direct handouts from a benevolent government. Humanitarian aid to "the least of these" would create dependency.

The dream of self-reliance is still alive, promoted by politicians, preachers and other hucksters who pretend that a man can get a place somewhere for free and live without roads, railroads, canals, harbors, airports, schools, places of worship, mail, medicine, healthcare, communication, police, firefighters, law, order, clerks, judges or other functions of government—if he has enough guns and ammo and is willing to kill multitudinously to enforce his own theory of law.

The Myth of Rugged Individualism:

E Pluribus Unum, "one of many," meant one nation of many peoples, the melting pot that America once bragged about. It seemed appropriate for a democracy; however, it did not include women and black people as equal.

"Rugged individualism" was a term used often by Hoover. The Constitution declared the Union was formed to "promote the general welfare," but he believed the "market" would take care of itself given enough time. As long as taxpayers subsidized the "free" (meaning unregulated) market, all would be well.

Western books and films promoted self-indulgent, self-seeking moralists who acted as enforcers, judges, juries and executioners. They are inappropriate, even harmful in a democracy or in a church. Shane don't need nobody or no law like "equal protection under the law" (use of vernacular for emphasis). Shane had a gun and he was itching to use it.

Rugged Individualism is a white-men-only virtue. No one wants a rugged individualist for a mother, wife, sister or daughter. Not one like Abigail Adams, Harriet Tubman, Sojourner Truth, Susan B. Anthony, Kate Chopin, Betty Friedan, Eleanor Roosevelt, Barbara Jordan, Michelle Obama.

Few want one for a father.

No one wanted rugged individualists to be black. 1955: Emmett Till, 14-year-old boy kidnapped, tortured and murdered. 1955: Lamar Smith shot dead on the courthouse lawn by a white man. Although dozens saw the murder the killer was never indicted. 1961: Herbert Lee shot dead by a white member of the Mississippi Legislature who was never charged with the murder. 1963: Medgar Evers, veteran of Normandy, shot in the back by a cowardly white supremacist who was found guilty 29 years later. 1965: Malcolm X murdered by members of Nation of Islam. 1968: Martin Luther King, Jr. assassinated.

Those and other black rugged individualists were murdered by those who were backed by mobs, Klans, middle class white supremacists including preachers, politicians, judges, local media and too often, local white society.

American Exceptionalism (aka American Impunity):

Because America, like Israel, was founded by God, we are exempt to the laws that all nations, except us, must obey. The Geneva Conventions: everyone except us. The Convention Against

Torture and Other Cruel, Inhuman or Degrading Treatment or Punishment: all nations except us. Some justices, law officials and government lawyers have excepted some Americans from our own Constitution.

Westerns as a Morality Play:

I mentioned earlier my first novel *North to Yesterday*. A group of old men who had missed adventure when they were young are determined to gather longhorn cattle and drive them to Trail's End to sell—although the trail has been closed for years and longhorns are worthless. I wanted to name it "The Days in the Wilderness" so that it would resonate with the desire of the Hebrews in the wilderness to return to Egypt, and because the "Old West" is a romance that plays in the imagination of some who wish they could return to those lawless days of anarchy when a man with a gun was his own law.

Yahweh set the Hebrews free. They were fed by Yahweh and guided by Yahweh day and night. And they were happy about as long as a child is happy with a new toy. Then they longed for those wonderful flesh pots and all the bread they wanted (Exodus 16). Fish, cucumbers, melons, onions and garlic (Numbers 11). Not that dreadful manna day after day.

When they reached the borders of the land given to them by Yahweh the Hebrews didn't want it. They wished they had died in Egypt or in the wilderness. They wanted to choose a leader to take them back to slavery (Numbers 14). Believers have a lot to complain about. (Intended irony.) But they have someone who hears their complaints. (Anecdotal truth.) I've told you a hundred times.

I thought *North to Yesterday* was an anti-western because no one in the book wins through violence. I sent the book to Knopf because they stated that they did not publish westerns. In the cover letter I wrote that the book was no more a western than Don Quixote was a western. The book received a Wrangler Award from the National Cowboy Hall of Fame.

I have written other "westerns," some of them contemporary. I have also received a second Wrangler Award from the National Cowboy Hall of Fame and two Spur Awards from Western Writers of America. I don't believe any of my books are "westerns" because they don't portray violence as being redemptive. Whatsoever you sow is what you will reap. Plant a carrot, you get a carrot. Plant bombs and you get box-cutters. Is that scripture quaint?

Once when I told Mother that Jean and I were going to Pampa to answer some questions I had about Uncle Boyd, she told me that she and Dad had worried about Uncle Boyd buying a gun. Pampa was in the heart of Panhandle oil fields, surrounded by oil field workers, suppliers, drivers, robbers, hijackers, con men and other sharpies. Money flowed like oil and Uncle Boyd, who was too good to live, needed a gun for protection.

From newspapers, court records and conversations we learned that, like Uncle Boyd, his killer was married. They had been friends but quarreled over a waitress they were both seeing. Uncle Boyd was squatting, changing a tire and his friend walked up behind him and shot him four times in the back. As Uncle Boyd slumped against the tire, the pistol he had showed me fell from his pocket. His killer swore that Uncle Boyd had threatened to kill him. In Texas that was self-defense.

Did Uncle Boyd's killer say he was too good to live? It wasn't in the official record or the newspaper but some people said that two or three men nearby had heard it. If so, it didn't mean what I thought it did.

The Redolent Flesh Pots:

The safety and goodness of the past is a delusion. During the Depression honest people stole to feed their families. Dad believed that about the tire thief he had shot. During the "Good

War," the "greatest generation" incinerated German and Japanese children. Bigotry was accepted, even in many churches. In some churches tolerance was not tolerated. I never attended a school in which an African-American would have been allowed to enroll. I never taught in a university department that included a black person.

The appeal of the safety and the goodness of the imagined past is powerful. Back to a time when life was safe, everyone believed as we did, all the children were loved. God's purpose was not to keep Jesus safe. The same may be true of God's purpose for you.

We don't know what new marvel or horror we will wake up to tomorrow. I think the first person who discovered how to make fire was condemned by others. "You're going to set the whole world on fire." I can imagine a mother and father weeping over a dead child and asking why God ever allowed a wheel to be invented.

Knowledge is not evil. Not even scientific knowledge. Our faith in God has to be big enough to embrace knowledge and technology that seems to explode every year. Our faith has to be wise enough to guide humans in using knowledge in ethical and creative rather than destructive ways. Instead of being the guiding star to the future, religions have become the reliquary of antique notions. Instead of embracing the future with faith and offering leadership we dream of the flesh pots of Egypt where we were safe from surprise.

Jesus was tempted by power, by control. And Jesus refused. His kingdom was not a kingdom of power but of love. The salvation of the world does not depend on our power or our willingness to kill but on God's grace.

What does lie in our power is total abstinence from the flesh pots of Egypt. They were never as piquant, as meaty as we remember. Only the memory is spicy. The taste is toxic.

You don't destroy evil by killing evil people. There are always others, perhaps worse than those you killed. You can't defeat evil by attrition. You can't destroy evil without destroying all of us or part of all of us. That's a lesson from the Garden of Eden. The penchant toward evil may be the God-part of us, giving us free will.

Violence may sometimes be necessary but violence can never be redemptive. Isn't that the lesson of the cross? It wasn't the violence done to Jesus that was redemptive; it was his sacrificial love.

CHAPTER ELEVEN

Cinderella, The Ugly Duckling, Snow White and the Twelve Dwarfs, and GodStory

You may have noticed that myths and stories are similar. The story of America is not so different from the story of Israel. God's chosen people escaped the tyranny of bishops, barons and pharaohs who told them how to live and how to worship, by crossing a body of water to bring form to a void and chaotic land. Winthrops and Lowells gained self-governance but only white males of property could vote or hold office. They declared freedom of religion for themselves and denied it to others.

With the benevolence of guns, skills, germs and cunning they defeated a Super Power and wrested the land from heathen savages. Laying claim to a sacred land that was worth more than human life, the powerful shaped the forests, rivers and mountains to their wants and used slaves and new immigrants for their profit. When the country neared dissolution God remembered Abraham Lincoln and Lincoln brought the people to a Promised Land but was not able to see it himself.

The despised Micks, Spics, Chinks, Bohunks and Wops followed the same path but found their freedom denied by robber barons and clergy who supported money and power. Without guns they fought against unnecessarily dangerous jobs and company stores and for their place in the land. Their grandchildren found their place with dangerous unregulated food, water, air and medicine and payday loan stores—and tried to deny entry to those following the same path as their grandparents. Together they formed a nation like no other.

Boy meets girl, boy loses girl who chooses the wrong guy, boy gets girl. Except for grandeur, scope and scale that isn't very different from God creates man, God loses man who has chosen evil, God saves man.

Cinderella was of noble birth and gracious character but is left by her father to live with her evil stepmother and the stepmother's two daughters, Scribe and Pharisee, who scorn her as a maid. A king invites all the young ladies of the land to a ball where he will choose a beloved. The stepsisters plan their wardrobes and leave Cinderella behind as a servant when they go to the ball but the Holy Spirit restores her nobility, transforms a pumpkin into a golden carriage and mice into horses to take her to the ball. When she enters the ballroom, the guests part and throw palm branches before her and everyone declares her the fairest of the fair.

The clock strikes midnight, instead of the king it is Judas who kisses her cheek, her golden crown is taken from her, she is carried from the palace in disgrace, tried for impersonating royalty and crucified. But on the third day the prince comes looking for the one the golden crown belongs to. A transcendent Jesus accepts the crown and returns to his royal throne.

Did that remind you of The Ugly Duckling? The frog that turns into a prince? Snow White and the Seven Dwarfs? There are many stories of America, some of them ugly. There are many stories of Christianity, Judaism, Islam, Hinduism, Buddhism, some of them ugly.

In Egyptian mythology Horus, the son of the God Osiris, was born of a virgin who gave birth in a cave. The birth of Horus was announced by angels and attended by shepherds. He was baptized by Anup the baptizer, who was later beheaded. He performed miracles and raised his dead father from the grave. Horus was crucified in some stories, descended into hell and was resurrected after three days.

The similarity doesn't reduce the story. It verifies the story that we were made for something better and fulfills the universal need for a story of redemption. The yearning for a relationship to something greater, more lasting than oneself is universal. That yearning produces the stories. The closer we get to the original stories, the more primitive they are. The refinement of the stories is progressive revelation. One story is essential, the sine qua non.

"Space seethes with an enormous enigmatic energy, and, each second, trillions of cubic light-years more of it materializes from nothingness" (Bob Berman, *Astronomy*, November 2007). A trillion is beyond my calculation, trillions beyond my comprehension. Light-years are trillions of light-years over my head and I understand neither the definition nor the meaning of "nothingness." But whatever Berman's statement describes is God. God is the enigmatic energy, God is the light-years, God is the nothingness.

When Moses asked God's name, God replied with a "to be" verb usually translated as "I am that I am," "I am who I am" or "I will be who I will be." I think "I am" is too passive for the enigmatic energy that every second creates trillions of cubic light-years of space out of nothing. I believe the translation of God's name should be IS. What IS. What IS to come. All that IS, and IS beyond all that IS.

But there's more. Is the universe infinite or is it hugely infinite? Both are possible according to physicist Brian Greene, author of *The Hidden Reality: Parallel Universes and the Deep Laws of the Cosmos*. If the universe is infinite and matter is finite, "there are only so many ways matter can arrange itself within that infinite universe. Eventually, matter has to repeat itself and arrange itself in similar ways. So if the universe is infinitely large, it is also home to infinite parallel universes."

That makes me very small on an insignificant planet, but it gives God the awesome and majestic divinity we claim for the Creator but are unable to imagine. Systematic Theology is to God's creation and intention what the multiplication table is to quantum physics.

Every day God becomes light-years bigger than anything my mind can conceive and it takes an enormous amount of faith to believe a God creating trillions of cubic light-years of stuff every second in one of what may be many parallel universes could care about my sore throat, the last drop of milk in your refrigerator, the most important thing I ever think, say or do or your little dog that is the sole survivor of those who love you. However, if you pray to the Creator who is creating cubic light years of matter every second you might have more faith that God can create miracles. Perhaps the tiny triumphs and tragedies that occupy our minds and consume our lives are not that important.

The Greek word *logos* means "word" as the expression of thought. It is translated as "sayings" (Mat. 7: 24), "communications" (Luke 24: 17), "treatise, book, account, narrative, discourse, story" (Acts 1: 1).

John 1:1 could be translated "In the beginning was the Story, and the Story was with God, and the Story was God." The story was not about God. God was not part of the story. God *is* the story. The story became flesh (John 1: 14) and walked among us.

As the presence of the story "that dwelled among us" faded, followers of the way neglected telling the story and seeking to enlarge the relationship in order to collect Jesus's words and codify his stories. To keep it from growing beyond them, they sought to enshrine it, embalming it instead. The story made flesh became institutionalized, embedded in tradition and dogma so that it would not change and grow even as the relationship changed and understanding grew.

Those in power held back the story privately from those who wanted to make it their story, reserved to a few, first the Jews, then the Greeks and the Romans, then a war between the Eastern story and the Western story. Debating the ownership of the Book of Jonah, they forgot the message of Jonah. They withheld the story from those who wanted to make it their story, the Buddhist story, the Hindu story, the Muslim story.

Rather than allowing the story made flesh to be reincarnated in other stories and creating a commonality that could make us a brotherhood, the Eastern story and the Western story chose exclusivity, warring over whose story would prevail, creating a new story of exclusivity with attendant wars and strife. Christianity became less a relationship with the story made flesh and more an approved way of thinking and acting. "Every thing begins in mysticism and ends in politics," wrote the French poet Charles Peguy.

The story made flesh cannot be entombed in one place or one time or one religion. The story that was from the beginning reveals itself and is resurrected by those who seek to know the Eternal. If we can get over ourselves as the stars in our story perhaps we can fulfill our part in GodStory, become a verb in GodStory, a footnote or a punctuation mark.

We are not at the end of revelation. Living in the story with the One who walked among us will lead us beyond devotion to commandments and beatitudes of stone, the Christmas tree, baby Dionysus in the manger to faith in our common parentage (our unique part in the story) until the story made flesh dwells with all of us.

When words do not avail, when prayers are beyond words, remember the story: God so loved the world. All of it. All of us. Happily ever after.

About the Author

Robert Lopez Flynn grew up in the small west Texas town of Chillicothe, attended Baylor University and Southwestern Baptist Theological Seminary (his "apprenticeship in hell") and worked as a war correspondent in Vietnam. He taught creative writing and literature for 40 years at Trinity University in San Antonio. His late wife, Jean, was the author of several historical works for children.

Flynn is the author of numerous books, including ten novels: *North To Yesterday* (Knopf, 1967), *In the House of the Lord* (Knopf, 1969), *The Sounds of Rescue, The Signs of Hope* (Knopf, 1970, TCU, 1988), and *Wanderer Springs* (TCU Press, 1987). He is also the author of a two-part documentary, *A Cowboy Legacy* (ABC-TV); a nonfiction narrative, *A Personal War in Vietnam* (Texas A&M, 1989); an oral history, *When I Was Just Your Age* (Univ. of North Texas Press, 1992); and several collections of stories and essays. His critical study/philosophical rumination, *Lawful Abuse: How the Century of the Child Became the Century of the Corporation* was published by Wings Press in 2013. *Burying the Farm: A Memoir of Chillicothe, Texas,* was published as a limited edition, fine press chapbook (Wings Press, 2008).

North to Yesterday received awards from the Texas Institute of Letters and the National Cowboy Hall of Fame, and was named one of the Best Books of the Year by the *New York Times*. (It is also the funniest cowboy novel [actually, it's an anti-cowboy novel] ever written.) *Seasonal Rain* was co-winner of the Texas Literary Festival Award. *Wanderer Springs* received a Spur Award from Western Writers of America. The list of awards is considerable. His work has been translated into a dozen languages. Flynn is a member (and past president) of The Texas

Institute of Letters, The Writers Guild of America, Marine Corps Combat Correspondents, and P.E.N. In 1998, he received the Distinguished Achievement Award from the Texas Institute of Letters.

Colophon

This first edition of *Holy Literary License : The Almighty Chooses Fallible Mortals to Write, Edit, and Translate GodStory*, by Robert Flynn, has been printed on 55 pound Edwards Brothers natural paper containing a percentage of recycled fiber. Titles have been set in Flat Brush and Nueva Standard type; the text in Adobe Caslon type. All Wings Press books are designed and produced by Bryce Milligan.

On-line catalogue and ordering:
www.wingspress.com

Wings Press titles are distributed
to the trade by the
Independent Publishers Group
www.ipgbook.com
and in Europe by
www.gazellebookservices.co.uk

Also available as an ebook.